PILGRIMAGE, PLACE, AND PLURALISM

PILGRIMAGE, PLACE, AND PLURALISM

Essays in Conversation with Diana Eck

Edited by
JENNIFER HOWE PEACE
· AND ·
ELINOR J. PIERCE

Afterword by
JAMES CARROLL

Red Elixir
Rhinebeck, New York

Pilgrimage, Place, and Pluralism: Essays in Conversation with Diana Eck
© copyright 2024 Jennifer Peace, Elinor Pierce, Diana Eck

All rights reserved. No part of this book may be used or reproduced in any manner without the consent of the publisher except in critical articles or reviews. Contact the publisher for information.

Paperback ISBN 978-1-960090-44-7
eBook ISBN 978-1-960090-45-4

Library of Congress Control Number 2023921926

Book design by Colin Rolfe

Red Elixir is an imprint of Monkfish Book Publishing Company

Red Elixir
22 East Market Street, Suite 304
Rhinebeck, New York 12572
(845) 876-4861
monkfishpublishing.com

CONTENTS

Editor's Preface	ix
Acknowledgments	xiii
Introduction and Gratitude | *Diana L. Eck*	xv

PART I
ENCOUNTERS: CO-PILGRIMS AND COLLEAGUES

1. Diana Eck: Apostle of Pluralism — 3
   \| *Karen Armstrong*

2. When Religion Turns Toxic: Mitigating Polarization through Poetic Tradition — 8
   \| *Ali S. Asani*

3. Encountering Ourselves: Diana's Pathbreaking Work in Service of a New Religious America — 16
   \| *Preeta D. Bansal*

4. At Home Where We Live: My Life in Parallel to Diana's — 23
   \| *Francis X. Clooney, SJ*

5. Concluding Lecture from an Introductory Course in Comparative History of Religion — 28
   \| *William A. Graham*

6. One Without a Second — 40
   \| *John Stratton Hawley*

7. Reflections on Learning from (But not Studying with) Diana Eck — 45
   \| *Lucinda Mosher*

8. Diana Eck's Overton Window — 53
   \| *Laurie Patton*

9. North Star, A Shining Light   59
   | *Simran Jeet Singh*

PART II
SACRED GEOGRAPHIES: CONSIDERING PLACE

10. Pluralism as *Nomos* and Narrative: Reflecting on Religious Land Use in Modern America   67
    | *Whittney Barth*

11. Religious Pluralism and Civic Engagement: A New Lens from LA to NY   73
    | *Chloe Breyer*

12. The Corridor   78
    | *Lawrence Cohen*

13. Like a River: Sacred Geography and Its Ecological Tributaries   88
    | *Rebecca Kneale Gould*

14. *Darshana*: Learning to See from Diana Eck   98
    | *Rahul Mehrotra*

15. Shifting Patterns of Epiphanies   103
    | *Vijaya Nagarajan*

16. Residing on the Hair of Śiva, Rising from the Foot of Viṣṇu: The River Gaṅgā in the Khmer Landscape   110
    | *Vasudha Narayanan*

17. Media and Memory: From Cambridge to Manzanar   119
    | *Susan Shumaker*

18. Somanath and the Rhetoric of "the Shrine Eternal"   130
    | *Neelima Shukla-Bhatt*

PART III
BEYOND COMMON GROUND: CONSTRUCTING PLURALISM

19. A Legacy of Embodied Scholarship: Stories of Pluralism in Practice at Harvard   141
   | *Halah Ahmad*

20. Diana Eck: Partner and Co-Pilgrim in My Interfaith Journey   148
   | *S. Wesley Ariarajah*

21. A Transformational Conference: "Women, Religion, and Social Change"   151
   | *Sissela Bok*

22. Braiding Epistemological, Theoretical, and Methodological Contributions   158
   | *Patrice Brodeur*

23. Diana Eck: She Who Changed My Life   165
   | *Dhammananda*

24. Beyond the Rules of Interfaith Dialogue   170
   | *Blu Greenberg*

25. Potentials of Pluralism: Eid on 9/11   176
   | *Nancy A. Khalil*

26. Diana Eck as Teacher   183
   | *Pranati Parikh*

27. Diana Eck: The Single Biggest Influence on Interfaith America   192
   | *Eboo Patel*

28. An Advaita Vedānta Theology of Religions: A Sketch   199
   | *Anantanand Rambachan*

29. Buddhism, Religious Pluralism, and Labor Strikes in Hawai'i   207
   | *Duncan Ryūken Williams*

Afterword   217
    |*James Carroll*

About the Contributors   223
Select Bibliography for Diana L. Eck   231
Endnotes   233

EDITOR'S PREFACE

This volume includes many stories of encounter—of engaging with and learning from Diana Eck. For many, this encounter is transformational: as one who has worked with Diana for many years, I often witness her indelible impact. I also hear regularly from those who have been inspired deeply by her work even if they have never met Diana in person but have encountered Diana through her writing.

I first learned about Diana Eck in a cramped seminar classroom on a snowy campus in St. Paul, Minnesota, when my professor introduced us to Diana as a gifted scholar, friend, and fellow traveler. We heard how Diana would ride her bicycle through the ancient streets of Banaras with one hand on the handlebars, the other grasping a cob of roasted corn. For me, this image was nearly as captivating as her powerful prose. Later, I would read *Darśan,* in which Diana described the task before us as "developing a hermeneutic of the visible." At an age—or stage—at which I was more inclined to a "hermeneutic of suspicion," this book helped to shift my approach away from reductive criticism towards a more expansive, appreciative engagement. Based on the faded pencil underlines, extensive margin notes, and effusive exclamation points, there was much I found compelling in that slim volume: even the extensive glossary and pronunciation guide signaled her emphasis on lived experience and making knowledge more accessible.

Many years later, when I found myself with Diana at a Hindu temple as part of the early "mapping" of the religious landscape of America, I recognized her real genius. As we took off our shoes and entered, I nervously imagined the conversation: *Would this be a test of my knowledge of Hinduism? Would the priest be in awe when he learned that this world-renowned scholar was visiting?* The priest offered a tour of the storefront temple, tucked behind a strip mall in central California, and told us the names and attributes of various deities—information we "knew." Yet Diana brought a genuine sense of wonder, and rapt attention, as if this was her first visit to a Hindu temple. She didn't hide her knowledge nor condescend; rather, she asked informed questions, observed closely and joyfully, and listened carefully. That day, I heard a version of a myth that I hadn't heard before, learned the history of the temple, and listened to some of the struggles of the local Hindu community. This abiding sense of respect for people and a nuanced approach to seeing, listening, and learning, in my experience, informs Diana's work and life.

My co-editor Jenny Peace has her own story to tell of encountering Diana:

> I first encountered Diana through an email exchange in the mid 1990s. I was a young, earnest seminary student who had just discovered I was a semester too late to take Diana's course, "World Religions in Boston." I was finishing my master's in theological studies at a seminary north of Boston and had come across her class description in the course catalog of the Boston Theological Institute (a consortium of seminaries that encouraged cross-registration). I dashed off an email to Dr. Eck explaining how much I loved her course description and that in fact, she was just the kind of scholar I wanted to be someday. I asked if she would meet with me so I could tell her all about my vocational goals. Never mind that I was not a student in her class or even at her institution.
>
> Years later, when I became a professor myself, with a full load of classes, a center to run, and administrative responsibilities to attend to, I realized more fully the generosity of Diana's response. She wrote back immediately. She would be delighted to meet me. I read once that you can judge a person's character by how they treat someone from

whom they have nothing to gain. From that first conversation in her warmly-lit office at Harvard, to consulting with her and wonderful colleagues like Ellie at the Pluralism Project, to my professional highlight of getting the chance to co-teach with Diana, I have appreciated qualities I see mentioned in so many of the essays in this volume. Diana always makes you feel welcome and valued, like there is nowhere else she would rather be than talking to you or working together for some greater goal. I admire Diana as a brilliant scholar, writer, teacher, and advocate in the civic arena. But beyond this, the care she took to encourage an unknown seminarian has had an indelible impact on my trajectory.

Together, Jenny and I have thought about how this *festschrift* might best reflect Diana's distinctive way of seeing the world and engaging others. When we asked her about putting together the volume, she demurred: "No one wants to write a *festschrift* essay; no one wants to read one." We countered: "But what if there are those who want to tell you something about the impact you've had on them, personally and professionally?" Diana agreed, hesitantly, with one caveat: to encourage everyone to write in their own voice about themes or topics of genuine interest to them. And so, we have an *Eckschrift* that brings together diverse voices, in divergent lengths and formats. We hope these nearly thirty essays offer a glimpse of Diana, beyond her scholarly achievements, as radically relational. We have imagined this volume as an extension of Diana's table—whether a seminar table or dining table—around which she regularly gathers others to listen and to learn. Diana's table is a place of hospitality, generosity of spirit, and graciousness.

There are many who cannot be at this table, whether because of conflicting commitments or limited space; there are those who are not at this table, or in these pages, because of their passing, such as Diana's beloved mother Dorothy Eck, her friend and esteemed colleague Peter Gomes, and her student and former teaching fellow Brendan Randall, to name only a few. There is also another voice who has been rendered silent: Diana's wife Dorothy, who is now living with dementia. Dorothy

Austin, for some fifty years, has been at Diana's side: brilliant, voluble, warm, sensitive, provocative, and often hilarious. When we imagine the essay Dorothy might have contributed in celebration of Diana, it is hard to suppress a smile: she would have crafted a beautiful essay, one that might push some boundaries or perhaps disclose more than Diana might prefer—all in a way that Diana would cherish. While this book is dedicated to Diana, it is also dedicated to Dorothy, Diana's wife and partner in this life.

ELINOR J. PIERCE

ACKNOWLEDGMENTS

Sincere thanks to James Carroll and to all of the contributors.

We are grateful to Neelima Shukla-Bhatt for her consultation and for thinking together about ways to celebrate Diana. We appreciate Nicole Malte Collins for her assistance, and wish to thank the many students, staff, alumni, and affiliates of the Pluralism Project. Thanks also to Catherine Brekus and Diana's colleagues at Harvard's Committee on the Study of Religion and the Harvard Divinity School.

Thanks to Jon Sweeney at Monkfish Book Publishing for his enthusiasm.

Ellie offers special thanks to Paula O'Connor and to all of those who have served as mentors and teachers, including Paul Axelrod, Jim Laine, and the Tri-Faith Gardeners.

Jenny offers special thanks to her late mother-in-law Edie Howe as well as all the students, colleagues, and activists from whom she has learned so much.

As always, we thank our families, especially Joel and Asheesh.

Our ultimate gratitude goes to Diana for inspiring and helping to shape this volume through her example, words, and vision.

INTRODUCTION AND GRATITUDE

Diana L. Eck

Pilgrimage has been my life in so many ways. There are, of course, the particular pilgrimages: the exhilaration of reaching a high mountain temple, a hilltop shrine, the headwaters of a mighty river. I think of standing in a crowded temple when the curtain was opened for *darshan*. I think of my journeys to the confluence of rivers, and especially the great confluence of the Ganga and Yamuna and the massive Kumbha Mela. It was a personal pilgrimage when I went to Jerusalem for the first and only time on my way home from Banaras. Pilgrimage is my way of learning, on my feet and the ground.

But more broadly, pilgrimage is not so much a particular journey, but a life journey in the company of each of you who have contributed your thoughts to this book. Among you is one of my oldest friends, Jack Hawley, whose journey with me began the day we started graduate school and who is uniquely able to write playfully and personally of the oneness and manyness of my life. Bill Graham's journey began about the same time when we met as graduate students and led interlocking lives as young teachers and colleagues, and his retirement lecture on the study of religion summed up so much of what we had learned together. It is an honor to have it here in this book. My colleague Frank Clooney has enabled me to see the many ways in which our intellectual and spiritual journeys have been driven by similar questions—different journeys to India filled with scholarly fascination and, at the same time, with spiritual reflection. Over the past two decades my own journey has intersected with that of Karen Armstrong, beginning at a conference at the turn of the millennium modestly entitled "God at 2000." We both presented our thoughts and have been together in Cambridge and London ever since. We discovered that both of us were influenced by Wilfred Cantwell Smith and Karen's essay here takes Smith's wide view of human religiousness as she articulates her signature ethos of compassion.

Students have also had life journeys in my company, and their paths have connected with mine in gratifying ways. I think of Ali Asani, a student when he first came to Harvard from Nairobi, later a colleague in the study of religion and a creative Muslim voice in interfaith relations. And Laurie Patton whose path has paralleled my own in many ways—from comparative studies to Sanskrit scholarship to public life and interreligious leadership. I have been moved by the journey of Lucinda Mosher who was not directly my student, but who found inspiration in my work and became a pilgrim teacher and leader in interfaith work, serving in countless local contexts.

Preeta Bansal was one of my first Indian-American students and only later did I become aware of her accomplishments—as a lawyer, as Solicitor General of New York and as Chair of the US Commission on Religious Freedom. Here she writes of the ways in which her journey led her back to Indian spirituality. One of my former students, Simran Jeet Singh, is a Sikh pilgrim from Texas walking the path of compassion. His remarkable book, *The Light We Give: How Sikh Wisdom Can Transform Your Life,* gives us narratives of his experience on the journey.

Actually, all of you who have written here have been pilgrim companions on the way. I hope our journeys together will continue as we enter the next stretch of terrain, whatever it may be.

■

Place has also been a theme for me. I grew up in a beautiful Montana valley where mountains and rivers had names. This impressed me from my earliest days. Bozeman was my home ground, and Banaras became a second home, and sacred in the complicated ways that a place becomes entwined with one's life. In your writings here, many of you have focused on places and have expanded and stretched my own understanding. Neelima Shukla-Bhatt revisited Somnath on the coast of Gujarat, with its long-contested history and its shifting and resonant symbolic importance, still today a vibrant and changing shrine. Vasudha Narayanan has taken us far and wide into Cambodia, a place I have never been, so filled with astonishing links to the places, the shrines, and especially the rivers of India—the Ganga in Cambodia. Vijaya Nagarajan has brought the sophistication of the ancient Indus sewage system home to us as we struggle with overwhelming waste production in a consumer society.

Susan Shumaker, who years ago coaxed me into multi-media and created the CD-ROM "On Common Ground: World Religions in America," went on to bring the power of film to our National Parks and monuments. Her contribution of a film script on Manzanar is a unique view into another form of scholarship and activism. I think of another early student, Rebecca Gould, whose journey from homesteading to sweeping her gaze across America and seeing the meanings of land and sacred geography and the movements that are creating ecological theologies and environmental practices.

Chloe Breyer was one of our first researchers at the Pluralism Project, writing about the struggles of a Vietnamese home temple in California, later becoming an Episcopal priest and now leader of the Interfaith Center of New York. Whittney Barth also began with the Project as a Divinity student and then served as our Assistant Director. Here, as Director of the Emory Center for Law and Religion, she has shown how the Religious Land Use and Institutionalized Persons Act of 2000 has become a vital part of the toolbox of civic life as religious communities create space for themselves in America.

Rahul Mehrotra has been such a gift as a colleague, a practicing architect, thinking about today's cities and leading students to the dense suburbs of Mumbai every January. He had invited me to join them when we hit on the idea of going to the Kumbha Mela instead. Thus began a venture that was interdisciplinary in the widest sense. The pop-up Ephemeral Megacity gave both of us as city-scholars a new sense of the "kinetic" city in our age. I didn't understand my old Banaras as a kinetic city, although I knew it was changing, perhaps in unrecognizable ways. However, Lawrence Cohen's exploration of the "Corridor" has made me see what I didn't want to see: a wide path of plazas and shops that the government of India created from the Ganga waterfront to Shiva's Vishvanātha Temple, all in the interest of development, hygiene, and mobility. The Corridor had been plowed through winding lanes, old neighborhoods, and tiny wayside temples where pilgrims had long made their way. I had seen sickening photographs of the bulldozers at work. The central city I had mapped so carefully was now full of dead-ends and the heavily policed walls of the Corridor. Lawrence has created a contemporary addendum to *Banaras, City of Light*.

■

Pluralism has been part of our work together, all of us. My earliest interfaith involvement was with the World Council of Churches (WCC). In the 1980s, I became a member of its working group on "Dialogue with People of Living Faiths and Ideologies," a long name for a process of engagement with people in multireligious societies where living together was increasingly imperative: Indonesia, India, Birmingham, Mauritius, and Malaysia. Wesley Ariarajah was my mentor and companion in this work and a theologian who spoke deeply to Christians living as neighbors with people of other faiths. Anant Rambachan was part of the global interfaith work of the WCC, bringing a Hindu perspective to so many of our contexts of dialogue and indeed to the General Assembly in Canberra. As the first Hindu professor of religion at the Lutheran St. Olaf College, he taught generations of students by his very presence as a Hindu philosopher in a religion department. Working from a starting point in Advaita Vedanta, his essay explores the ways in which this non-dualism speaks to the meanings of pluralism.

My work with the WCC led me to a lifelong interest in the many dimensions of interfaith relations. In 1983, I worked with Devaki Jain to convene a weeklong conference on Women, Religion, and Social Change with women from around the world who identified in some way as religious and were committed to foundational social change. Among those who helped us think this through was Sissela Bok, a philosopher who was keenly attuned to the tensions between the Gandhian and Quaker participants who advocated for non-violence and the participants from South Africa and Guatemala who lived in the midst of violent upheavals and could not find non-violence as a way forward. We reconvened twenty years later, older and still living in a world of upheaval and polarization. As a "practical philosopher," Bok's analysis of the value of deep dialogue in the midst of conflict is a profound affirmation of what I had hoped we were doing. Blu Greenberg, founding president of the Jewish Orthodox Feminist Alliance, joined in many of our women's meetings and her essay here appreciates from a personal point of view the importance of opening a space for dialogue in the midst of conflict. Dialogue is not easy which is precisely why it is important.

Chatsumarn Kabilsingh was at both conferences, speaking of the importance of Buddhist women taking on roles of religious leadership in Thai society. In 1983, she was professor at Thammasat University, but by 2003 she had stepped into that Buddhist leadership role and been ordained as a *bhikkhuni*. Her name is now Dhammananda, and she has broken barriers in Thai Buddhism and gone on to create an international community of Buddhist women.

The Pluralism Project began in the early 1990s at a time when the focus on fundamentalism and terrorism was preeminent in the minds of many scholars. The Fundamentalism Project at the University of Chicago was an important landmark in public understanding of conservative and radical movements around the world. It sparked my countervailing interest in exploring where people were coming together in local initiatives, in organizations, and in the growing movements I would call the "interfaith infrastructure." Eboo Patel met me on my patio in 1999. We agreed that interfaith dialogue needed to move from the circle of international elders and leaders to become the work of young people. The Interfaith Youth Core (IFYC) caught the imagination of college students. It grew exponentially and, as the young leaders grew, it became Interfaith America. The Pluralism Project, a research project with its base in the University, grew alongside IFYC.

Patrice Brodeur was an early participant as a student, then as a young professor where he started the Pluralism Project at Connecticut College. His scholarly research led to a major center for pluralism in Vienna and then to a Canadian Research Professorship in Montreal. He here has suggested "pluralism" as pedagogy and epistemology for studying religion in a world in which all of us are co-located. Duncan Williams began his research in American Buddhism with the Pluralism Project and has become a Sōtō Zen priest, a distinguished scholar and professor, and author of *American Sutra* on Buddhists in the internment camps. Nancy Khalil came to the Project as a doctoral student in Anthropology and has been involved in the case study initiative from the beginning. Her fearless research is on display in her trenchant critique of "inclusion" in the rush toward "diversity, equity, and inclusion" as the gold standard for institutions of higher education today.

It is a joy to have two of my more recent students in this volume. Halah Ahmad, a Palestinian Muslim student from Wisconsin, recalls times in our journey together at Harvard when she realized how much pluralism, the encounter of commitments, requires the energetic willingness to gain knowledge of the other. From her experience of feeling "invisible" during the 2014 war in Gaza to her summer work with volunteers in a refugee camp in Greece, she learned that general respect for diversity is insufficient. Listening and learning is critical, as I myself found as former faculty advisor to the Palestinian Solidarity Committee. Pranati Parikh, an Indian American Hindu, had started to learn Sanskrit as a high school student in rural Missouri and I knew her from her very first days at Harvard. She enrolled in "Hindu Worlds of Art and Culture" which I thought might be superfluous for Pranati. On the contrary, she writes about the excitement of discovering, as a Hindu, forms of Hinduism defined not by a set of principles, but by a "dazzling and complicated multiplicity" of images, narratives, questions, and answers.

Elinor Pierce and Jennifer Howe Peace have worked with me over many years now and are cherished partners in the work of the Pluralism Project. Ellie was one of our first researchers working in Fremont, California where a Methodist Church and an Islamic Society had purchased property together and were building side by side. So began the kind of longitudinal work that culminated in deciding to create case studies for teaching. Over the years, Ellie has researched and written all of our Pluralism Project cases, at every step embodying the care, diligence, and dialogical method that has been our ethical compass. Through these case studies, Ellie has essentially been teaching with me for the past decade. Since her days as professor of Interfaith Studies at Andover Newton Theological School, Jennifer Howe Peace has been at the forefront of creating the field of interfaith studies in the American academy through her publications and leadership in the American Academy of Religion. Her work spans theological thinking and interfaith engagement. As senior advisor to the Pluralism Project she has taught case studies with me at Harvard Divinity School. While she will continue to advise the Project, Jenny is now pursuing her passion for the arts and social change through ceramics. She is on a new path, but still we travel together.

Gratitude is the first and last word that I offer to all of you who have come this far with me.

· PART I ·

ENCOUNTERS:

CO-PILGRIMS AND COLLEAGUES

· Chapter 1 ·

DIANA ECK:
APOSTLE OF PLURALISM

Karen Armstrong

What first drew Diana and me together was our admiration and love for Wilfred Cantwell Smith. Diana had been his prize pupil, but I never had the good fortune to meet him. Yet his books had radically changed my life. I was brought up as an Irish Catholic in England—a very un-British minority; I had then spent seven difficult years as a nun and had left my convent feeling for years very hostile to religion. But Smith's books gave me an entirely new understanding of the nature of faith. Diana, of course, had a very different experience. Her deep study of Hinduism, her love of India, and her devoted commitment to the Pluralism Project, has never diminished her heartfelt devotion to Christianity. She must have made Wilfred really happy. I shall always remember the gusto, joy, and commitment in which she sang in the Memorial Church—hymns that I, with my inbuilt love of the austere Latin Gregorian chant, would always find difficult.

Diana has fully embraced Smith's ecumenism, which urged us all to pursue truth in communion with others. This could never simply be a matter of bonhomie. Smith insisted that the shift from understanding "others" as *they* rather than *we* required "erudition, critical acumen, imaginative sympathy and penetrating understanding" as well as "time, effort, and dedication."[1] We have, he said, to approach religion in humility and love, pursuing truth in communion with others: "To know is to love and true knowing requires loving."[2] But, as we all know, loving is difficult. Ecumenism is never simply an exchange of theological notions. It cannot merely be a nice idea. We are living in an increasingly dangerous and hostile world, linked together more closely than ever before by modern communications. But instead of bringing us together, our sense of self seems to be drawing us perilously apart so that we can sometimes feel oddly estranged. We prefer chatting on our mobile phones to people we like rather than reaching out with sympathy to those who challenge us. But pluralism is now an urgent necessity, and throughout her lifelong pursuit and passionate cultivation of this diversity, Diana has made an incomparable contribution to this crucial quest.

Part of our problem these days is that we still fail to regard one another as equals. In the West, we pride ourselves on the egalitarianism which, we sometimes insist, is the hallmark of our society; it has, we claim, been a gift to humanity making it more fair, just, and equitable than the civilizations of the past. These are fine words, but the West has also done great harm in the world and our own societies are still dangerously stratified. I live in a very pleasant part of London but every day I see people sleeping rough on the streets near my home. And, I believe, matters are even worse in some cities of the United States. Despite our commitment to egalitarianism, we still see ourselves as special and in a separate category and seem to find it impossible to regard some of our neighbors as equal to ourselves.

In the West, we tend to assume that we were pioneers of egalitarianism. But this, of course, is not the case. Long before the modern period, archaeology makes it clear that for millennia in the distant past human beings assiduously cultivated an equality that puts us to shame. Anthropologists argue that for about 40,000 years humans experimented with different forms of social organization. Sometimes they tried to create social hierarchies but always, it seems, they eventually became disillusioned and dismantled them. Indeed, it has been suggested that instead of being less politically committed than we are today, people who lived in stateless societies may have been even more so. Amazonian chiefs, for example, have been calculating politicians, maneuvering in a social environment that seemed deliberately designed to ensure that nobody could ever exercise real political power or lord it over others.

Our societies may pride themselves on egalitarianism without having considered indigenous models and worldviews. When humans are not regarded as special and privileged, or as the dominant species, plants and other animals are understood as equals. Humans are part of that natural world—not its masters. Indigenous societies might be seen as models of egalitarianism in their prohibition of overbearing behavior and the quiet but firm refusal to bow to the authority of others. Among the Inuit, moodiness is equated with hostility and control of temper is a cardinal virtue. So, their egalitarian ethos is conscious, deliberate, and carefully cultivated; its aim is precisely to prevent and forestall the eruption of hierarchical and egotistic tendencies.[3] This ethos is shared—and a matter of individual responsibility. As a member of the !Kung tribe explained to an anthropologist: "Of course we have headmen . . . each of us is headman over himself."[4]

So clearly egalitarianism involves hard work, far beyond bland assertions of equality in the West. Anthropologists have noted the self-effacing behavior of the tribal headman, who is a facilitator rather than a governor or ruler. While self-assertion may be expected in warfare and hunting expeditions, which are essential to their survival, they are also expected to be generous, kind, and free from bad temper. In these contexts, leaders do not issue commands; they simply present their ideas as suggestions. They may try to avoid prominence, giving away possessions and becoming virtually impoverished. The leader's authority and skill are appreciated, rather than an order of prestige and dominance.[5] The leader is called to practice what the Greeks called *kenosis,* the "emptying" of self.

But these principles of indigenous egalitarianism were side-lined during the so-called Axial Age (c. 900 to 200 BCE), when the great civilizations of India, China, Greece, and Rome came into being and these societies became highly stratified. This, however, was also the period of the Buddha, Socrates, the Hindu Upanishads, and the Greek philosophers, who all, in very different ways, tried to revitalize the older egalitarian ethos in what would become the great world religions. In fact, the insights of these Axial sages challenged what we sometimes call "religion" today. As Wilfred Cantwell Smith argued, it was not a question of "belief" or accepting certain theological doctrines. If the Buddha or Confucius were asked if they "believed" in God or the divine, they would probably have courteously replied that this was not an appropriate question. What mattered was how you behaved. The sages all preached a spirituality of empathy and compassion—an ethos that is not always apparent in religion today. Furthermore, you could not confine your benevolence to your own people. Your concern must somehow extend beyond it—ultimately to the whole world. This egalitarian ethos is desperately needed today. Each tradition developed its own version of what is called the Golden Rule: "Do not do to others what you would not have done to you." It requires you to look into your own heart, discover what gives you pain, and then refrain from inflicting this distress on anybody else. For the Axial sages, respect for the sacred rights of all beings—not orthodox belief—was religious. If people behaved with kindness and generosity to their fellows, they could save the world.

We need to reaffirm the original Axial ethos, and perhaps, extend it. In our global world, we must learn to live and behave as though people in remote and less developed countries are as important as ourselves—as indeed they are. Our world is imperiled by the possibility of catastrophic warfare, torn apart by violence and terrorism on a scale that is perhaps unprecedented. But the scriptures tell us to love our "enemies." We cannot simply confine our benevolence to those who are congenial. Each of the Axial traditions developed in societies like our own that were torn apart by warfare and arrogance. Indeed, the first catalyst of religious change was usually a principled rejection of the aggression that the sages perceived all around them. We need to realize that this violence also exists within our own selves and work to transcend it.

The texts also insist that compassion must extend beyond our own people and our own selves to reach the entire world, not omitting a single creature from our radius of concern. Even our so-called enemies. It was this extension of a sympathy that knew no bounds—*not* an intense introspection—that, some of the scriptures tell us, enabled the Buddha to achieve enlightenment. And he did not spend the rest of his life in the yogic position (as the statues of the Buddha might suggest) but spent the next forty years of his life tirelessly helping people—and animals—to deal with their pain. Similarly, the Gospels present Jesus as besieged by desperate suffering people so intensely that he had no time for prayer or relaxation. All the great religious traditions insist upon the importance of empathy and compassion rather than yogic expertise because it takes us beyond our rabid egotism.

A prayer attributed to the Buddha, if repeated, and meditated upon daily, can help us achieve this. He had been approached by forest people who wanted to follow him but who had neither the time nor the capacity to practice yoga. The Buddha smiled and gave them this prayer that would mitigate the egotism that debars humans from the sacred dimension of life:

> Let all beings be happy! Weak or strong, of high, middle, or low estate,
> small or great, visible or invisible, near or far away,
> alive or still to be born—may they all be entirely happy!
>
> Let nobody lie to anybody or despise any single being anywhere.
> may nobody wish harm to any single creature out of anger or hatred!
> let us cherish all creatures, as a mother her only child!
> May our loving thoughts fill the whole world, above, below.
> across—without limit; a boundless goodwill toward the whole world,
> unrestricted, free of hatred and enmity![6]

· Chapter 2 ·

WHEN RELIGION TURNS TOXIC:
MITIGATING POLARIZATION
THROUGH POETIC TRADITION

Ali S. Asani

In her extraordinary study, *Encountering God*, Diana Eck recounts her visit to Nairobi, Kenya, where she met with my parents. After lunch at a local Gujarati restaurant and a quick tour of the city, they took her to the railway station so that she could catch the overnight train to her next destination—Mombasa. As they sat in her compartment waiting for the train to depart, they heard the Islamic call to prayer. My father, always punctual in his prayers, looked at his watch and said to Diana, "It's time to remember God, excuse us." As my parents began the Arabic prayer, Diana, recognizing the beginning of the first chapter of the Quran, *Bimillahir Rahmanir Rahim* ("In the name of God, the Most Compassionate, the Most Merciful"), bowed her head. Although she did not understand Arabic, she joined them in "the spirit of the prayer" for, after all, they were praying to the same God.[7]

Sometime later, during one of her sermons at a church in Lexington, Massachusetts, Diana reflected on this incident, pointing out to the congregation that the God of three great monotheistic faiths—Judaism, Christianity, and Islam—was in essence one God, and that the word Allah did not mean a specifically "Muslim God," noting that Arab Christians use the same word when they pray. She recounts that after the service, one of the congregants challenged her claim that God and Allah were one and the same: "[O]ur God includes Christ and the Holy Spirit. Allah could not possibly be the same God."

As she and the congregant discussed the issue further over coffee, they explored three possible ways to think about this: the exclusivist ("there was only one God, the Christian one, so the Muslim one was false"); the inclusivist ("Christians see God in God's fullness while Muslims have only a partial less clear idea of God"); and the pluralist ("there is only God whom both Christians and Muslims understand only partially because God transcends our understanding"). They concluded that the third, the "pluralist," was most satisfying since "it would leave room for the self-understanding of both Christian and Muslim," a fact reflected in the Arabic phrase—*Allahu Akbar*, or, literally, God is greater than any human understanding of God.[8]

For decades, through her teaching, research, preaching and personal example, Diana has been an eloquent and powerful advocate for pluralism, engaging with and understanding difference: "building bridges instead of walls." At the same time, she acknowledges that religiously exclusivist forces have also become a dominant form of expression in political and social life in various parts of the world and therefore pose a major barrier to the nurturing of pluralist societies. This is especially true in South Asia where, under British colonialism, peoples, notwithstanding their ethnic, linguistic, social, and sectarian differences, were categorized into distinctive communities based on European definitions of religion.[9] As categories, such as Mohammedanism (the common European term for Islam in the late nineteenth and early twentieth centuries), Hinduism, Buddhism, and so on, became entrenched and infused with nationalist ideas and sentiments, Hindus and Muslims came to be conceived of as two distinctive nations, leading to the demand for Partition.

Since their creation, both India and Pakistan have succumbed to forms of exclusivist religious nationalism that seek to marginalize and even eliminate "the religious other." Particularly egregious has been the dramatic rise of forms of nationalism invoking religion as the yardstick to determine who belongs to the nation. The two nations have also witnessed growing hostility and intolerance, both between as well as within religious communities, resulting in widespread political turmoil and societal ruptures. The resulting marginalization and violence have become an existential threat for religious minorities in the region.

The hatred, mob violence, and pogroms unleashed by political and social forces that seek to "Islamize" Pakistan or "Saffronize" (Hinduize) India, have led to widespread critique of religion. For example, journalist Ziauddin Sardar writes,

> Allegedly Pakistan was created in the name of Islam. But Islam in Pakistan is not a faith or a worldview, but an ideology. Like all ideologies, it is an inversion of truth: whereas Islam, in theory at least, is about justice and equality, in Pakistan it functions as a mechanism for oppression. In other words, it has gone toxic . . . almost everything that carries the adjective "Islamic" in Pakistan is associated with puritanism, intolerance, chauvinism, and phobia of the Other.[10]

Sardar's comments on Pakistan are equally applicable to the recent situation in contemporary India where Hindutva ideology, promoted by the Bharatiya Janata Party (known as the BJP) and its partners, prevails in political and social circles, resulting in the marginalization and disenfranchisement of large segments of the population, not to mention rampant Islamophobia.

How does one create bridges of understanding and practice pluralism in such a deeply divided and polarized context? In South Asia, many are turning to the rich heritage of the region's precolonial poetic traditions. Although excluded from the formal curricula of colonial and post-colonial educational systems—since they do not conform to notions about what constitutes religion or "proper" literature—these poetic traditions have for centuries played a central role in shaping ethical, moral, philosophical, and spiritual life in South Asia.

Often boxed into distinctive categories, such as Sufi, Bhakti, and Sant, these traditions actually share many overlapping characteristics. The poetic knowledge they embody and convey through a diverse range of languages is not only discursive but, unlike Western poetry, is also meant to be felt or experienced through musical performance. Hence, Nosheen Ali has aptly referred to it as *mannkahat* ("heart-mind" knowledge).[11] These traditions are also characterized by a strong discourse of dissent in which poets reject identity markers that discriminate between people based on religion, class, and caste. They critique and defy religious authorities—Hindu and Muslim—who arrogate power for themselves on the basis of their learning and thus promote ritualistic, legalistic, and intellectual orthodoxies that restrict salvation to only a few. Instead, these ancient poetic traditions invite audiences of all backgrounds to understand what it means to be human and the human-divine relationship through the all-encompassing lens of love. They extol the transformative powers of *ishq* or *prem*, a multi-faceted term interpreted as passion, devotion, ardor, commitment, longing or yearning for the Divine Beloved. For these poets, *ishq* is a primordial link that connects the divine to all of creation. Tasting or experiencing the nectar of *ishq* is the central purpose of worldly existence and draws each of us closer to the divine so that we may be enlightened by beholding "the face of God" that surrounds us and exists deeply within all of us.

One can easily understand how the non-binary worldview of these ancient poetic traditions and their key messages—self-empowerment, critique of those in power and their hypocrisy, social inequity, the importance of individual inner search—would resonate with those who are alienated by contemporary movements of religious exclusivism and their discourse of hatred and "othering." In this regard, Anand Taneja has remarked on the phenomenal rise of interest in Urdu—a language that has been marginalized in North Indian state-run schools because of its "Muslim" roots—and Urdu poetry in contemporary Delhi among Muslims and non-Muslims. As one student attending an Urdu workshop put it, it "allowed her to understand and express the complexities of being human."[12] This upsurge, Taneja observes, is "happening at the same time as an authoritarian government committed to religious nationalism tries to mold India into a homogenous Hindu country and attempts to crush all dissent in the name of the nation."[13]

By way of example, I would like to turn to Salman Ahmad, a Pakistani guitarist and vocalist and his mobilization of the poetic traditions of Pakistan as a means to counter the rise of religious fascism.[14] Salman, who was born in Pakistan, developed a passion for rock music during his teenage years when his family lived in Rockland, New York. In the 1980s when Salman returned to Pakistan to study medicine, the government of military dictator General Zia ul-Haqq launched its campaign to "Islamize" the country through highly controversial legislation that marginalized Muslim and non-Muslim minorities and impinged on the rights of women. Unfortunately for Salman, "Islamization" entailed a ban on music and musical instruments, elements essential to his being. Therefore, Salman and some of his fellow students, choosing to ignore the ban, arranged an "unofficial" concert on campus. Consequently, a student militia of *Jama'at-i Islami,* a right-wing political party allied with Zia's military regime, stormed the concert, and smashed his guitar. This incident forced Salman to confront the divisive forces that were dominating Pakistani society through a control of cultural and religious expression. Undeterred by this "religious fascism," Salman continued playing at underground concerts.

Salman's talents as a guitarist brought him to the attention of the renowned Sufi musician, Nusrat Fateh Ali Khan, who in the 1990s was experimenting with incorporating western instrumentation and music into the *qawwali,* the iconic Sufi music of South Asia. Although some purists regarded Nusrat's experiments to be a blasphemous betrayal of tradition, Nusrat himself favored this fusion of musical traditions since he believed that it was a powerful way to celebrate and express human diversity through music, an impulse he believed was in accordance with the Quranic precept that God loves diversity.[15] The two years Salman spent under Nusrat's tutelage sparked an interest in learning more about Sufi and other poetic traditions, particularly those associated with Bullhe Shah, the eighteenth-century Sufi saint, popularly acclaimed as one of the greatest mystic poets of the Punjab. Bullhe Shah's poetry was infused with the love of God and humanity, and challenged narrow and intolerant interpretations of religion, as well as labels related to caste, religious creed, and gender. Under Nusrat's tutelage, Salman also began to appreciate the poetry of the iconic poet-philosopher, Allama Muhammad Iqbal. Salman's newly-found appreciation of Punjabi and Urdu poetry inspired the creation of a new genre of Muslim devotional expression, Sufi Rock, which fused western rock music with lyrics from traditional South Asian Sufi poetry. About Nusrat's influence, Salman writes:

> Nusrat paved the way for my band Junoon to take the risks we did when we married electric guitars to *bhangra* drums and *dhol* grooves while chanting traditional Sufi texts considered sacred by the orthodox.[16]

The lyrics of his first Sufi Rock song, *Saain* ("Lord, Master") were written in collaboration with Sabir Zafar and performed by his band, Junoon. Musically, the piece opens with the notes of the *adhaan*, the Islamic call to prayer, followed by lyrics representing the pleas of a yearning lover to God. Some segments of Pakistani society, particularly those who regarded western culture and, in particular, its popular music as being non-Islamic reacted negatively to this composition. "Why are you using the word of God in a westernized way? You are not showing respect!" were some of the criticisms leveled. The lyrics of Junoon's first major album, *Azadi* ("Freedom"), dedicated to Nusrat, not only referred to traditional Punjabi Sufi mystical themes, such as the famous Sohni-Mahival folk romance, but also contained excerpts from Sir Muhammad Iqbal's famous poem on *"khudi"* ("the self"), which focuses on the importance of each individual developing their own divinely bestowed potential so that they could truly become God's vicegerents on earth.

Alongside mystical themes, Junoon's songs, inspired by the well-established Sufi tradition of speaking truth to power, addressed issues such as political corruption. In 1998, when India and Pakistan set off nuclear explosions, Junoon released *"Sayonee"* ("Friend"), a song calling for peace between the peoples of India and Pakistan. By highlighting the similarities and affinities of the cultures and traditions of the two nations, the song provided an alternative to the discourse of mutual demonization favored by nationalist politicians of both countries. Although, for a while, members of Junoon were labeled as traitors and accused of blasphemy and corrupting the country's youth by some right-wing religious groups, the band's compositions were enthusiastically received by audiences all across South Asia and the South Asian diaspora. *Azadi*, for example, was the highest selling album in Pakistan, Bangladesh, and India in 1998 and 1999. With over 25 million albums sold, Junoon won several awards and distinctions, including UNESCO's Award for Outstanding Achievement in Music and Peace in 1999.

The widespread appeal of Sufi Rock is undoubtedly based on its remarkable capacity to bridge various divides and differences in a highly polarized society. Among the youth in Pakistan, it bridged the class divide between *burgers* and *mailas*. The *"burgers*," who were economically well-off, westernized, and spoke predominantly English, identified with Sufi Rock as it expressed their composite identities—cosmopolitan yet embedded in a culture with distinctively Pakistani roots. For the so-called *"mailas,"* who were economically less well-off and primarily spoke Urdu, it affirmed the value of their culture and traditions by casting them within a broader global context. Junoon's use of Sufi poetry resonated deeply across the border since many Indians, Muslim and non-Muslim, are well versed in Sufi and related poetic traditions. For example, Bullhe Shah, whose Punjabi poetry formed the basis of some of Junoon's compositions, is a poet who enjoys universal popularity among Muslims, Sikhs, and Hindus in India, especially in the Urdu-Hindi-Punjabi belt. Finally, Sufi Rock gave public voice to popular Sufi poetry and music, a tradition that had been silenced by culturally dry and politicized Islam promoted by the regime of General Zia, and later the Taliban and their allies.

Junoon's success with fusing different musical and poetic traditions to create Sufi Rock inspired the creation of several other rock bands in Pakistan, including Noori, Mekaal Hasan Band (MHB) and Fuzon. Following in its footsteps, Coke Studio, a highly successful popular Pakistani TV show and international franchise sponsored by Coca-Cola, continues to bring together performers representing the diversity of Pakistan's different poetic traditions, in studio performances. Coke

Studio embraces the belief that many gaps within a highly polarized society can be bridged through powerful and meaningful music, emphasizing common values. Significantly, the show promotes itself as the "Sound of the Nation," alluding to its unifying role in a fractious nation.

The poetic arts can play an important role in humanizing what political discourses of colonialism and nationalism have destroyed, and dehumanized. They do this by connecting us with ancient poetic wisdom on what it means to be human and teaching us ways of thinking, seeing, and acting in the world, conscious of our shared values and histories. Such ancient traditions have survived for a reason which we would do well not to forget. In a highly polarized world, they remind us that ultimately, notwithstanding our many differences, we remain existentially one soul, from one universal source. As my friend and mentor, Diana, writes:

> God is at the center of our very being, and the heart of the believer, so Muslims say, is the throne of the Compassionate God. If we glimpse God in this way, there is no reason we cannot stand together, all of us, in prayer.[17]

· Chapter 3 ·

ENCOUNTERING OURSELVES:
DIANA'S PATHBREAKING WORK IN SERVICE OF A NEW RELIGOUS AMERICA

Preeta D. Bansal

Diana Eck was one of the first people—indeed, perhaps the first person—who made it safe and enlivening for me to begin exploring my Indian heritage in any real way. Having grown up in Nebraska as part of the first wave of Indian immigrants to America after passage of the 1965 Immigration Act (the year of my birth), the only seemingly viable option up until the time I came to Harvard in 1982 was to "assimilate or die." And assimilate I did—even to the point that at some level (no kidding!) I thought I was blonde like all the Nebraskans of Germanic-Scandinavian stock around me.

I may be misremembering, but I've always recalled that my class entering Harvard in 1982 had only about six Indian Americans—though there were several more international students who had gone to high school in India. That's hard to believe now, just a few decades later, when Indian Americans and Asian Americans are so numerous on Ivy League campuses—so much so that the US Supreme Court just a few months ago struck down Harvard College's admission policy because, among other reasons, its race-conscious criteria disadvantaged Asian Americans who would otherwise be a dominating presence on campus absent the policy.

But 1982 was just one generation after the passage of the 1965 Immigration Act, which had eliminated the last remaining color line in US law—the bar on immigration from Asia—following the Civil Rights

Act of 1964. And so second-generation Indian Americans (or the 1.5 generation in my case) were still mostly young, were barely entering college in small numbers, and remained somewhat of a novelty.

In that context, I came across the Core Curriculum course, "Foreign Cultures 12—Sources of Indian Civilization," taught by Diana Eck. Though I entered a detailed, seemingly obscure world of story, myth, and iconography that felt as strange and unfamiliar to my overly rational mind as anything else that I might have randomly encountered, I was mesmerized by Diana's light, gracious presence—especially by the vim and vigor with which she pronounced Hindu and Sanskrit phrases, spoke warmly and comfortably with students of all backgrounds, and conveyed her passion for encounters with the Divine in all their many forms. Diana's presence and being-ness planted a seed in me that would ripen many decades later, in my journey to myself.

9/11: A NEW RELIGIOUS AMERICA

Fast forward nearly two decades later. Following the terrorist attacks of 9/11 and the pending talk of a "clash of civilizations," Diana's book *A New Religious America* recognized that there was a "marbling" of civilizations rather than a clash. She pointed out that two generations after the passage of the 1965 Immigration Act, America had become the most religiously diverse nation on earth. "Just as the end of the Cold War brought about a new geopolitical situation," she wrote, "the global movements of people have brought about a new geo-religious reality." And those new arrivals to America were connected to their homelands and cultures as never before, given the changing telecommunications landscape.

America had always been a religiously diverse nation, she noted—comprised originally of indigenous peoples, European settlers from diverse religious traditions (Spanish and French Catholics, British Anglicans and Quakers, Sephardic Jews, and Dutch Reformed Christians), and enslaved African Americans of various indigenous and Muslim backgrounds. That initial diversity had been supplemented by the early 1900s' wave of immigration—comprised of Chinese and Japanese miners who brought with them Buddhism, Taoism, and Confucianism;

Eastern European Jews; Irish and Italian Catholics; Christian and Muslim immigrants from the Middle East; and Punjabi Sikhs from India.

Now at the turn of the twenty-first century, drawing on her research from the Pluralism Project at Harvard, Diana wrote that following the post-1965 wave of immigration, there were new arrivals dramatically changing the religious and cultural landscape of America: Buddhists from Thailand, Vietnam, Cambodia, China, and Korea; Hindus from India, East Africa, and Trinidad; Muslims from Indonesia, Bangladesh, Pakistan, the Middle East, and Nigeria; Sikhs and Jains from India; Zoroastrians from both India and Iran; new Jewish traditions from Russia and the Ukraine (adding to intra-religious diversity); and new Christians (consisting of peoples from Latin America and the Philippines; Vietnamese Catholics; Chinese, Haitian, and Brazilian Pentecostal communities; and Korean Presbyterians).

I remember reading Diana's book soon after 9/11, feeling invigorated and "seen" more fully than I'd ever felt seen before. She recognized the diversity of America's new arrivals not only in terms of skin tone, but in terms of their broader culture, deepest sources of meaning, and sense of the sacred. At that point, the American political dialogue around diversity focused largely on racial categories defined as either black or white or Hispanic, and here was Diana recognizing a whole new form of diversity coming from post-1965 immigration. Hers was an important insight that touched my heart, because increasingly I was seeking a more solid ground of belonging.

On that fateful day of 9/11, I was winding up my service as New York Solicitor General, where I had an office with a beautiful straight-on view of the Twin Towers. My life up until that point—without really intending or planning it to unfold in quite that way—had turned out to be the classic Indian American immigrant story of achievement and hyper-achievement—perhaps in part as a protective response to early experiences as an extreme minority and "outsider" growing up in the heartland. I had graduated from Harvard College and Harvard Law School. I had worked at the highest branches of the US government—as a law clerk for a

Supreme Court Justice, in the White House, and in the Department of Justice. I had been an attorney for one of the nation's top law firms. And when I became New York State Solicitor General, I became one of the highest ranking Indian American public officials in the country at the time, and I became the first Indian American to argue a case before the US Supreme Court.

And yet, with all the achievement-based expectations of the emerging Indian American community, and as a public face of it, I knew that a life of achievement was not by itself a life of meaning—or even belonging, for that matter. I had honed the tools and prepared myself to serve, but I had not yet become the vessel for something deeper and greater than me. And so, I stepped away from my coveted post—a decision I had actually made and announced several days before 9/11. I took a sabbatical, returned to Nebraska, and began by reading as many published works by Gandhi that I could, as well as studying and teaching American constitutional law. As a lawyer, I was drawn to Gandhi's background in law and turn to spiritual activism, his vision of social justice and sense of service. I sought to understand how best I could serve with the skills and tools I had developed. And at this time, I read Diana Eck's book, *A New Religious America*.[18]

A NEW INTERRELIGIOUS AND SPIRITUAL AMERICA

For the next decade, I deepened my study of many other religions. I read as much as I possibly could. I returned to the East Coast after my sabbatical in Nebraska—around the same time that the first Hindu temple was built in Omaha, Nebraska (with my parents among the founding leaders)—marking a dramatic shift in the religious landscape of the American heartland, as presciently foreseen by Diana Eck.[19]

Seemingly serendipitously, but perhaps providentially, I was appointed by the US Senate in 2003 to serve on the Commission on International Freedom, a bipartisan federal human rights agency, and later became its chairperson. In that capacity, I had opportunities to meet with extraordinary people of faith (lay people as well as leaders) from across the world—from Catholic cardinals and archbishops in China, Bangladesh, Iraq, and the US, to the Dalai Lama, to Falun Gong practitioners, Jewish leaders, political prisoners and persecuted religious minorities, Southern Baptist convention heads, members of the Bahá'í faith, and leading Imams in Saudi Arabia, Afghanistan, Uzbekistan, Syria, and Turkey. I advised on the drafting of the Iraqi and Afghan constitutions to ensure human rights and religious freedom guarantees.

Like most people in these official policy settings, I was working, serving, and seeking greater meaning during this period with the tools that were well-developed within me—my left-brain analytical skills. I hadn't learned yet to tap into a deeper, more sacred, and enduring source of wisdom beyond the intellect alone.

There's an old parable where someone is intently searching the ground for dropped keys near a lamppost. A constable comes up to the person and starts helping with the search, unsuccessfully. Finally, the constable asks, "Are you sure you dropped the keys here?" And the searcher responds, "No, I dropped them across the street." To which the obvious reply: "So why are you looking over here then?" "Because," the searcher says, "the light is much better here."

The human tendency that this parable illustrates has actually come to be known as the "streetlight effect"—an observational bias where people only look for whatever they are searching for by looking where it is easiest or where they know to look. The truth is, answers to the deepest questions (including religious and spiritual questions) require us to look in the dark. But we lack the tools to search inside the unlit spaces where the key really can be found—inside ourselves.

For me, this tool came in 2012 when I came upon my first ten-day silent meditation retreat in the Vipassana tradition. Like all transformative experiences, I didn't even know what I had been looking for over so many years until I found it. There's a saying that "when the seed is ready, the fertilizer appears." Now that I was ready, I found that in those ten days of simply observing respiration and body sensation, I experienced for the first time what sages and mystics of all faith traditions have been saying for millennia, and what modern science and quantum physics have only finally verified in the past century—that all matter (including our bodies) is illusory in that it is constantly shifting, dissolving, and reforming into a new mass every nanosecond. Matter is comprised of ever-changing wavelets.

By focusing entirely on and observing bodily sensation, I caught a momentary glimpse and *an embodied knowing* of the reality of a dissolved self and a dissolved ego. I was blessed to receive a fleeting but deeply felt sense that the same forces and the same subatomic particles that are swishing inside and outside of our bodies—and constantly arising and passing away—are the same forces and subatomic particles that comprise the cosmos and all other living beings. We are an interconnected organism, and every interaction I have with a so-called "other" is an interaction I am having with myself.

Think about that for a second as an ethical precept—every interaction I have is with myself. It's not just that I am my brother's keeper, or that I should do unto others what I would have them do unto me. More fundamentally, it's that I *am* my brother, and what I do to others I am in fact doing to myself.

At long last, I experienced a profound sacred or divine encounter when I was least looking for it! The spiritual seeds that Diana had planted in me by her warm, embracing presence when I was a student in 1982 found safe space for nascent expression. I personally had accessed a spiritual home—not in the stories, myths, iconography, or stone figures of religion—but in a living Vedanta (not unlike a living Christ, a living Dharma, or a living *Qi*). I found it in the practice of silence, surrender, and non-attachment, especially through meditation and yoga—practices which in turn point me to a life of service.

As Diana reminded me when we met in more recent years, I have the privilege of coming from a spiritual tradition in which these tools are at the core, not simply at the fringe—and where a direct personal relationship with the Divine spirit, unmediated by priests or others, is encouraged and not simply tolerated. It is a set of tools that does not lead us away from the world, but in fact draws us to a more engaged, peaceful, and effective interaction with and service in the world. And, above all, it leads us to embrace the spiritual "other" as a brother or a mother.

I am grateful for the planted seeds and encouragement Diana has offered throughout the years to me—and to so many other students of Indian American or other origins—at critical points of our lives, as both immigrants seeking belonging and as spiritual seekers. She has been instrumental in my journey home—encountering both the Divine and myself.

· Chapter 4 ·

AT HOME WHERE WE LIVE:
MY LIFE IN PARALLEL TO DIANA'S

Francis X. Clooney, SJ

Diana Eck has been a welcome and gracious colleague during my nearly twenty years at Harvard. An experienced and insightful faculty colleague, Diana has been easy to work with in Admissions, on doctoral committees, in Divinity School searches, and on the Committee on the Study of Religion. Even earlier, of course, during my twenty-plus years at nearby Boston College, we met a few times, and certainly I knew of her scholarship—*Banaras: City of Light* was a groundbreaking book, and so many of us in those days used in class that wonderful little book, *Darśan*.

We have lived and worked in Boston/Cambridge our entire professional lives, Diana at Harvard, myself neatly dividing my decades into half at Boston College, half at Harvard. I'd like to think that the synergy goes deeper: there is a certain synergy in our views of our vocations as writers, teachers, and builders of community.

I am a few years younger than Diana. I was in high school in the mid- to late 1960s, graduating from college in 1973, and started my grad program in South Asian Languages and Civilizations at the University of Chicago only in 1979, after the long seminary training of a Jesuit and my ordination as a Catholic priest.

Diana has written vividly of her earlier and later stays in Varanasi. My own first immersion in an Asian and Hindu-Buddhist culture began in 1973 when, at age twenty-two and a month after college graduation, I flew from New York to Delhi to Kathmandu to begin two years of teaching at St. Xavier's School. I was already five years into Jesuit training at that point, but quite unprepared for immersion into the fascinating culture of the Kathmandu Valley. All at once, I was in the classroom every day, teaching Hindu and Buddhist boys in a variety of subjects, watching over them in study halls, at meals, out on the playing fields—and, most importantly, learning from them. They took me off campus, to celebrate Siva Ratri by a night trek over to Pasupati, and to visit the great stupas in Bodhnath and Swayambhunath. We went together to the grand coronation in 1975 of Nepal's Hindu king, Bhirendra. All this was a mix of basic human encounters and friendships, person to person, at a time when I, future text scholar, had given even the *Bhagavad Gita* only a cursory reading. I was deeply changed by my two years in Nepal, even if I was only getting started on my lifelong learning from Hinduism. Like Diana, I've had a sense that life is a journey, a pilgrimage on which we can only map our time and place at the moment, but with a sense that we are heading toward a sacred, holy goal. Banaras in her life, Kathmandu in mine, holy places whence sprang ideas and insights for a lifetime.

AT HOME AND ABROAD

Diana is blessed with a sense of space and place. We see this of course in her first book, *Banaras: City of Light*, all the way to *India: A Sacred Geography*. She mapped her own life in terms of places, from Bozeman all the way to Banaras; travel, over time, is always a theme. My own journey might, I suppose, be labeled the less resonant, *From Brooklyn to Mylapore: On Pilgrimage*. It would not be impossible to write interestingly of the Borough Park neighborhood where I was born. In my father's childhood there it hosted a great mingling of Jews and Irish Catholics. But I was only a month old when we ferried over to Staten Island, a quiet and homogenous place in those days, hardly interreligious at all.

Even on a local level, Diana has paid attention to place, in her work at the Pluralism Project. She took to heart what many of us knew and then passed by, the fact of many religious spaces near at hand when we walk the campus and venture into neighboring cities and towns. *A New Religious America* was a pioneering project that shed light on the changing nature of the United States, as the "religious other" has become our neighbor, co-worker, friend wherever we are. Add to all that Diana's collaborative work on the Kumbh Mela, in Harvard's multidisciplinary study of that astonishing festival, millions of people descending on one holy site in so short a time. As I recall, during that admirable project I was entirely immersed in directing the Center for the Study of World Religions, and trying, rather idealistically, to help Harvard Divinity School realize that it needed the Center to be a center, hearth, home to the school community. I was too much concerned about cultivating a home *here* to participate in learning *there*.

For me, a sense of place—of home—has played out in various ways. Ever since I went to Kathmandu in 1973 and returned to New York two years later, the metaphor of journey-forth, crossing-over, and return-home had real life force to it. I was at home in New York; by grace, I felt at home in Kathmandu, and later in Madras. But I could always still return home, where I had begun. New York and then Boston were still home, but now with a difference. Even in my writing in the field of comparative theology, I often use the metaphor of crossing over. For me, reading commentaries in a Sanskrit or Tamil theological tradition is a manner of crossing over, intellectually and spiritually, into other great traditions which, after visiting, one returns home surely changed.

Though Diana and I have both traveled a lot, we are also deeply rooted in the places where we live. She was for some twenty years Master (now called Faculty Dean) of Lowell House, again and again building community among every new group of students. I have helped out in a single Catholic parish, Our Lady of Sorrows in Sharon, Massachusetts, for over twenty-six years, working with six pastors over that time, and witnessing a generation and more of parishioners come, settle in, bring the parish to life, and then quietly draw back into retirement and old age. The ceremonies of college life are marked by comings and goings; a parish witnesses baptisms and confirmations, marriages, and in the end anointings for the sick and dying, and funerals.

I was never a faculty dean, but I have taken up some opportunities to build community at Harvard. As I already hinted above, when I was

Center Director, my key metaphor was that of the "center," rather than the themes of our many discussions, lunches, and dinners, visiting lecturers, conferences, etc. My sense of place meant that the lovely, contemplative space of the Center really was a center—hearth, home—a place to gather for all conversations and just ordinary talking, for meals and feasts, for prayer and contemplation too. One of my first acts as director was to turn the director's office into a meditation room, finally restoring to the Center a contemplative space such had been lost nearly fifty years earlier. The third-floor space above the Center's living space had in the 1960s been turned into a library, in those early days deemed to be more necessary than a meditation room.

Like Diana, I live in Cambridge, and I was happy to have hosted many a Center festivity at my home, and also monthly Mass and supper gatherings for the Catholic students of Harvard Divinity School and beyond.

THE TIMES OF OUR LIVES

Diana and I have both been inspired to speak of our journeys along the broad and narrow pathways of interreligious learning. We both know that we have to be somewhere, be rooted, at home, if we are to teach, write, gather community, our feet on the ground.

I welcomed her book-length autobiography, *Encountering God*, when it appeared in 1993, and was pleased to be a member of the panel we arranged at the meeting of the Society for Hindu-Christian Studies at the AAR that same year. In 1996, I published a short autobiographical essay, "In Ten Thousand Places, In Every Blade of Grass: Uneventful but True Confessions about Finding God in India, and Here Too,"[20] a glimpse of my life in Hindu-Christian studies up to that relatively early moment in my career, only twelve years into a now nearly forty-year teaching career. The essay was my story, but just a passing moment in the 500-year history of the Society of Jesus, of which I am but one member. The parallels in recollecting and writing of our journeys have continued: I was pleased to have read recently Diana's typically lucid and vivid essay, "Autobiographical Reflections on Anthropology and Religion,"[21] after completing a third draft of my own autobiography, entitled, *Hindu and Catholic, Priest and Scholar: A Love Story*, a small book which should be in print soon if all goes well.[22] I'd like to think of our recollections as parallel witnesses to personal, intellectual, and spiritual journeys traveled largely in the Boston area where we have lived, studied, and taught from the 1970s on.

Our careers are a bit like parallel lines that have touched now and then—so much in common, but always with a bit of difference: Protestant and Catholic; Montana and New York; North India and South India; Harvard for a whole career, Harvard as the latter part of my career already rooted in Boston College; the geography of pluralism, Catholic life, on campus and in the parishes, in an ever-changing Boston.

Deep down, perhaps my strongest bond with Diana has had to do with balancing Christian identity and a deep commitment to Hindu studies, and in seeking the balancing act as a lifelong work in progress that also holds its own at Harvard. Both of us early on in life found our ways into Hindu wisdom that became part of who we are. Neither of us is an evangelist, neither of us a convert, and yet neither of us has been merely a neutral spectator on worlds of faith.

All along the way Diana has been an inspiration for me in the vocation of a sacramental and incarnational witness, God present now, here in the lives we live, the people we meet, the faiths that enrich our lives, and all this as lived out in the present moment of our journeys, wherever we live, work, love, grow old. I am grateful to Diana for confirming, in her scholarship, teaching, and way of life, how being here and now, grateful for the graces and challenges of a long life, is the basis for whatever wisdom we actually might share with others.

· Chapter 5 ·

CONCLUDING LECTURE FROM AN INTRODUCTORY COURSE IN COMPARATIVE HISTORY OF RELIGION

William A. Graham

After sharing a half-century of academic life at Harvard with Diana Eck, it is a pleasure to contribute to this volume honoring her. Beginning in the late 1960s as PhD students in comparative study of religion and affiliates of the Center for the Study of World Religions, then continuing as members of the Faculty of Arts and Sciences and later also the Faculty of Divinity, we worked, often together, with undergraduate and graduate students in various capacities, including as masters of undergraduate residential colleges. Our most important shared work was in (1) shaping and guiding the undergraduate concentration in the Comparative Study of Religion from its inception in 1974 and (2) teaching undergraduate and graduate students in both comparative and Hindu- or Islamic-studies courses. Among the comparative courses, the first lecture course offered in service of the new concentration was one we taught jointly with our senior colleague Richard R. Niebuhr for nearly a decade from the mid-1970s: Religion 10, "Pilgrimage: A Thematic Introduction to the Study of Religion." In many ways that course established patterns that have marked the varied introductory religion courses that she or I, or others, have offered in Harvard College ever since.

Given this long-shared concern for teaching, it seems appropriate to proffer here the text of my final Harvard lecture in 2018 for my own introductory course, "Scriptures and Classics,"[23] which I offered with small variations some nine times between 1987 and 2018.[24]

As the text of a lecture (slightly condensed and supplied with minimal footnotes), there are many references to texts and issues treated in the course's preceding twenty-four lectures and twelve weekly discussions. Most of these will be clear from context, but it may help to note the texts from which readings were drawn: Upanishads, Bhagavad Gita, Lotus Sutra, Virgil's *Aeneid,* Torah, New Testament, Qur'an; or which were read in their entirety: *Gilgamesh,* Dhammapada, Confucian *Analects* (*Lunyu*), Lao Tzi's *Daodejing, Zhuangzi,* Basho's *Okunohosomichi* (*"Narrow Road to the Deep North"*).

RELIGION 13: "SCRIPTURES AND CLASSICS: ICONIC TEXTS OF RELIGION AND CULTURE," CONCLUDING LECTURE (NO. 25, APRIL 24, 2018)

As we have seen this term, the Jewish and Christian scriptures have defined the category of "scripture" for the Western world since early in the Christian Era. We have also noted how the term "scripture" was, in later centuries, gradually extended to apply to the principal religious texts of other major traditions—beginning at least as early as the twelfth century CE, e.g., by Peter the Venerable, d. 1156, who contrasts *"sacra scriptura"* (Bible] *with "nefaria scriptura"* (Qur'an).[25]

On the other hand, the traditional literary classics of the West include culturally important texts, but rarely ones that are overtly religious in content, beginning with the Greek and Latin classics, gradually including later Western vernacular literary masterpieces and ultimately masterpieces from literatures worldwide. Such "classics" have been formative, even *defining* achievements of particular linguistic, ethnic, regional, national, or cultural traditions. As such, they have also been important as part of the wider intellectual and cultural context of many religious traditions—something that one could argue whether speaking of the masterpieces of Homer or Hesiod, Aeschylus or Euripides, Plato or Aristotle, Ovid or Virgil, Shakespeare or Milton, Cervantes or Pascal, Goethe or

Melville, etc. To these we must add today wider-world texts such as the Ancient Near Eastern (Akkadian and Sumerian) epic of *Gilgamesh;* in Arabic, *The 1001 Nights;* in Persian, Ferdowsi's *Shahnameh;* in Sanskrit, the *Mahabharata, Ramayana,* and Kalidasa's *Shākuntala;* in Chinese, *Journey to the West* and Cao Xueqin's *Dream of the Red Chamber;* or in Japanese, Murasaki's *Tale of Genji.*

In addition, just as most religious scriptures are also cultural classics, some cultural classics that by most criteria are clearly *not* scripture are nonetheless indisputably religious and quite important to major religious communities. For example, Augustine's *Confessions,* Dante's *Divine Comedy,* Teresa of Avila's *Interior Castle,* Maimonides' *Guide for the Perplexed,* Rumi's *Mathnawi,* the Japanese *Kojiki* and *Nihongi,* and Dogen's vernacular *[Kana] Shobogenzo.* (And as we have seen, the three Chinese texts—all classed as *jing* in Chinese—that we read this term (*Analects, Daodejing,* and *Zhuangzi*) also fall easily into this "religious classic" category, if you don't want to call them "scripture").

Our purpose this term has not been, however, to refine categories of text, or even to delineate our two types, scripture and classic, as themselves fully adequate terms for describing the wide variety of truly great texts, religious or literary, around the world. In particular, the examples just cited of religious classics show us that the line between texts that have been what we might call iconic for religious traditions and those that are iconic for cultural traditions is very fuzzy, even sometimes nonexistent. By addressing both clearly *scriptural* texts and clearly major, but arguably *non-scriptural,* texts in an introductory course in the history of religion, I hoped that we might see in the end how much the dichotomy between religion and culture, or religious and secular, fails to be itself a fully useful typology for studying human religiousness in its many forms and sites.

I have at the end of our time together no magic formula that can formally delineate religion and culture as two isolated, separate dimensions of human affairs: I would argue that historically they are even harder to separate than scripture and classics specifically. It is a serious question whether anything of human significance can be *merely* cultural or *merely* religious; so let's not try to distinguish too sharply where the religious and the cultural part ways, whether in our Western traditions, *where we generally think it is clear how they divide*, and much more so in other traditions *where traditionally it has not even been thought important to distinguish religion from culture or "religious" from "secular."* As we have seen, for religious persons, being religious is not something apart from their cultural identities, since being religious is finally about being fully human, and everyone comes to their self-definition or self-awareness with particular cultural as well as religious and psychic backgrounds and predispositions.

Ultimately, while it is useful in studying religion to understand the importance of texts that have functioned historically as scripture, it is less useful to worry too much about whether some foundational texts—the *Analects*, Laozi's *Daodejing* and *Zhuangzi* being prime examples—be called classics or scriptures (in my judgment they have been both), than to recognize that they have functioned both culturally and religiously as defining or iconic texts in a particular historical setting or tradition.

Here a suggestion by James Watts may be helpful: He argues that a scripture is a text "ritualized along three different dimensions:" the semantic, performative, and iconic.[26] This is useful in that while scriptures generally exhibit all three dimensions, most classics lack at least one of them—usually the performative. This tallies with my own sense that Johannes Leipold and Siegfried Morenz got it right in their 1953 book on sacred scriptures,[27] by identifying ritual and especially liturgical functions as the key characteristic of scriptural books, at least in the ancient Mediterranean traditions that their study covered. By contrast, texts that we term "classics," even "religious classics," usually lack most performative (ritual or liturgical) functions that scriptures typically have—even though, as texts to be memorized, recited, and referenced, classics typically take on semantic and iconic roles much the same as scriptures do.

Now all of the preceding can be considered a lot of scholarly pedantry, I realize. (It's said that there are two types of scholars, those who divide everything into two categories, and those who don't. I'd frankly rather be one who doesn't.) Nonetheless, my acknowledged discomfort throughout the term with too neat a distinction between our two types of text was not meant to question the inescapable, necessary work of creating categories and typologies as part of the analytical task of *making sense of the world*—which I take to be the ultimate goal of scholarly endeavor. In scholarship, we seek always better to comprehend, describe, and, yes, imagine, the nature of things, from atomic particles to human societies to ethical imperatives. In doing this we have inevitably to categorize, compare, and contrast; *the question is, how seriously do we take the ultimate validity of these activities?* In studying religion,

- Can we rest with Rudolf Otto's dichotomy of "rational" and "irrational" religiousness?[28]
- Can we agree with Mircea Eliade (or Émile Durkheim) on a categorical division of time, space, and human action into "sacred" and "profane?"[29]
- Are the Weberian distinctions between "world-affirming" ("inner-worldly") and "world-denying" religious orientations generalizable enough to be helpful in comparing religious data?[30]

Many such binary typologies or categorizations are suggestive, sometimes helpful, and often quite seductive. Here one thinks especially of the anthropologist Claude Lévi-Strauss, who used identification of binary oppositions as a key to interpreting the myths underlying human, especially pre-literate human, cultures.[31] Another famous example of such binary divisions would be Isaiah Berlin's contrast (following that of Archilochus) of "hedgehogs," persons who view everything in terms of one great idea, with "foxes," who draw upon a multiplicity of ideas.[32] Such schemas can be instructive: You will remember that I discussed both Franklin Edgerton's binary distinction between "ordinary" and "extra-ordinary" norms in Indian traditions,[33] and also—to take a typology with multiple types—William James' four attributes of mysticism.[34] I do hope, however, that you have taken these always as *provisional* ways to help us think more adequately about phenomena we encounter, *not* definitive or final categories on the order of Platonic ideals.

In the main, I have found very few typologies fully satisfying, even though some are clearly good to think with. I don't want you to leave the course thinking either that scripture and classic, any more than religious and secular, or religion and culture, are binary absolutes that work for historical cases everywhere, even if they seem *apropos* in some, possibly even many, particular instances.

Perhaps I can make this more vivid with a humorous typology suggested to me long ago to highlight the seductiveness of neat classifications, especially binaries, by Harold McCurdy, a psychologist who applied it to theories of personality.[35] This typology comes from that great student of humanity, Ogden Nash, in his poem, "Are You a Snodgrass?"[36] Here he divides humanity into Snodgrasses ("kind" and "intelligent" innocents) and Swozzlers ("ruthless egotists"). These two groups cannot be distinguished "by their outward appearance," but only by their "treatment of the cream and sugar on cereal and berries" (Swozzlers first apply the sugar, then swozzle it away with the cream, while Snodgrasses pour the cream on first, then sprinkle on the sugar to keep it in place).[37] Even if this schema appeals to you more than many a scholarly binary, it still warns against taking any categorical typology as a general truth.

I hope that, if nothing else, this course has problematized the very idea of humanity's (or any smaller grouping) being divided into two (or five, or ten!) main divisions. We have certainly made a number of generalizations here about Buddhists, Hindus, Christians, Jews, ancient Mesopotamians, Romans, Chinese, Japanese, Muslims, etc., but I trust you won't leave this course imagining that you can really understand any of these groups, even in a delimited period or place, in terms of some general set of traits, characteristics, or even beliefs, let alone in terms of some typological category of thought, motivation, or *mentalité*. I hope in particular that the complexities, ambiguities, even contradictions—in short, the all-too-human messiness—of the many human things we have encountered in each of our texts and traditions will have made you not just cautious, but skeptical, of easy typologizing or theorizing, of drawing simple comparisons in order to pigeonhole any person or text, let alone the broader tradition to which he, she, or it belongs.

That being said, let's *not* give up trying to compare and contrast things we encounter or trying to organize them into categories that we can use at least provisionally—ones that we can test or think with as ways of understanding our subject matter. We just can't let neat schemes determine how we see things ultimately; all schemes have to remain expressly provisional, tentative possibilities, hypotheses, trial balloons, *essais de compréhension*—not reliable final conclusions.

This means being open to having our categories, typologies, and comparisons or contrasts "broken"—that is, altered by new facts or insights, or even by more refined typological or comparative efforts. This also means recognizing that scholarly theories and explanations, including historical accounts and literary critiques, are all products of particular periods and contexts as well as particular minds and sensibilities, and thus it is to be expected that every generation has to rethink and reinterpret all theories and accounts in the light of its own time, context, and attendant concerns. *Scholarship is a process, not a product*, and if you have found me tentative, even wishy-washy, about absolute judgments, it's because I am acutely aware of being involved primarily in the *process of refining* description and analysis, *not* in some *ultimate resolution*, let alone in reaching the ultimate (and ultimately unreachable) goal of fully adequate understanding of religious or other human phenomena. Certainly, this holds in all arenas of humanistic study, if nowhere more clearly than in that of the vexed and vexing, but always fascinating study of human religiousness.

But so much for typologies, categories, and academic study of religion—I want in the time remaining to take a brief backward glance at our broader purpose in this course beyond the obvious goal of exposure to major texts and traditions. That broader aim has been to offer a general introduction to religion as a global phenomenon presenting many different faces and forms, past and present.

At various points we have looked at different aspects of religious thought and life; however, because we focused on formative texts rather than many other ubiquitous and equally important religious phenomena, our bias has been toward ideas and problems that present themselves verbally (and thus philosophically or theologically) in the traditions we have considered. Similarly, it has meant a bias toward literate rather than non-literate traditions.

I am keenly aware just how many aspects of religion we have *not* dealt with sufficiently, from ritual acts to social movements to religious institutions to everyday practices. At the same time, we *have* managed to identify and even tackle to some degree some significant ideas and issues that religious persons have wrestled with for millennia:

- *Gilgamesh,* the necessity of dealing with mortality and death, but also the possibility of meaningful human relationships and personal growth or maturation,
- in the Upanishads, the compelling idea of the identity of the human Self and the Transcendent and Eternal,
- in the Bhagavad Gita, the hard discipline of one's *svadharma* and the variety of paths to the realization of some kind of intimate encounter with the Divine,
- in the Dhammapada, the ethical demands of the Buddhist Dharma that in a suffering world can help our progress toward release, or *nirvana,*
- in the Lotus Sutra, guidance for transcending the suffering world through the Bodhisattva path of infinite compassion and enlightenment,
- in the *Analects,* cultivation of virtues such as human-heartedness and filial piety that can transform individuals as well as society,
- in the Daoist texts, the renunciation of average morality and temporal goals for a simpler, deeper, purer, more natural life in alignment with the Way, or Dao,
- in Basho, the proximity, even identity, of aesthetic and religious sensibilities that can find in the phenomenal world multiple openings to enlightenment,
- in *The Aeneid,* the conflict between one's personal desires and one's larger, moral or religious and communal duty and destiny,
- in the Tanakh, God's promises to, covenants with, and demands upon, his erring but ultimately faithful chosen people,

- in the New Testament, the New Covenant as fulfillment of the Old in the good news of the Messiah's self-sacrifice to redeem sinful humanity,
- in the Qur'an, God's enduring mercy and guidance that, together with His moral demands upon His servants, offer salvation beyond the grave.

We could add many other ideas and issues that each of these texts has raised for us; these are only salient examples. And even though the emphases in each of the traditions and texts we have encountered are different, each of them does offer at one point or another some response to shared, universal human dilemmas:

- How do we live a moral and meaningful life?
- What are our responsibilities to our families/communities/fellow human beings?
- Why is suffering such a fundamental fact of existence?
- Whence are we come? And where are we going?
- Is this world of sense perception all there is? Is there a larger reality or order, a something more, that transcends this world and our brief moments in it?
- If so, can we know it? How can we align ourselves with it?
- How do we face death? Is there anything beyond death?

And so on, and on.

I have deliberately shied away from *definitions* of religion, but in the end we might at least say that religion, or religiousness, is that dimension of human experience or activity that has to do with these kinds of questions—fundamental, finally personal questions that no one, not even our own tradition, can answer for us, questions that even scientific inquiry cannot answer for us, questions that have to remain open ones this side of death and eternity.

As I've said more than once: *religiousness* might be said to be, most simply put, the conviction of the reality of Something More beyond our ken—namely, the conviction that there is more to life and the world than meets the eye. That conviction can lead to a quest for answers to fundamental questions such as those just broached. In other words, religiousness has to do with living life in light of a realization of, and commitment to, something that transcends our mundane existence and reality, however that transcendence be conceived—as Truth, as God, as Brahman, as Dharma, as Dao, as Heaven.

I noted how difficult it is to separate scriptures from classics, or religion from culture, and that was really only to say that, in the end, religious thought and action are not divorced from everyday living, moral reasoning, philosophical inquiry, or artistic sensibility, except in the crucial matter of their overt reference to something Transcendent and Eternal upon which our mundane existence is contingent or, in Schleiermacher's terms, "absolutely dependent" (*schlechthinig abhängig*).[38]

The perceived problem for, or obstacle to, finding meaning and living a moral or pious life may be differently identified in different religious and cultural traditions: as suffering, sin, mortality, evil, inequality, ingratitude, blindness, selfish desire, pride, greed, ignorance, contingency, the randomness of fate, etc. But however the problem be identified, it is one that every religious orientation strives to confront and to overcome. In other words, a religious tradition represents the cumulative effort of a given community of persons over time to find a satisfactory way to live, and to live uprightly and abundantly, in the face of the harsh facts of earthly existence and the ultimate questions these inescapable facts raise.

Indeed, religion might be said to be the human activity that tries to give positive answers to Robert Frost's blunt challenge in his little poem entitled "A Question"[39]: "A voice said, Look me in the stars / And tell me truly, men of earth, / If all the soul and body scars / Were not too much to pay for birth." Religious persons have answered this question by saying that the price is not unreasonable because there is something more, something beyond suffering existence and human fallibility—be it beauty, truth, nirvana, or God.

Of course, this does not by any means make the answers of religious traditions perfect. Because they are human affairs, religious traditions are all too flawed and imperfect, as their checkered histories show: inspiration or prophecy is inexorably followed by organization, and with this come efforts to establish an orthodoxy, which leads inevitably to dogmatism and conformity, intolerance, and schism, which create the need for reform or even creation of a new religious vision—and so the cycle begins again. This pattern can be seen as corroboration of Weber's notion of charismatic inspiration being inescapably followed by routinization (*Veralltäglichung*) and bureaucratization, which offers a plausible historical model for the life-cycles of religious traditions.

In the traditions we have considered, we saw how different historical strands of religious thought follow this recurring pattern of inspiration, organization, dogmatization, ossification, then reaction in reform or the creation of new inspiration, and so on. Many examples of this kind of historical progression come to mind, such as that from Vedic and Brahmanic sacerdotalism to the radical questioning of Upanishads and Gita, or from Veda to Buddhist rejection of Veda, and thence to differing traditions of Buddhist religious life; or that from Israelite Pentateuchal religious tradition to the successive emergence of Jewish, Christian, and Muslim traditions; or that from classical Chinese traditions to Daoist, Neo-Confucian, and even Chinese Buddhist and Japanese traditions and their complex histories. . . . (To be sure, things do not fall out so simply in direct lines of influence but involve myriad cross-currents of influence and varied historical circumstances; so, this typology of religious development is itself meant to be suggestive and heuristic, not in any way absolute or universal.)

More could certainly be said, but in closing let me repeat something I spoke about in our very first class, when I said that this would be a course at one level about how we have constructed religion as a discrete entity to be studied (too often apart from culture, or even over against it)—however diverse its manifestations have been, and also a course about how we grapple with our own presuppositions and preconceptions, which we have projected onto our notions of religion vs. culture as well as scriptures vs. classics.

I hope finally that we have tried to cultivate what my own teacher, Wilfred Smith, called "a critical self-consciousness" about how we use terms and ideas, and that we have understood how easily, unless we are vigilant, we can objectify phenomena such as religion and culture and dehumanize whoever and whatever is "other" than we are—religiously, culturally, linguistically, ethnically, or however. I hope you agree that reading the transformational texts of other persons and other traditions alongside our own is one way to recognize both the shared humanity and powerful thinking of persons in historical traditions seemingly wholly foreign to us.

The most compelling argument for studying not only our own culture's various forms of religiousness, but also those of the rest of the world, is that only by seeing the variety of human thought and action can we really see our own particular views and practices with some kind of clarity and perspective, and possibly some degree of objectivity. This, as I believe I noted at the outset this term, might best be summed up in a French aphorism that I once heard the late Victor Turner cite, using it to describe the act of pilgrimage as *voyager loin pour comprendre le prochain*—"going afar to understand one's fellow human (what is near, one's neighbor)."

It's been great to "go afar" with you all this term, and I hope you found our textual romp around the world enjoyable, maybe enlightening, and, still more, perhaps in some way challenging—or even better, unsettling.

· Chapter 6 ·

ONE WITHOUT A SECOND[40]

John Stratton Hawley

Every human person is unique and inimitable, even twins, but I can think of no one for whom this is truer than Diana Eck. It seems a grand conundrum. This, after all, is the person who so loved the "pressing crowds" she encountered in north India that my wife Laura Shapiro sometimes found herself x-ing out a few when Diana asked her to give her Harvard dissertation a pre-submission edit. These Banaras crowds might press upon the reader once or twice, Laura felt, but should they do so again and again? Still, it did make sense. Diana perceived that a deeply Indian way of honoring the singularity of things was precisely to celebrate their multiplicity. If one was so miraculous, how much better to have it many times over! Or as she put it inversely early on, "the bodies of the gods sometimes convey multiplicity in oneness."[41]

Then there was the Pluralism Project, which Diana founded to reflect back America's own religious diversity to a nation resistant to seeing it. So many of her fellow citizens seemed determined to celebrate the *unum* part of *e pluribus unum* rather than the *pluribus*. Not Diana. Yet this was the person whom fate had conspired to name Eck. It's Swedish, of course—Ek (meaning "oak")—before the American immigration officials told her grandfather they thought that was a little short for a proper name. Diana would often celebrate both her Swedish ancestry and the fact that her Americanness came so late in the game. But the true meaning of her name was revealed only once she got to India. In Hindi the syllable *ek* designates the number 1. Diana loved it if a gaggle of children shouted out hopefully "one rupees!" as she passed. Well, they got it right: Diana *Ek*, one without a second.

But it doesn't take India to see her in the midst of those swirling crowds. It could also happen at home. For twenty years, Diana and her partner-then-wife Dorothy Austin shared the title of Master at Lowell House, one of the undergraduate complexes that have given Harvard College its special flavor since the 1930s. Each such "house" is a house, in fact—the master's house—and for two whole decades, when school was in session, Diana and Dorothy could be found in their dining room every Thursday pouring tea from a giant silver urn for hordes of students. They loved them all and took an interest in each one of them—all 400—to whatever extent was humanly possible. In 2016, the title Master was revised to Faculty Dean, but I like to recall that Diana and Dorothy were Harvard's first lesbian Masters.

We see Diana again amid the pressing crowds when we catch a glimpse of her every June at Harvard graduation. There she is on a little platform high in the trees that hover above a Harvard Yard jammed with students, parents, and dignitaries. Like a sports announcer she's interpreting the proceedings over a local-access television channel so that fans unable to join the throng can tune in. And who better? Diana had a well-practiced, professionally developed taste for public ritual, and she knew everyone—every single one—who played on the team.

Personally, though, I like to think of Thanksgiving—*pluribus* of a different sort. Often this took place at Lowell House, where there was room to seat some twenty-five at the table. A few Lowell students might appear, unable to travel as their peers dispersed, but the rest were family—not perhaps family in the usual sense, but family because Dorothy and Diana had made them so. Laura and I and our daughter Nell were often among them, and Diana and Dorothy took particular delight in welcoming Laura's almost 100-year-old father, a longtime veteran of the Boston Symphony and teller of many Boston tales. Yet the diversity that came so naturally, even essentially, to Diana's world wasn't just generational. There were different races, different nationalities, different religions—and none. All of us were family by adoption, and some even more so than others. Here I'm thinking of the Zejnullahu children—Amella, Aida, Kreshnik, and Sokol—since Diana and Dorothy became their legal guardians when the four of them were orphaned in the Kosovo war of 1999. In time they were joined at the Thanksgiving table by their mates and their mates' families. Thanksgiving at Diana and Dorothy's has been a Pluralism Project all its own. When the plates and glasses are filled, Diana or Dorothy will tap a glass and raise a toast and ask everyone to say something about what has happened in her or his life since the Thanksgiving before. No silent partners allowed. Around the table we go until the circle is complete, and so is the year.

This singular instinct for manyness—plurality in every color and form—has been the generating force of Diana's intellectual and institutional life. I've often asked myself where it came from. Surely her parents had a great deal to do with it. Her mother, another Dorothy, was a prominent leader of Montana's Democratic Party and utterly committed to causes of social inclusion and justice. She served in the Montana State Senate from 1980 to 2000. Was there anyone in Montana who did not know her? And there were crowds at home, too. Dorothy Eck's natal family, the Fritzes, fitted themselves (again some twenty of them) into a house and barn on the Olympic Peninsula of Washington State every summer for the sheer joy of mixing it up together. They called it The Hills, and there too you had diversity. I recently came across a letter from July 19, 1973 in which Diana remarked that "Aunt Irene is coming up tomorrow and is having 30 Republican country chairmen up here Sat. for a get together. Alas! I think we'll disappear for a hike."

Diana's father, Hugo Eck, taught architecture at Montana State University and took family and students year by year to Pátzcuaro, Mexico, to participate in a bilateral, bilingual UNESCO-sponsored project on community development. There Diana discovered the Virgin of Guadalupe, forecasting Hindu goddesses to come. Hugo was a great builder with massive hands who, by late afternoon on the day before Diana sent me a letter from The Hills, "had the scaffolding up on the little barn and we had torn half the old mossy rotten shakes off the roof. The roofing project began full scale this morning, with daddy nailing, cousin

Steve holding, Ike supervising and Letty and I carrying shakes and hoisting them up on the roof. And I spent a good bit of time clambering around the rafters, washing off the old shakes, pulling out 70 yr. old nails and whisking away the squirrelings of a dozen generations of squirrels." Diana went on to generalize as follows: "I couldn't help thinking you'd have enjoyed a day like today as much as I did—a nice substantive project with immediate results—for once!"

Looking back, I would generalize a little differently—toward the Diana who was yet to be. Here was a person who loved to see life as a project of gathering, repairing, and rebuilding. Here was someone who took strength, even then, from a certain inbred fearlessness ("clambering around the rafters") and exhibited an intrinsic fascination for a geographically sedimented past. No wonder that, when she pursued her "spiritual journey from Bozeman to Banaras," as she put it in the subtitle of *Encountering God*,[42] it was the structure of this ancient city as understood by those who lived there that captured her attention—that and its endlessly unfolding pageant. No wonder she went on to contemplate India in 559 pages as *A Sacred Geography*[43] where "the term *tirtha* . . . signals the linkage of place and space," the one being "finite and specific" while the other is "wide, expansive, and ultimately ungraspable." Then too there was the whole world, as we see in the vast terrain she surveyed in her Gifford Lectures of 2009 on "The Age of Pluralism." The house kept growing and needing repair.

Two images come to mind as I conclude. One is of Diana's distinctive handwriting, gently tilted and effortlessly proportioned, marching confidently forward with plenty of circular motions to suggest a generous sense of life along the way. If you'd like to see a sample, you can turn to the cover page of *India: A Sacred Geography*. Someone on the staff of Harmony Books, New York, had the brilliant idea of reproducing Diana's signature beneath her printed name. It's beautiful and legible— values she never doubted in an age when other scholars in the humanities often stood for very different things. If it draws attention to itself, it's not because this was its purpose.

The second image is rather different. This is Diana the warrior (her

Greek goddess legacy, I suppose) getting ready to play Holi in Banaras in the spring of 1974. She's going over to the home of the Mankhands, whom she's known since 1972, where she'll join family members in throwing colored powder and squirting colored water from the syringes that are special for the season. And be powdered and squirted back, of course. Diana can't very well play Holi out in the streets: that's a man's game, and it can be truly dangerous. Still, she has to get from her apartment in Gurudham Colony over to where the Mankhands live in New Colony. Well, she'll take her bike. The neighborhood boys are sure to be waiting for her to emerge on this day of upside-downs, though. They'll be ready to attack the well-connected, wealthy, feminine foreigner they've seen so many times. Nonetheless, she sets out. She pedals off to the crossroads, and sure enough there's a gang of three or four. They have handfuls of colored powder ready to throw, and a determined look in their eye. What's a foreign woman doing out on the streets of Banaras on a day like this? What chutzpah to show herself in public!

Diana is prepared. She has carefully filled a little mountain of balloons with water before leaving home, and has stuffed them into the basket in front of her handlebars. The boys don't suspect, and certainly have no inkling of the baseball arm that's ready to lob them in their direction. I'll never forget the stunned expression I saw when the first of these balloons hit its target. *Holi ki jay!* Victory to Holi! These boys received a liquid blessing, a true *abhishek*, from the person who would go on to write their city's best-known biography, *Banaras: City of Light*.[44] Diana L. Eck, it says on the cover—Diana *Ek*, one without a second.

· Chapter 7 ·

REFLECTIONS ON LEARNING FROM (BUT NOT STUDYING WITH) DIANA ECK

Lucinda Mosher

I no longer remember exactly how and when I became aware of Diana Eck. I suspect that the conduit was *New York Times* religion correspondent Ari Goldman. His bestseller, *The Search for God at Harvard,* was released in 1991. At the time, I was in the middle of earning a master's degree in religious studies, which—when it was conferred in October 1992—enabled me to teach religion as well as music and, eventually, to chair the recently re-established religion department at the boarding school whose faculty I had joined in 1977. A reviewer asserted that Goldman's account of his year as a Harvard Divinity School student would affirm that one could indeed honor the truth of one's own religion while being genuinely open to the worldviews of others. That was my stance already, but further support would be very welcome. I dove into Goldman's book, skimming at first. However, I soon had reason to slow down. On page 33, he introduced his readers to his World Religions instructor. I paid attention. Diana Eck was doing what I wanted to do. Perhaps she could show me how. She could; she has. I have never been her student in any formal sense. Yet I do believe that she has had a bearing on who and what I have become.

PLACE

Diana Eck and I are contemporaries. During the years she was training as a religion scholar, I was doing likewise as a musician. Some three decades later, I would earn religion-scholar credentials myself. I was now a neophyte in a discipline closely related to that in which Diana Eck was already a well-established exemplar. My professional circumstances have always contrasted sharply with hers. Her career as a scholar of religion has been characterized by rootedness: living and working in Cambridge, Massachusetts. At best, mine has been peripatetic: playing out in at least eight states plus Haiti, and (for many years) involving regular commutes between New York City, Hartford, and northeast Florida. She has held a tenured professorship; I have had a great many gigs. During the nearly half-century that Diana has taught at a single institution, I have offered courses and workshops at some fifteen schools, a federal prison, and various churches and agencies—often teaching at multiple institutions in a single term. My professional location is now quite settled. Yet, my place in higher education remains non-traditional. In short, our *locations* have contrasted sharply; yet, for both of us and for a very long time, it has been clear that our *place* is among students. Whether standing behind a podium or seated at a table, Diana Eck and I are women who love to nurture a community of learners.

PUBLIC SPEAKING

I have never been an enrollee in a course taught by Diana Eck. I have never sat in front of her in a university classroom; but I have indeed heard her speak formally. In my experience, her public presentations are beautifully crafted and rich in content. Her presidential address to the American Academy of Religion in 2006 is a fine example. It included a clarification of the theologian's task. I, a theologian by training, appreciated the approach she took:

> A theological argument utilizes the language, the symbols, and the authoritative sources of one's own religious tradition. It is plainly evaluative and interpretive. It speaks from the tradition to the tradition. In distinction from civic discourse, the focus of theological discourse is not on the civic "we," but on the "we" of a particular community of faith. This does not mean that our religious discourse is private,

whereas civic discourse is public. Rather, both religious and civic speech are quite public, but different.[45]

The compelling aspects of Diana Eck's public speaking are, I imagine, also characteristic of her classroom presentational style. Ari Goldman had, after all, taken note of the many hours she invested in polishing the lectures she delivered during the "world religions" class in which he had enrolled. His observation grabbed my attention. At that moment in time, my classroom practice was to lecture from notes rather than a script. By contrast, when I, a lay theologian, was called upon to preach, I would always write out my sermon in full. When invited to give a public lecture, I would take the same approach, leaving nothing to chance. It seemed to me that Diana's method of course-lecture development and delivery was closer to my preparation for the pulpit and podium rather than the classroom desk.

When I transitioned to online teaching, Goldman's description of Diana's lecture preparation resurfaced in my imagination. More than two decades had elapsed. Had her approach remained as fastidious and deliberate as he had implied? That was not a question I asked. Rather, I simply determined to follow suit. As the instructor for asynchronous courses, my lectures needed to be prerecorded for mounting in an online course management system. I have colleagues who sit down in front of a camera, talk extemporaneously for as long as the topic requires, then post the resulting video without further ado. I, by contrast, rarely record a lecture in a single take. Rather, determined to present my very best self to my online students and motivated in part by Diana's example, most of my online lectures are carefully scripted and benefit from careful audio-visual editing.

PILGRIMAGE

As a twenty-year-old undergraduate student, Diana Eck went to India to study pilgrimage sites. As a thirty-seven-year-old secondary-school educator, I left my husband and our four children under the age of ten to fend for themselves while I spent seven weeks in Europe visiting all of the places that Johann Sebastian Bach had lived or worked (plus quite a few associated with George Frederick Handel and Heinrich Schütz). Both ventures were research trips; they were also, in fact, pilgrimages: deliberate journeys with potential for self-discovery, self-transformation, or deep engagement with the divine.

During the first two decades of the present century, I facilitated systematic exploration of religious manyness in New York City, Greater Detroit, Greater Chicago, Hartford (Connecticut), Houston and its suburbs, Owensboro (Kentucky), Philadelphia, Greater Pittsburgh, and the District of Columbia and its surroundings. I became adept at designing opportunities for intensive experiential learning: the Worldviews Seminar, the Religious Diversity Leadership Workshop, the Spiritual Journeys project. About these offerings students often declared: "I expected this to be an academic course; but in reality, it was a pilgrimage!" Diana Eck would not have been surprised. She had already determined that the one who would study pilgrimage sites does this best—not as an aloof observer—but by becoming a pilgrim oneself.

Occasionally, I would hear reports about Diana's "pilgrimage course"—which, it seemed, was wildly popular among Harvard students. I often wondered: just what did the syllabus entail? Given what she had concluded about the study of pilgrimage, were her students encouraged or required to self-identify as pilgrims? The online Syllabi Collection maintained by the Wabash Center for Teaching and Learning in Theology and Religion provides some clues. Therein can be found Diana's description of her Fall 1999 course on "Hindu Myth, Image, and Pilgrimage"—in which students learned to make sense of the "web of meaning and reference" created by what she has termed India's "myth-image-pilgrimage complex." From this syllabus can be discerned a plan for investigating the interplay of story, image or architecture, and place that can be adapted to study of religious and cultural life in multireligious North America.

Preaching at Harvard University's Memorial Church in 2020, Diana asserted that she had long been a professional pilgrim. That is not a label I have applied to myself. However, I was once described as "the ideal companion when one deliberately walks into difference." It is an apt description of her as well.

PLURALISM AND PEDAGOGY

As a professional companion to people endeavoring to walk deliberately into difference, I am well aware of the slipperiness of the term *pluralism*. Diana Eck defines it as "a dynamic process through which we engage with one another in and through our very deepest differences." It is a definition I have used for two decades. For me, pluralism is a theological response. Hence, I follow Diana in seeing it as an attitude toward, rather as a name for, the phenomenon of religious manyness. However, even when a definition is stipulated, clashing usages can complicate a conversation. I then follow her lead in encouraging caution when comparing one religion to another, preferring to emphasize the unique aspects of each. I concur with her assertion that "religious pluralism is not primarily about common ground. Pluralism takes the reality of difference as its starting point. The challenge of pluralism is not to obliterate or erase difference, nor to smooth out differences under a universalizing canopy, but rather to discover ways of living, connecting, relating, arguing, and disagreeing in a society of differences."[46]

Diana Eck launched the Pluralism Project in 1991. Speaking to the American Academy of Religion in 2006 she described this initiative as "part history, part ethnography, part immigration studies, part cultural geography, part what we used to call civics."[47] Through it, she gave educators like me access to a continually expanding storehouse of pedagogical resources, each of which is a means for giving students an insider's view of communities of belief and practice: a database of religion sites around the US; a library of site-visit reports; the CD-ROM called *On Common Ground: World Religions in America* (1997, 2002, 2008; online version 2013), with its myriad narrated slideshows (each about four minutes in length); her book, *A New Religious America: How a "Christian Country" Has Become the World's Most Religiously Diverse Nation* (2001); documentaries such as *Fremont USA* (2009); the coining of the term "America's interfaith infrastructure"; and a plethora of decision-based studies of cases of multireligious America's conundrums. These resources were instrumental in my development of a participant-centered approach to course design that has been effective in face-to-face instruction at every level from middle school through doctoral study, and more recently, in online courses (both synchronous and asynchronous).

I am honored to be included by the Pluralism Project in a cohort of educators who have helped to further its Case Initiative as a means of teaching about America's religious manyness. I am well aware that effective decision-based cases are fiendishly difficult to compose. Yet, for years, Diana has encouraged her students to try. Axel Takács, editor-in-chief of the *Journal of Interreligious Studies,* first encountered the case method in one of Diana Eck's graduate courses. Her style of mentorship, he says, imbues her students with confidence and proficiency, empowering them by giving them the tools, methods, and strategies to research and produce a case study of their own.

The Pluralism Project has informed my teaching methods. It has also influenced my research. Certainly, it played a role in shaping my interview-driven publications. Among Diana's recurring lessons about religious diversity, as noted above, are that deep differences can be sources of delight, and that wise comparison-making will not insist on tidy parallelism between different religion-communities' beliefs and practices. My books on America's religious manyness endeavor to pass these lessons along.

PUBLIC SCHOLARSHIP

The voice with which one speaks or writes is modulated by context, audience, and task. It will vary from one arena to another. Diana Eck has made it clear that, among other options, scholars of religion have at their disposal a public voice. She urges them to put it to regular use—not only because bringing a scholarly perspective to an issue is valuable, but because it is an act of good citizenship.[48] All scholars may exercise their public voice; but to function as a public scholar is to be an academic whose research and teaching is directed at, is readily accessed by, and has a palpable impact on communities beyond the university. Because of the reach of the Pluralism Project, "public scholar" is an appropriate title for Diana Eck. Furthermore, she is a public scholar who has inspired—indeed, has participated in the formation of—other public scholars. To name but three of her former students who play that role, we might acknowledge the entrepreneurial Eboo Patel, founder and president of Interfaith America, who works at the intersection of faith and social action; Simran Jeet Singh, a columnist for Religion News Service whose pieces often address matters of religion and race; and Axel Takács who, as editor-in-chief, has dramatically expanded the readership of the *Journal of Interreligious Studies* beyond the academy, such that this open-access, peer-reviewed publication reaches grassroots practitioners and community organizers as well.

Public scholars, like other sorts of professional educators, scatter seeds of information, attitudes, and skills. But seeds fall and take root where they will. Public scholars sometimes have opportunity to see and enjoy some of the fruit of their sowing; but the produce of their teaching, writing, and activism may be cultivated beyond their gaze. So it is that I, although I have never studied *with* her formally, can count myself as a public scholar in whose formation Diana Eck has had a hand—and I am quite certain that there are others.

PERSPECTIVE

Eventually—at AAR annual meetings; at an interfaith event held at Harvard's Lowell House, where she lived; at gatherings aimed at shaping the nascent field of interreligious studies; at a convening on pedagogy—I got to spend time with Diana Eck. In *The Search for God at Harvard*, Goldman describes her as "enchanting" and "enigmatic." I have found her to be earnest, engaging, and genuinely interested in and affirming of the contributions of other interreligious scholars and educators. I have come to know that, not only is she a gifted instructor, she is one who loves to accord her students radical hospitality—delighting in serving them food and drink as well as ideas. I share that propensity with her.

Indeed, I have been learning from Diana Eck for a long time. Just when it was that I first became aware of her work, I cannot say with certainty; nor can I say when I first realized that she was aware of mine—but I am grateful that she is. Through her indications of respect for what I do in the arenas of interreligious studies and online learning, she has given me a fresh perspective on my own progress as a scholar. Her affirmations have enhanced my confidence that my choices during that unfolding were, in fact, the right ones: I have, in fact, landed where I ought to be, doing what I ought to do. That has been a lovely lesson to have received from her—a gift that I treasure deeply.

· Chapter 8 ·

DIANA ECK'S OVERTON WINDOW

Laurie L. Patton

In 1983, undergraduate religion majors at Harvard had to take general exams in order to receive the degree. I remember studying for them vividly. There was a group of us who spent hours together, who founded an undergraduate journal, who walked the streets, day and night, discussing issues in comparative religion. We had found our fellow nerds, and we were all taking generals together. Diana Eck and her fellow faculty in the Department of Religion provided an oasis of genuine undergraduate education in an otherwise less supportive institutional landscape.

Those of us in that group would go on to varied careers in the life of the mind—a professor of Hebrew Bible, a professor of Indian religions, a professor of anthropology, a professor of Islamic studies, a Rabbi, and a CIA officer. But then, at that moment, we were just a group of undergraduates quaking in our boots. No matter how much fun we had together, generals were serious business. As I entered Harvard Hall, walked to an unfamiliar classroom, and opened my blue book, the possibility of becoming a professor was not on my mind.

Before I began writing answers to the questions, I looked up. There was Diana (everyone knew her as Diana, even then). She looked different than she usually did. We normally beheld her perfectly poised, wearing an Indian shawl, lecturing from close to perfect lecture notes and commenting on gorgeous slides. Everyone wanted to be Diana Eck, but no one thought they could ever accomplish it. This morning, however, she had glasses on. She looked tired and her clothes were a little more wrinkled than usual. As she handed out the questions, she said, "I'm a little messy this morning. I've been up all night writing a grant proposal."

I suppose it would have struck someone else as the human side of Diana Eck. But her words made me even more filled with awe. The discipline it showed—that she would be up all night in the spring term, not just teaching us, but writing a grant proposal! I also asked her what it was about, and she said religious pluralism. It may have been a grant about religious pluralism in India. And it was years before the Pluralism Project would be born. But even then, the topic itself seemed so vast, and so important, so public, and so courageous. It was almost as if she was taking our training—our glorious, generalist training—and making it relevant in the world.

I already had identified Diana Eck with all things Indian. She had authored an authoritative book on Banaras, a city where I was set to live and do research only months later.[49] But that morning, I was suddenly introduced to the idea that knowledge about religion could be relevant to the world. That you could write a grant proposal about such knowledge, and it might even be funded. At that moment, as I was about to be tested on my own generalist knowledge, Diana Eck stood in front of me, fearless, tired, and even more inspiring. That moment instilled in me a respect for general knowledge and its power. We simply had to know a lot of things about world religions. Because of that experience, I never turn down an opportunity to learn about a religion that I am technically not "trained" in, and to try to teach it at an introductory level.

It would not be surprising to anyone to hear that that sensibility went underground when I trained for my PhD in the 1990s, when proving one's mettle in a specialist field was paramount. That decade was also the moment when local knowledge and the new historicism reigned over the study of religion as well as South Asian studies. Even as my mentor Wendy Doniger insisted on the staying power of the comparative approach, many of my peers were focused on undoing the comparative impetus in the study of religion. They wanted the most situated, historically, contextualized portraits of religious community as possible. To be sure, much of this intellectual trend was a good correction to a field whose distortions were just becoming visible. This move to respect the local was the moral grounding for so much of our work. Just as any young scholar with a recently minted PhD often thinks, in my mind and at that moment, the general only had its place in the introductory course or in the basement classrooms of an adult education course.

But that memory of Diana persisted, and I remember perusing the early accounts of the Pluralism Project with deep curiosity. It was almost a secret pleasure as I slogged through Sanskrit philology looking for poetic inspiration. We cannot put too fine a point on it: the Pluralism Project emerged during a time when the intellectual trends were, in fact, the opposite. That alone showed courage of conviction. As I think about it now, I would argue that the deep value of the Pluralism Project was to create an "Overton window" for open conversation about religion in the public square. Overton windows are forms of thought which make it possible to have public discussion about something that has been forbidden, or inchoate. The Project introduced the possibility of talking about certain forms of being religious in America that had not been discussed previously. In particular, while members of Asian religious traditions or new religious movements had been living and practicing in America for decades, the Project's naming of them made them not just *in* America, but *of* America. They were no longer exotic visitors, but American in their own right. Long before her book, *A New Religious America*[50] appeared in 2009, the Pluralism Project made it impossible for any leader to ignore the religious pluralism that made up the fabric of all of America—even rural, southern or midwestern farmland America. Pluralism became deeply American, not a phenomenon just on the coasts.[51]

It might be helpful to elaborate. First, in a decade when fundamentalisms were on the rise, and the culture wars we are still fighting today were ascendant, the Pluralism Project showed the dire need for the straightforward documentation of America's religious landscape. Once that documentation occurred, it was close to impossible to contradict or change the history of America. Most importantly, it allowed all sorts of smaller communities—states and counties and towns—to tell their own stories. Without the Pluralism Project's first publication, *World Religions in Boston: A Guide to Communities and Resources*,[52] the smaller more local maps of religious diversity in America would not have been possible. Once the Pluralism Project established itself as the Ur-source of documentation, projects like the 2001 *Buddhism and Barbecue*,[53] which showed all the Buddhist communities in North Carolina for example, became commonplace.

Second and relatedly, the Pluralism Project has helped to make politics and political life different. Without the Pluralism Project, Nikki Haley's Sikh roots or Vivek Ramaswamy's Hinduism would not have been comprehensible to the public. At the moment in 2006 when the first Muslim Congress person, Keith Ellison, was sworn in on a Qur'an, the Pluralism Project was there, documenting and collecting the reports.[54] The Project opened not only the Overton window of American history and demography, but the window of American public discourse and political life.

Third, the Pluralism Project has had several direct and indirect scholarly legacies. Young scholars became braver about describing religious pluralism in their hometowns, and in the United States. Such descriptions became legitimate topics in their own right. Relatedly, the Pluralism Project's emphasis on cooperation between religious groups made interfaith studies, now a vibrant field in the study of religion, imaginable.[55] What would it look like to study the intersection of religions in history and in contemporary life? That's the question that the Pluralism Project posed, and one that many scholars coming of age in the 90s and early 2000s were able to answer without worry that their topics were not "legitimate."

Fourth, the Pluralism Project kept the idea of a general study of religion alive. In its insistence on the general idea of pluralism and its role in public life of a nation, the Project kept methodological, comparative, and public concerns at the forefront of the study of religion. My guess is that many students like me, who spent much of their early careers in the focused specialization that lends legitimacy to a scholarly career, were still able to keep at the back of their minds the possibility that one could pursue a larger, more courageous and risky idea at a later point in one's professional arc.

Fifth, and relatedly, the Pluralism Project kept alive the idea of the religious studies scholar as a public intellectual. If Diana Eck's legacy had not given me courage, I would not have pursued a secondary interest in interfaith studies and religious encounters that I have called "pragmatic pluralism."[56] Even more importantly, I would not have pursued my third book project, *Who Owns Religion? Scholars and their Publics in the Late Twentieth Century*. Eck has insisted that religious identity belongs at the center of American public life. Because I had carried this intuition with me throughout my career, I was able to study theorists of that public life and write about episodes when that public life ruptured. The members of the Religion and Public Life section at the American Academy of Religion would all hail Diana Eck as one of the founding thinkers of this new and vibrant area of thought in religious studies.

Finally, the question of public intellectual life is directly related to the role of liberal arts & sciences. Unafraid of the general idea, and the impetus to describe and redescribe public life, Diana Eck has also opened the Overton window on the relevance of the humanities for today's college. Note this testimony to Diana Eck in the context of the revised General Education curriculum at Harvard from the *Harvard Crimson*, 2013:

> Dhruv P. Goyal '16, whose work for the Undergraduate Council's Education Committee has also given him reason to think about Gen Ed more closely, is quick to recount the story of how Diana Eck's Culture and Belief course, "Hindu Worlds of Art and Culture," changed his perception of Indian politics. Although Goyal is from India and has focused his studies on government and politics, the Gen Ed system injected a new and surprising perspective into his studies, reshaping the boundaries with which he approached the topic at hand. "[CB 28] helped me understand one more facet of Indian politics, which is really the intersection between religion and politics—in my own country," he says. "That's the beauty of a Harvard education."[57]

Diana Eck has pushed us to claim the humanities as fundamental vehicles for rethinking what it means to be a citizen.

Let me return, then, to the memory of that tired professor and mentor who had stayed up all night but nonetheless showed up to proctor a general exam for nervous college seniors. Diana Eck was introducing the idea to all of us that we can and should be brave enough to be intellectual citizens of our country. Now, as a college president, a job which requires one every day to be a generalist *par excellence*, I think about her example with profound gratitude. I am inspired by the power of intergenerational knowledge. I have the courage to continue to advocate for liberal education. I have hope for public intellectual life in America.

· Chapter 9 ·

NORTH STAR, A SHINING LIGHT

Simran Jeet Singh

They don't teach us much about grammar in American public schools, so it probably wasn't until high school that I learned what plural nouns were. Imagine my confusion when I got to college and my religion professor began talking about pluralism. I had no idea what he meant, which wasn't so much of a surprise. Despite being a religion major, and despite my attempts to feign interest, I often sat there quietly, wondering what the hell was going on. Some college students take religion courses to find themselves. I took them and felt perpetually lost.

That day, as my professor continued his riff on pluralism, he described a vision that felt both foreign to me, yet strangely familiar. He described a view where there is no singular, exclusive claim to truth; that there's a way of appreciating people's views without putting them in rank order. It felt strange because this was not my experience of the world, especially growing up in South Texas where evangelizing was as prevalent as iced tea. It felt familiar, though, because it's how I grew up in my Sikh household. My parents taught us that everyone has their own path, and that it's not our place to judge one another. In the mornings, as we got ready for school, we often sang the words of Guru Nanak, including one line that's always stuck with me: "*Hum nahi changay, bura nahi koi.* I am not good, and no one is bad."

I hadn't encountered many people outside my family and community who shared this worldview, and it's something I cherished about my Sikh faith. Now, in a classroom, I was realizing for the first time that there were many others seeing the world through a similar lens. Then, my professor peeled back the next layer. He turned on the projector and opened a website—a novel teaching method back in 2004. The screen flashed in bright, bold letters: "the Pluralism Project." Dr. Brown scrolled through the pages, showing us the diversity of religious life and the various kinds of issues that different communities were navigating. I was caught off guard. Five minutes ago, I didn't even know other people viewed the world in this way. Now, I was realizing scholars were studying pluralism and how people all around us are living into it.

Dr. Brown then boasted that the founder of the Pluralism Project was a classmate of his at Harvard. "Professor Diana Eck," he said. "She teaches at Harvard now. Who knows? Maybe some of you can study with her when you graduate." His comment seemed far-fetched to me. I dismissed it, as I'm sure my classmates did, too.

I couldn't imagine that within the year, I'd be applying for graduate schools, and my top choice would be Harvard Divinity School (HDS). By this point, I was even more familiar with Professor Diana Eck's work, including *Darśan* and *A New Religious America*. I wanted nothing more than to study with her.

Dr. Brown encouraged me to visit the school to bolster my application and see if the school was a good fit. He also offered to arrange a meeting with his former classmate while I was there. I wanted to say no. I'd never been more intimidated. But I was also scared of Dr. Brown, so I said yes to the meeting. And the rest was history.

I met Professor Eck in her office. She probably has no recollection of this. But I told her I was a prospective student and that Dr. Brown was my adviser.

"Ah, Cheeeeeeverrrrr!" she exclaimed. She must have seen the confusion on my face, because she immediately explained: "That's what we used to call him in school. Good old Cheever!"

I must have still looked confused, because she followed up quickly: "Cheever Brown, right? That's your professor." Suddenly it clicked. I'd only seen his name as C. Mackenzie Brown.

"Oh yes, of course," I responded. "I'd go by my middle name too if my name was Cheever." I regretted the joke before I even finished it. *I didn't know this professor. What if she was offended? What was I thinking?* But the roar of laughter brought me sudden relief.

"That's so funny," she said. "You're going to fit in just fine here." My relief turned into comfort, as we had a delightful conversation about life, scholarship, and service. That discussion assured me that Harvard Divinity School was the right next step for me.

A year later, I joined as a graduate student, along with three other classmates from Trinity University. I knew going into graduate school that I was different from many of my peers. For one, I was a Sikh going to seminary. How often does that happen? Well, often enough at HDS, it turns out. Two other Sikhs had attended in the years prior to me, and they had both worked with Professor Diana Eck, among others. Second, I didn't quite buy into the scholar/activist binary. Many of my classmates at HDS described themselves as following a path of academia or justice work. I understood that, but it didn't make sense for me. My interest in scholarship was grounded in a desire to do good in the world.

I had a clear sense of why I wanted to do this work. Growing up on the margins of society, I wanted to ensure that religious minorities had equal rights and opportunities. I especially wanted to ensure that kids growing up in this country wouldn't have to go through some of the challenges that I endured. But I wasn't quite sure of what I wanted to do, or how to do it. Sometimes, you need models of people to help imagine what's possible. That's what Professor Diana Eck was for me. And she played this role without even knowing it. In a moment where I was endeavoring to imagine what my life and career could look like, and in a time when very few people were breaking the mold, Professor Eck was my North Star. If she could leverage her scholarship to make our world more just and compassionate, couldn't all of us do the same?

I took a pair of wonderful courses with Professor Eck during my time at HDS, but what I enjoyed even more was our one-on-one advising sessions. We would sit in her office, just the two of us, and she paused her busy life to be fully present with me. She listened to every word and engaged with me as a peer. She responded to my ideas and reflections, and offered guidance when I sought it. I reveled in those moments, knowing that I had the attention of one of the foremost scholars of religion. That she made me feel respected and deserving speaks to her authenticity and integrity. That she connected with such warmth and kindness reflects her compassionate nature. And that she continued to engage with my thoughts, despite so many of them being elementary and inane, speaks to her humility.

In a word, Professor Eck was a consummate teacher, someone who gave of themselves whatever they could. Selflessly. Heartfully. Constantly. In the Sikh tradition, we learn that there are very few people like this in the world, and that when we find them, we cherish them, celebrate them, and try to emulate them. I take this wisdom to heart, and over the years, I have continued to walk a path that Professor Eck helped open up for me. I continue to challenge the scholar-activist binary, convinced more than ever that my journey, like hers, is one that bridges those two worlds and helps people see humanity in one another. We have each done this in our own ways—though I didn't have the courage or vision to pursue this path until Professor Eck came into my life.

It's also no coincidence that my work in the world has become centered around that concept I was introduced to in the formative stages of my journey: pluralism. During graduate school, I volunteered with civil rights and racial justice organizations, and I began writing publicly to help enhance religious literacy and cross-cultural understanding. These engagements have evolved over the years, and it's only in retrospect that I've come to understand that what I've been doing—often intuitively guided by lived experience—is the work that Professor Eck has been teaching us about all along: pluralism.

This understanding reveals another way in which Professor Eck has influenced the trajectory of my career. Now that I'm explicitly working on religious pluralism, I see how all of us in this space are building upon a foundation that she laid decades ago. The sturdiness of that foundation reflects the strength of her scholarship. The continued relevance of her work reflects her perceptiveness. As our world falls into tribalisms and nationalisms, and as so many of us struggle to figure out what it means to live alongside difference, Professor Eck's work on pluralism offers us a way out of our plight. It's a framework and a vision, but it's also more than that, because she has done the hard work of showing what pluralism looks like in real life, ethnographically, across traditions, community by community.

It's incredible work, and so easy to take for granted. But when we pause to remember, it's impossible not to appreciate what those of us who work in this space know, yet often forget: We stand on the shoulders of giants. Thank, you, Professor Eck, for lifting us all up.

· PART II ·

SACRED GEOGRAPHIES:

CONSIDERING PLACE

· Chapter 10 ·

PLURALISM AS *NOMOS* AND NARRATIVE: REFLECTING ON RELIGIOUS LAND USE IN MODERN AMERICA

Whittney Barth

In her 2001 book, *A New Religious America: How a "Christian Country" Became the World's Most Religiously Diverse Nation,*[58] Diana Eck vividly maps the changing religious landscape of the US—a result of increased immigration following changes to the law in 1965. In particular, Eck's work highlights the growth of Muslim, Hindu, Buddhist, and Sikh communities across the United States. Over the years, these communities established themselves in unexpected places, like a retired Friendly's restaurant turned *mandir* in Holbrook, Massachusetts.[59] Others, like the Sikh community in Niskayuna, New York,[60] have purchased property from different religious communities,[61] often a church. Sometimes these efforts to give a house of worship new life are met with vocal and hostile opposition from neighbors and government officials alike, as I will elaborate on below. This essay[62] argues that pluralism, as defined by Eck, can be a useful normative and narrative framework for religious groups, local officials, and broader communities encountering the sale of religious property. Eck describes pluralism as the "energetic engagement with diversity," "active seeking of understanding across lines of difference," an "encounter of commitments," and "based on dialogue."[63] Employed in this way, pluralism both stands alongside law as a tool in the toolbox and informs it.

When animus toward religion seeps into government decision-making about land use, religious groups are protected by the First Amendment of the US Constitution and by federal law. In 2000, a year before Eck published *A New Religious America*, Congress passed the Religious Land Use and Institutionalized Persons Act of 2000 (RLUIPA),[64] a landmark piece of legislation that sought, in part, to protect the religious liberty of individuals and organizations from substantially burdensome land use regulation. RLUIPA contains several provisions prohibiting different types of discriminatory land use regulation, including a provision that requires "equal treatment" of religious and nonreligious uses,[65] and this essay is concerned primarily with the nondiscrimination provision that prohibits discrimination on the basis of "religion or religious denomination."[66] Part of the Congressional record includes a joint statement by Senators Orrin Hatch (R-UT) and Edward Kennedy (D-MA) describing subtle and overt discrimination in zoning, often targeting "new, small, or unfamiliar" religious communities and sometimes with explicit references to "race or religion" as a reason for exclusion.[67] In a 2012 UNC law review article, veteran government civil rights litigator Eric Treene noted that churches and synagogues were the types of spaces most frequently referenced in the record.[68] In the decades following September 11, 2001, RLUIPA became an important tool for challenging anti-Muslim backlash playing out at the local level.

In his remarks upon signing RLUIPA into law, President Bill Clinton thanked the Coalition for the Free Exercise of Religion "and the civil rights community for the central role they played" in crafting the legislation.[69] "Their work in passing this legislation once again demonstrates that people of all political bents and faiths can work together for a common purpose that benefits all Americans," he continued.[70] Melissa Rogers, General Counsel for the Baptist Joint Committee on Public Affairs, highlighted the diversity of that coalition in a July 14, 2000 letter submitted into the Congressional record on behalf of the Coalition for the Free Exercise of Religion in which she names the American Civil Liberties Union, the Christian Legal Society, Americans United for Separation of Church and State, the Family Research Council, People For the American Way, and the National Association for Evangelicals all as RLUIPA supporters.[71] Not included in the letter but also in the record is evidence of support from the Union of Orthodox Congregations and the American Jewish Committee.[72]

RLUIPA was not the first major religious freedom law enacted during President Clinton's tenure. In 1993, the Religious Freedom Restoration Act (RFRA)[73] was passed with the stated purpose of restoring the "compelling interest test" for determining whether government action could substantially burden an individual or organization's religious exercise. RFRA was a direct response to the US Supreme Court's decision in *Employment Division v. Smith*[74] that held that the Constitution did permit religious exercise to be burdened under a neutrally applicable law. In his remarks at the signing of RFRA into law, President Clinton also thanked the Coalition for the Free Exercise of Religion and echoed Vice President Gore's acknowledgment of the "broad coalition of Americans [that] came together to make this bill a reality."[75] After noting the bill was passed on a voice vote because it had such high numbers of support in the House, he remarked:

> I'm told that, as many of the people in the coalition worked together across ideological and religious lines, some new friendships were formed and some new trust was established, which shows, I suppose, that the power of God is such that even in the legislative process miracles can happen.[76]

A few years later, in *City of Boerne v. Flores*,[77] the US Supreme Court declared RFRA unconstitutional as applied to the states, leading to the legislative moment that produced its "sister statute," RLUIPA.[78] While trust and collaboration among the diverse coalition that lobbied for RFRA began "fraying" as early as the *City of Boerne* decision,[79] both have plummeted precipitously in recent years as RFRA has become a flashpoint in the "conscience wars."[80]

RLUIPA, on the other hand, continues to enjoy bipartisan support (although, to be sure, some groups have expressed misgivings from the start).[81] Why has RLUIPA not shared RFRA's fate? To start,

RLUIPA is more targeted in its purview; as Baptist Joint Committee Executive Director Amanda Tyler and former Director of the White House Office of Faith-Based and Neighborhood Partnerships Melissa Rogers observed in their essay marking the statute's twentieth anniversary: "Congress did not address every religious liberty problem with RLUIPA."[82] This naturally provides less opportunity for innovation and expansion. Tyler and Rogers also observe that the US Department of Justice has been responsive to the needs of minority religious communities that face "a disproportionate level of discrimination in zoning matters," according to a 2016 Justice Department report.[83] Further, RLUIPA was explicitly tailored *not* to interfere with other civil rights statutes (unlike the earlier-drafted but never-passed Religious Liberty Protection Act that did not contain such protections[84]). I also suspect that support for RLUIPA is a result not just of its self-imposed limits, but also from the fact that it recognizes that *having a place* is important and it attempts to curb animus-infused efforts to make others seem *out of place* (local, grassroots interfaith efforts can also combat animus in this way, as I began to sketch out in this 2015 essay in the *Journal of Interreligious Studies*[85]).

Controversies over the establishment of certain houses of worship are not new. In 2000, just months before RLUIPA's passage, controversy erupted in Palos Heights, Illinois, when word spread that a local Muslim community intended to purchase a church building belonging to the Reformed Christian community in town.[86] Although the building had been up for sale for two years, it was not until the Muslim community's intention to purchase was made known that two city council members led a campaign to convince the city to purchase the property for a recreation center. Amid vocal opposition and anti-Muslim public statements, the proposal was made to offer the Muslim community $200,000 to walk away from the deal, a proposal the mayor—appalled by the controversy—vetoed.

A 2010 report from the Institute for Social Policy and Understanding describes opposition to the building of mosques since the 1980s, often resulting in Muslim communities spending years "searching for developments before finally succeeding... [it's also] not unusual for them to settle for parcels that were undesirable but more likely to be approved [by planning and zoning boards], or to make considerable compromises in their original plans" due to opposition.[87] The report describes a shift in the expression of that opposition, visible by 2010, wherein the controversies over mosque-building that had previously been largely confined to local, public sessions "and within the framework of public debate," had given way to "vocal and organized opposition in the streets with placards and bullhorns, shaping public opinion through national media coverage."[88]

Although RLUIPA is an important tool for protecting religious groups from discrimination, challenges remain. Outcomes are uncertain with litigation. Once in court, plaintiffs face a host of legal obstacles to surmount,[89] not to mention that federal circuit courts are inconsistent in analyzing RLUIPA claims. There are also financial concerns.[90] A Sikh community in Oyster Bay, New York, filed suit against the town in 2016, alleging that for years, the town created roadblocks as it sought to build its new *gurdwara*, purportedly influenced by the animus toward Sikhs expressed by some of the temple's neighbors.[91] The parties settled later that same year, with the temple's attorney citing legal fees as a burden that contributed to the Sikh community's decision to settle.[92] Protracted legal challenges also cause groups to run out of money before their new house of worship is completed, as was the case for a church in South Hackensack, New Jersey which, at the time of a 2017 profile in *The Atlantic* continued to worship in unfinished space.[93]

The late Yale University Law Professor Robert Cover wrote that "[o]nce understood in the context of the narratives that give it meaning, law becomes not merely a system of rules to be observed, but a world in which we live."[94] That world (or *nomos*, as he called it), is normative and those very narratives not only imbue law with meaning but shape the world(s) in which we live. To find those meanings, different sources might be consulted. For example, social and political debates leading to a bill's proposal and adoption or executive statements when signing a bill into law offer windows into the moral, social, and legal imaginations of the individuals and groups involved. Even photographs taken at the signing lend weight to particular narratives about who had a seat at the table. Over time, the effects of a law—what it prohibits, protects, and encourages—can also be a source for its narrative and, by extension, the normative world that it builds.

From her work mapping the religious landscape of America, Diana Eck articulates a vision for religious pluralism that is comprised of four key components: 1) pluralism is not diversity alone, but the energetic engagement with diversity; 2) pluralism is not just tolerance, but the active seeking of understanding across lines of difference; 3) pluralism is not relativism, but the encounter of commitments; and 4) pluralism is based on dialogue.[95] In this context, pluralism speaks to the civic, rather than theological domain, and is "not primarily about common ground" but takes "the reality of difference as its starting point."[96] For Eck, pluralism is at once a normative and descriptive enterprise—or, put in Cover's terms, pluralism is crucial as both *nomos* and narrative.

The crafting and passage of RLUIPA itself arguably fits within this framework of pluralism. And while the passage of RLUIPA held—and continues to hold—great promise, it should be seen as one tool in the toolbox of civic life. As religious communities grapple with the future of the physical spaces and potential buyers may be new neighbors or long-established but previously less visible groups, local officials and community members might turn to Eck's framework of pluralism as instructive for building and maintaining partnerships around physical space that might otherwise be considered largely within the private sphere of a particular religious community.

· Chapter 11 ·

RELIGIOUS PLURALISM AND CIVIC ENGAGEMENT:
A NEW LENS FROM LA TO NYC

Chloe Breyer

In the summer of 1991, I set off as an early undergraduate researcher to document the Buddhisms of Los Angeles. My professor, Diana Eck, had pitched her new project during one of my comparative religion classes explaining how she sought to document the changing religious landscape of the United States since the 1965 Immigration and Nationality Act. My own assignment that summer brought me to Zen centers in Compton, a Cambodian Temple in Long Beach, and the 100,000 square foot North American Capital of the Fo Guang Shan Buddhist Order located in Hacienda Heights. My summer with Diana Eck's Pluralism Project provided me with a new lens on Los Angeles and a lifelong interest in civic engagement among immigrant faith communities.

Diana Eck's faith in her undergraduate foot soldiers and the open-ended research questions and guidance that she gave us shaped the award-winning multi-year mapping project outlining the changing contours of American religious diversity. They also impacted the course of our work and lives as well.

In my own case, now as an Episcopal priest and executive director of the Interfaith Center of New York (ICNY), there are at least three different ways in which I am indebted to Diana Eck and her work. These include an appreciation for religious pluralism and civic engagement; an understanding the key roles of mapping, place, and municipal rules; and a recognition of the importance of religious imagination in adaptation.

CONNECTING PLURALISM AND CIVIC ENGAGEMENT

Among the neighborhoods in and around Los Angeles in the summer of 1991, I ended up frequenting the Vietnamese "Home Temples" of Garden Grove, Orange County. In this historically conservative area, waves of Vietnamese refugees began arriving in the 1980s and it was here that I got the idea for my undergraduate thesis: "Religious Liberty in Thought and Action: Vietnamese Home Temples and the First Amendment."[97] I drew inspiration for my research from the conflict between zoning rules that appeared to discriminate against Vietnamese Buddhist home temples, essentially Ranch-style houses where monks lived, in favor of a Judeo-Christian model of worship space with car parks, and much more. Vietnamese Home Temples were regularly shut down for fire safety, parking, and zoning-related reasons. This conflict was one of the several "case studies" featured in the "On Common Ground: World Religions in America."[98]

Thirty-two years later, as I direct a socially engaged interfaith organization in one of the most religiously diverse cities on the planet, zoning, parking, and fire safety regulations are still critical matters in religious pluralism and civic engagement. As the ICNY seeks to equip diverse houses of worship to shelter and support migrant New Yorkers, showers and fire safety rules are the greatest barrier for Muslim, Sikh, and Buddhist Temple participation in a city-wide initiative to shelter migrants—as it is for storefront Christian Churches.

MAPPING AND MUNICIPAL RULES

Municipal codes can also be the measure by which civic engagement in newly arrived immigrant religious communities can be assessed. For example, my colleague and director of programs at ICNY, Dr. Henry Goldschmidt, sometimes opens his Religious Pluralism in NYC classes with the "alternate side parking list" issued by the Department of Transportation. NYC street cleaning rules require that residents with cars move their vehicles at least once a week for an hour or more at a time to make way for the street cleaner. The rules are suspended, however, for certain holidays. Traditionally, these holidays have included Memorial Day or the 4th of July and religious holidays like Christmas, Easter, and the High Holy Days. In recent years, however, as my colleague is quick to point out, both Eids, Diwali, and Vesak have been added to the list of alternate side parking exemptions. It is the result of engagement and lobbying efforts of Muslim, Hindu, and Buddhist communities at City Hall.

Before Google Earth, Professor Eck was putting marginalized and overlooked religiously diverse communities on the map. Not every scholar of religion takes such a grounded approach—her own predecessor Wilfred Cantwell Smith, for example, did not emphasize the importance of place. For Eck, location has always mattered. What is Hinduism without Banaras? Or Queens? In *A New Religious America*,[99] she sought to not only show the new contours of religious America—one of the most diverse countries in the world—but also to invite people of different faiths to find each other. For people asking the question, "Who is my neighbor?" The answer can be located—at one level—on the Pluralism Project's website.

Eck has written that pluralism is the "energetic engagement with diversity . . . the active seeking of understanding across lines of difference . . . the encounter of commitments . . ."[100] The Interfaith Center of New York has embraced this understanding of pluralism with our NEH Summer Institute Teacher-training program, "Religious Worlds of New York." We have brought over one hundred and fifty K-12 public, private, and parochial schoolteachers from around the country to hear from diverse faith leaders, travel to their houses of worship, and develop their own place-based "lived religions" curriculum that they then bring home to Nevada, South Carolina, Texas and Massachusetts. The Pluralism Project has long been a partner in this work.

During the pandemic, when our shared community space was virtual and Zoom was our only way to connect, ICNY's Interfaith Civic Leadership Academy (ICLA)—a nine-month civics education and interfaith dialogue program for emerging faith leaders of New York—found inspiration from the Pluralism Project. Hanadi Doleh, ICNY's director of community partnerships, built community among our ICLA fellows across religious divides during that time that included Reconstructionist and Modern Orthodox rabbis, an African American Muslim, a Latter-day Saints Bishop, and an Afro Caribbean Priestess—by inviting each person to present about their faith community by sharing their screen using the street-level option in Google Maps to give a virtual tour of their neighborhood. Barring a walking tour, this use of online mapping was the next best thing.

RELIGIOUS IMAGINATION OF IMMIGRANT TRADITIONS STRENGTHENS DEMOCRACY

Going back to that formative summer in 1991, it occasionally seemed disjointed to encounter recognizable Buddhist temples against a backdrop of concrete, car parks, and fast-food restaurants. As a comparative religion and government major, I had been first introduced to Buddhism while traveling in northern India and the Himalayas during a study abroad semester. Los Angeles was not the single seamlessly woven monochrome tapestry of religion and culture—like Catholicism in the layout of Italian hillside villages or Islam in mosques and minarets of Morocco. The Buddhist Temples of LA were often located in a shopping mall off the 101 Highway, or by the sloping concrete shores of the Los Angeles River. Buddhism in Thailand was different from Buddhism in any large American city.

But many of the new the Buddhist Temples of LA—like those of New York City or in other parts of the country—applied religious imagination to problem-solve and adapt to a new context. Before I left Cambridge, Diana Eck suggested I visit a Cambodian Buddhist temple in Long Beach. At that time, gang involvement was a significant problem among the second-generation Cambodian youth. When I arrived to meet the abbot, who had a degree in psychology and counseling, he introduced me to a young monk—born in California—who had recently returned after spending a decade meditating and living in a Theravadin monastery in Thailand.

This white American-born monk re-introduced the Cambodian Buddhist practice of young boys in the community "becoming monks for the summer." In Cambodia, this took place during the rainy season; in LA, it coincided with school vacation, when gang-related crime increased. The film *Becoming the Buddha in LA*,[101] now on the Pluralism Project's website, documents the ritual shaving of a ninth grader's hair as well as his stepping into saffron yellow robes. The reintroduction of this ritual was an act of religious imagination and cultural adaptation.

The engagement of an ancient religious tradition, adapted to address the challenges of life in a diverse democracy is on display every day in New York City. For example, in the wake of "A Common Word Between Us and You," and with the help of then Community Partnership Director Dr. Sarah Sayeed and the GHR Foundation, we catalyzed a series of local dialogues and service partnerships between Roman Catholic and Muslim faith leaders in the Bronx, Manhattan, and Staten Island from 2008–2012. The joint service project participants included Muslim and Roman Catholic women volunteering together at a soup kitchen in the Bronx and then meeting with their State Assembly representatives to advocate for more Federal food assistance in the Bronx. In Staten Island, Roman Catholic, and Albanian Muslim Youth visited each other's houses of worship and helped to clean them. Other community projects included an Afro-Caribbean faith leader translating domestic violence prevention materials into Creole and Buddhist and Latter-Day Saints leaders together doing outreach to Chinese students at Columbia.

In her writing and work, Diana Eck has left open the possibility that the greatest contribution of immigrant religious traditions in the United States may be to the strength of our democracy—rather than to the art or architecture of the culture it left behind. Her conviction that US democracy is strengthened with interreligious engagement is something that we at ICNY have staked our work on for more than a quarter century.

· Chapter 12 ·

THE CORRIDOR

Lawrence Cohen

CITY OF THIEVES

Mrs. Ganguli cursed me again. There is no need, she said, to abandon me for *that* city: you can live with me. "*That* city" was Varanasi (or Banaras, or Kashi, its plenitude of names reflecting the layered panegyrics that Diana Eck has so carefully read).[102] It was 1983 and I was staying with Mrs. G in Calcutta. Her daughter, an MIT professor, had years earlier rented rooms from a woman who was a friend of my mother, and that tenuous connection served for my parents as hope that I would be adequately looked after. But I was Dr. Eck's student and was enroute to Varanasi, *Banaras: City of Light* in hand, where I planned to spend a year studying contemporary ethics of aging. I had memorized the book and was eager to get there. Entrusted with my care, Mrs. G attempted to disabuse me of expectations. It is a backward place, she told me: they are all thieves there. Stay in Calcutta.

Such a claim, of the danger and duplicity of the sacred city, admits a dense modern genealogy: resonating with modern Hindu reformers' denunciation of "priestcraft" in a colonial context,[103] or with the transformation of the cities and towns of eastern India into benighted sites of an imagined feudal backwardness set against a rising and reformist Calcutta.[104] Mrs. G's was not the only evocation of Varanasi as the city of thieves offered to me over subsequent years. Indeed, Varanasi as a city that in its material and social enactment radically diverges from its ideal form as a sacred *tīrtha* or place of crossing-over[105] and that must be restored is a familiar depiction. One of the central mythic cycles in the mid-fourteenth century *Kāshī Khanda*, the story of King Divodāsa, elaborates Lord Shiva's loss of the city and the complex efforts of all the gods to reclaim it.[106] The city's continual divergence from its idealized conception in the *māhātmya* or praise literature has served as perennial ground for its rebuilding and reform, most notably in the eighteenth- and nineteenth-century transformation of the Ganges riverfront spearheaded by Maratha and other Hindu sovereigns and across a range of current schemes.[107]

This brief essay engages a widely publicized and widely admired twenty-first century scheme to reform Varanasi, known colloquially as "the Corridor." The project has replaced an area of narrow lanes and buildings in the city's core with an architectural assemblage dominated by a series of open plazas linking the Ganges riverfront to the Vishvanātha (or Vishveshvara) temple which has dominated Hindu pilgrim itineraries over the modern life of the city.[108] I was caught by talk of the Corridor in the summer of 2022, during the pilgrim month of Shrāvana, as I stood with persons queuing in line to visit the Vishvanātha temple. Pilgrims spoke less of seeing the deity or the temple and more of having "*Corridor ka darshan.*" To have *darshan* as Eck has famously discussed is both to see and be seen by a charismatic or sacred presence.[109] The primary deity housed in the temple is Shiva as Vishveshvara, the Universal Lord or Lord of All. But what excited some Shrāvana pilgrims' visual devotion in 2022 was the form of the Corridor itself. A year later, returning to the city for Shrāvana in 2023, I found that discussions of *darshan* I elicited or overheard had reoriented to deity and temple, in a context where an intensively publicized legal suit centered on the relation between the Vishvanātha temple and the adjoining Gyan Vapi mosque had come to dominate public discourse on Hindu worship in the city.[110] But talk of the Corridor remained ubiquitous.

PATHS TOWARD A CLEARING

Corridors have been figures organizing regional, national, and transnational planned development globally since at least the 1970s: a corridor is a design (such as one centered on a highway) for appropriating land to improve the mobility of markets, capital, people, animals, or migrants (and in the case of the Varanasi Corridor of offerings, deities, and crowds).[111] Detlef Müller-Mahn has in a sub-Saharan African described development corridors as "dreamscapes of modernity" oriented toward the creation of "desirable futures."[112] Thus, not surprisingly, at stake in most state representations of the Corridor (as in the Varanasi conversations I elicited in 2022 and 2023) has been a claim for enhanced mobility. The subject of such mobility is rendered as both an individual body and a crowd. Varanasi is framed as having become dirty and a risk to individual health and as lacking the spatial infrastructure to move and manage devotional crowds.

Discussions of dirt (as opposed to crowding) were more common among English-speaking outsiders. A woman from Delhi, like me an academic, in 2023 described her experience of Varanasi in terms of disgust, centered on recounting her passage through filthy lanes to reach the *antagriha*, the sacred core around modern Vishvanātha. She understood the Corridor as an overdue modernization, as "development." Many Banarsi Hindus across class and caste with whom I spoke, though they did not foreground similar effects of disgust, did associate the Corridor with their sense of Prime Minister Narendra Modi's pronounced executive capacity to engender *vikās*, development, in the city. They spoke of *vikās* as a form of care, both sovereign gift and biopolitical rationality, giving city residents health and life.

Such a gift was palpable in the lanes surrounding the corridor both years during Shrāvana. Municipal sanitation workers (some from the Dalit slum in the south of the city where I have long worked) were ubiquitous, deftly threading wheelbarrows laden with garbage through lanes crowded with pilgrims. Dalit labor becomes hyper-visible in the city's lanes during Shrāvana, both a form of inclusion within this apparatus of sovereign gift and perhaps a painful association of Dalit identity with the disgust noted by many middle-class visitors. But key to the proliferations of wheelbarrows is a condition of hygienic mobility: garbage here is on the move and quickly. All that which elicits disgust is moving.

The Corridor's chief architect Bimal Patel and others responsible for its disseminated publicity have linked sanitation, security, and the removal of "encroachments" in narrating a commitment to the rationalization of the city's space and forms of life.[113]

The *crowd* in the publicity and talk of the Corridor is not merely the collective biopolitical form of population. If scenes of disgust like that narrated to me by the woman from Delhi linked narrow lanes, crowds, and garbage together, impinging painfully on subjects with modern hygienic sensibilities, they open to the possibility of a second, better crowd to be enabled. We might call this possibility the crowd yet to come. The Corridor is precisely that opening or clearing to enable this new crowd to come into being and to know itself. To anticipate the form, feeling, and reason of the crowd yet to come, I turn to two of its registers that emerged during time spent inside the Corridor in 2023: the visual and the commercial.

Visual: Entry into the Corridor is policed. Pilgrims and tourists are directed to one of several gates into the complex: each affords a distinct spatial regime for Corridor *ka darshan.* As the dominant publicity stresses the Corridor's linking river to temple, one might begin from a monumental Ganges gate constructed at the river entrance. From here, the Corridor is designed as a linear series of plazas opening to views of the golden roof of the Vishvanātha temple ahead. As the temple nears, one shifts from the individuated form of the walker in the crowd to the controlled and collective form of the queue. It is as if in the opening of the Corridor engenders the surprising apperception of a form of being, a crowd yet to come.

Official renderings of the view ahead center on the opening up of sightlines to the golden temple roof. Explicit in discussions I had with temple priests at Vishvanātha and with one of the local designers of the Corridor who worked with Patel was an account that these sightlines had earlier been occluded as a protective response to the iconoclasm of the Mughal Emperor Aurangzeb, that the labyrinthine form of the city was a once-necessary stratagem to hide its remaining shrines from destruction.

A presumptive Muslim iconoclasm, that is, is present both in the experience of the old crowd—the unsanitary lanes revealed as the improvisation of an early age—and the crowd yet to come, the shock of a collective *darshan* long denied. And as one moves up from the river through the Corridor approaching Vishvanātha, one experiences the Gyan Vapi mosque as a continuation of *darshan* denied. The crowd yet to come comes to being, that is, in relation to the one encroachment neither Patel's rationalized destruction of the space of the old crowd nor the Prime Minister's extraordinary executive capacity can eliminate. For Varanasi to be returned to an imagined scopic regime of radical openness, for God in the universal form of Vishvanātha to be fully seen, something else in excess of this rationality and this capacity must be brought into being. This something else is the crowd yet to come, assembled in anticipation of a visual and hygienic order which the mosque will no longer interrupt.

Religious structures were allegedly bulldozed to create the Corridor, a claim progressive left media have amplified and center-right media discounted.[114] The family responsible for one set of shrines to be displaced sought guidance on the ritual conditions for a deity to be properly moved: their relocated shrine now sits just beyond the Corridor's heavily policed walls. Several colleagues and I sat in the new space with members of this temple trust. One member was a designer who had helped Patel's team with the research on the area. He was smart and charismatic and offered what we might term a near-secular vision of the Corridor's rationality, centered on the production of health and the value of development. Some of my colleagues were university students, taken with the dreamscape of modernity he offered. The atmosphere in the room became marked by their excitement. We walked up to the roof of the translocated temple to take in its impressive view of the Corridor. The designer called our attention to the mosque, sharply delineated like golden Vishvanātha next to it, without saying anything to offend. Gazes followed his lead; excited smiles were replaced with looks of concern. I cannot and will not offer an interpretation of the atmospheric shift, beyond noting that the scopic order of the Corridor, its capacity for a new *darshan*, seemed to bring the mosque into focus as the target of a collective apperception of what prevents *vikās*.

VIPs (including visitors willing to pay for a swifter entry into the Corridor evading the long Shrāvana queues) enter not from the river or the gate closest to the pre-Corridor entry point, but from Gate Number Four adjoining the mosque. Here the experience is opposite to that of those entering from the riverside. One sees nothing, and must thread a path around the barbed wire enclosure surrounding the mosque in order to see Vishvanātha and be seen. Here the experience is not that of engendering the crowd yet to come. One has the status or capital to evade crowds, old and new. Here the mosque is immediate, a different sensorial ordering but nonetheless one that capitalizes on the mosque's disruption for those who do not need to be shown how to see it.

Despite the elicitation of disgust against which the Corridor is narrated, crowds in the surrounding lanes—those despised old crowds—have only multiplied with the great upsurge in Varanasi's popularity as a national destination under the Prime Minister's care. Banarsis living near the Corridor on several occasions shared with me the creative tactics they used to move freely despite a new reality they describe of impasse.

Commercial: In a resonant chapter of *Banaras: City of Light* on Varanasi as a center of artisanship and trade, Diana Eck develops a theme of the close interrelation between temple and bazaar in the cultivation of the city as an affectively intoxicating milieu.[115] Nita Kumar in *The Artisans of Banaras* historicizes this artisanal culture, and its present and future emerge as more uncertain.[116] The bulldozing of much of the dense urban core of the Vishvanātha *antagriha* and the creation of a security perimeter around the new Corridor erased many urban lanes with stores and artisanal workshops, space owned by or leased to families with multi-generational rights in the city, accentuating this uncertainty. Businesses negatively affected included many that offered services and materials to worshippers. Displaced businesses were offered participation in a lottery to receive new rights of long-term rental of commercial space *within* the Corridor. A third major gateway into the complex, not from the river nor the VIP entrance by the mosque, brought queuing worshippers entering the Corridor through a long arcade lined with those relocated businesses that won the lottery.

The growth of worshipping crowds has benefitted many shops along routes leading to the new Corridor gateways. Pilgrims and families often travel as part of larger groups whose guide or local contact will negotiate with a given merchant along these routes for goods that include appropriate offerings for the deity, guide and ritual services, the storage of footwear, and the securing of belongings not allowed inside. Merchants who lost their shops and were relocated to the Corridor arcade have in contrast regained little of their former trade. One shopkeeper in the arcade emphatically praised the Prime Minister's commitment to the city and to *vikās*. But the arcade, he said, was a failure. Most pilgrims settle their material requirements for worship before entering. Once inside the Corridor they form a queue that passes through the arcade, an anticipatory form focused on moving on and joining the more open spaces that I have described as potentiating the crowd yet to come. In the several hours I spend in conversation with this and other merchants almost no one broke free from the slowly moving queue to view the religious phantasmagoria on display. And indeed, the displays in the Corridor arcade were for the most part meager in distinction with the shops outside, bearing an air of hopelessness and failure.

The Prime Minister was above reproach, but the merchant with whom I was speaking reserved sharp words for local politicians and administrators. Despite decades of building relations with these officials, he was unable to get any of them to address the arcade's failure of concept. His abandonment by officialdom seemed as surprising to him as it was painful. It was as if the tissue of belonging in the city for him had been altered.

The oddness of the arcade—the tensile force of the queue moving along its spine, the inactivity in the shops lining the walls—was both mirrored and contrasted by the more celebrated new commercial spaces in the Corridor: its shopping areas and a food court that lined several of the open plazas. These were more suggestive of the wondrous "tableau of consumption" described by Sanjay Srivastava in his writing on the in some ways similar Akshardham temple complex in Delhi, in which a food court and other shopping experiences are enfolded within the playful form of a theme park. Like the Corridor, Akshardham is heavily secured with uniformed guards and metal detectors, and like the Corridor, movement through the complex is organized to enable the passage of large crowds. The Corridor is less subject to accusations of what Srivastava terms "Disney-divinity" than is Akshardham. Its studied seriousness as a presumptive national shrine does not permit the latter's intensive play and experiment in the sublime and monumental[117] or wondrous.[118] Both complexes emerged through executive claims on urban space set against all that can be rendered as encroaching and that can be bulldozed out of sight.

Srivastava makes the observation that Akshardham does not permit an easy distinction between the experience and aesthetics proper to a sacred interior versus a secular and commercial exterior. The temple complex as a vehicle of what Srivastava terms surplus consumption enables its visitors a form of mastery over commodity forms associated with modernity: such mastery is what makes surplus consumption densely "moral" and helps one understand the place of food courts in the Corridor:

> The making of a moral middle class, one that has control over the processes of consumption, and hence modernity, is . . . located in the processes of (surplus) consumption itself. For, it is only through consumption that one can demonstrate mastery over it. So, one consumes a wide variety of products of contemporary capitalism . . . in combination with "spiritual" goods such as religion and nationalism . . . the activities of a class that sees itself as "truly" Indian because it is not defined by foreign modernity, but is rather, able to define its own version.[119]

The *antagriha* in the lanes around Vishvanātha is replete of course with all the shops of religious goods not bulldozed to make the Corridor. For more elite visitors, like the woman from Delhi, these shops were of a piece with the disgust she felt walking through lanes encroached by filth and the presence of undesirable others. The Corridor for her offered an alternative milieu: the arcade for buying basic goods for respectful worship, the food court for its promise of hygienic eating, and the high-end stores for the examination of bespoke and branded handicrafts. Her experience of the Corridor combined the world-class pleasures of food courts with worshiping in ancient India via ersatz architectural rendering. But it maintained a sharp distinction between a devalued exterior marked by encroachment and an almost-entirely-purified interior of the temple (almost given the problem of the mosque that the Corridor's engineering of *darshan* reveal).

The Corridor, that is, is less a phantasmagoria of moral consumption for an emergent and vernacular middle class—it includes that, to be sure, following Srivastava—but depends as well on a graduated design: different gates, different points of view toward God, different relations to participation in or near the crowd yet to come. This graduation, this sense that the scene of consumption here is fragmented, comes out most sharply in the dual register of shops in the corridor: the cubbyholes for the relocated traders in the adjoining arcade versus the more "five-star" experience of shops girding the main spatial progression of the Corridor.

And yet, at least during my most recent 2023 visit, these five-star spaces, no less than the arcade, betrayed an air of abandonment. Many spaces reserved for elite shops were unused; the food court was far less exciting than the area of worship. The commercial scene that did bustle lay as it had before in the precincts just beyond the (now considerably enlarged) sacred complex. Some of these areas, most notably the nearby crossing known as Godowlia, had been given their own facelifts, both modernist and ersatz-ancient in design. The relation of temple to bazaar was not yet entirely spoken for. To put it otherwise, the world outside the Corridor's walls had not yet been entirely purged of the order of encroachment that forever girded the exciting executive capacity of this Prime Minister.

CODA: CITY OF WINDOWS

I had read of the Corridor, but did not understand the extent of the accompanying will for destruction until late December 2019, months before pandemic lockdown. I was back in Varanasi after some years, using bodily memory to find a friend's house in the tight lanes of the *antagriha*. But I kept coming up against brick walls, literally, that my body did not remember. Once I had learned to walk these lanes from *Banaras: City of Light*, having escaped Calcutta and my beloved Mrs. G. But now every path seemed foreclosed. I kept asking passers-by where a certain long-standing *paan* shop was and was told repeatedly I could not get there from here "because of the Corridor." Finally, at one unexpected brick wall with a locked door set into it, a man seated nearby took pity. He astonishingly produced a key and opened the door, telling me to be quick about getting across. What the opening revealed was a vast field of rubble, onto which I stepped. This was my first encounter with the affective machinery of anti-encroachment. It was the week when nationwide protests against the Citizens Amendment Act had activated apparatuses of state security, and the *antagriha* was on high alert. Two police officers spotted me trying to cross the rubble in search of that orienting *paan* shop and took chase. I fled back to the wooden door, but it was again locked. A nearby window opened: a voice cried out to me, get in. I found myself in a silk shop, with a young man asking me surreally if I had stopped by with a given purchase in mind.

Banaras, city of light, city of all the gods, city of silk saris and *paan* and every manner of consumable, had been reformed. No longer just a dirty place, no longer a city of thieves, it beckoned to a nation reformed, it offered a return to an imagined past cleansed of encroachment. On the cusp of that reform, I sat on a proffered chair in the silk shop, still shaking with visions of the police, their lathis swinging, and accepting tea and sweetmeats.[120]

· Chapter 13 ·

LIKE A RIVER:
SACRED GEOGRAPHY AND ITS ECOLOGICAL TRIBUTARIES

Rebecca Kneale Gould

In her 1992 theological memoir, *Encountering God: A Spiritual Journey from Bozeman to Banaras*, Diana L. Eck offers her readers a guiding metaphor for how to think about religion:

> Religious traditions are far more like rivers than stones. Like the Ganges and the Gallatin, they are flowing and changing. Sometimes they dry up in arid land, sometimes they radically change course and move out to water new territory. All of us contribute to the river of our traditions. We do not know how we will change the river or be changed as we experience its currents.[121]

I take up this fluvial metaphor, not so much to refer to religious traditions *themselves*, but to investigate the concept of sacred geography as it pertains to my own work in the subfield of "religion and ecology." In particular, I am using the idea of sacred geography as an occasion for reflection on where we—in the deeply troubled United States—now find ourselves, religiously and environmentally. Where have we been and where are we going? What good work can we celebrate and what challenges remain? The concept of sacred geography helps us to make these assessments because, while fluid in terms of where it shows up and how it is understood, it also can serve as an eco-spiritual *marker* of sorts. We know it when we see it and we know when it is "almost but not quite" culturally present. That presence or absence can make a transformative ecological, political, and spiritual difference.

When I first heard the term "sacred geography" I was a wide-eyed, in-over-my-head Harvard-Radcliffe sophomore utterly entranced by a class on pilgrimage jointly taught by Professors Diana Eck, William Graham, and Clarissa Atkinson. I remember responding to the term with the kind of full-bodied "yes!" that is typical of an undergraduate. My own long held, innate sense that mountains and rivers of Massachusetts were inherently sacred was suddenly being validated as true! At the same time, it was clear to me that I was entering another world entirely, an Indian context that was at once utterly foreign and at the same time, made both entrancing and familiar by the way Professor Eck artfully illuminated the pilgrim's experience. In that first course—which fatefully led me to a life-long study of religion—Eck's uncanny capacity to describe Hindu pilgrimage as if she were a pilgrim herself made me momentarily wonder if she were somehow Hindu, while also thoroughly Montanan. When I later heard her speak about Jesus from the pulpit of the Harvard-Epworth church, I began to perceive what I would later come to call "the classic Diana Eck" approach to teaching and scholarship: the magnetic ability to draw her students and readers into any number of religious worlds, giving each person within that world her careful attention and utter respect. On so many occasions, Professor Eck would describe herself humbly as "a student of religion," emphasizing the extent to which compassionate curiosity drove her research. That curiosity always came with an expressed willingness to grow, change and re-think—a scholarly posture that has profoundly shaped my own work as a teacher, scholar, and writer.

For example, within the realm of sacred geography, Eck describes how her own sensibilities significantly evolved over twenty years, from her initial focus on Varanasi (Banaras, Kashi) as a "sacred center" to her emerging understanding that this "sacred center" focus reflected Western biases that were not fully faithful to the Indian context. "It became increasingly clear to me," she writes in her introduction to *India:*

A Sacred Geography, "that anywhere one goes in India one finds a living landscape in which mountains, rivers, forests are elaborately linked to the stories of gods and heroes."[122] Eck goes on to describe the geographic repetitions, duplications, circles, and networks that are inscribed with sacredness by the footsteps of centuries of pilgrims. The stories and gods affiliated with these destinations underscore what is deeply important for those who seek contact with sacred places. "[All] of this," she explains, "constitutes a vivid, symbolic landscape characterized not by exclusivity and uniqueness, but by polycentricity, pluralism and duplication."[123] In underlining this polycentricity, Eck reminds us of what has been comparatively absent in the religious traditions of the West.

Along with the pluralism and polycentricity, we might also add something like "ecological intimacy." For the term *sacred geography* captures the reality that for millions of people all over the planet, nature and divinity are not separate, but co-existent, such that even the English word "incarnation" (of the divine) is not quite adequate, implying an initial separation that is ultimately overcome. Eck's work has long taught us that in India, particular mountains and rivers are worshipped not simply because they are the *abodes* of gods, but, in some instances, because they are fully embodied, physical *manifestations* of divinity.[124] Through Eck's eyes—and her vivid, evocative prose—pilgrimages and rituals that may seem extraordinary or odd to an uninitiated reader become, after a time, simply "the way things are" in the Indian context: the devout approach the Ganga as both mother and goddess, honor her with *arati*, bathe in her waters, tell her their troubles.

While India was my starting place, I was already attuned—experientially—to the possibility that the sacred could emerge in whatever lands and waters we call home. In North America, for instance, sacred geography is *everywhere*, although often veiled: Mark Twain's Mississippi, Henry David Thoreau's Walden Pond and Musketaquid river, the Navajo/Diné's *Tsoodzil* (Blue Bead or Turquoise Mountain, later called Mount Taylor by white settlers). But as the Diné example reveals, in the US context, the matter of sacred geography remains vexed and fraught. The history of North American colonial settlement after all, is a history defined by the stubborn—and politically expedient—refusal to recognize the sacrality of the lands and waters that stretch from the San Juan Islands to the coast of Maine.[125] By extension, this cultural stance has also included the refusal to recognize the inherent sacrality of the living beings (otters and loons, moose and sheep, sweetgrass and pine) that dwell there. As the founder of the Wild Church movement, Victoria Loorz, tells us in her narrative of joining indigenous Water Protectors at Standing Rock in 2016: "Defending a river for her inherently sacred existence was not the typical call to action of the white liberal environmental movement, much less the practice of any white religious community I knew."[126] Finding herself on new religious territory, a territory that she had long sought, Loorz then worked to uncover the latent ecological roots of her tradition. She went on to create the emerging Wild Church Movement, seeding new possibilities for Christian—and "beyond Christian" nature-based worship.[127]

Loorz's complaint against the "other worldly," nature-ignoring evangelical Christianity of her young adulthood captures the dominant (colonial) American religious story in a nutshell. The consequences of that story pervade my days. As I write this, in the summer of 2023, the signs of our exponentially growing climate crisis are visceral. In June, thick smoke from climate-induced wildfires in Eastern Canada shrouded the beauty of my customary view of the Vermont landscape: green mountains, lush fields, and vibrant wetlands. The smell and taste of climate devastation were literally up my nose and in my mouth. A few short weeks later, unprecedented downpours suddenly transformed river-valley villages into sites of utter devastation. With a bright yellow life jacket in my back seat, I drove past vegetable fields that had turned overnight into muddy lakes filled with acres of ruined crops. I gazed down at Montpelier, our state capitol, rendered inaccessible to everyone but rescue workers in swift-boats, readying themselves for door-to-door searches.

Not for the first time, I asked myself: "If the European colonizers had understood mountains and rivers, wetlands and mesas as being inherently sacred, would we be in the existential situation in which we now find ourselves?" The answer is actually quite complicated. As the scholarship of both Kelly Alley and David Haberman clearly reveal, affirming the sacrality of a river does not necessarily neatly line up with environmental protection. Certain Hindu notions of purity, for example, can even allow for a kind of unconscious permissiveness as far as pollution is concerned.[128]

Nevertheless, the last four decades of scholarly history (both shaping and shaped by a larger cultural history) give me a modicum of optimism. While Loorz's analysis reflects a common experience, the histories of both eco-theology and the rise of religious environmentalism tell us that a cautious cultural openness to nature's sacrality has been afoot for quite some time. Back when I was that sophomore in the pilgrimage class, eco-religious rumblings of change were already beginning. These rumblings were rooted in a long, although distinctly "underdog," history of religious concern for the natural world, a concern voiced not only by the Transcendentalist triumvirate of Margaret Fuller, Ralph Waldo Emerson and Henry David Thoreau in the mid-nineteenth century, but also by a range of mid-twentieth century theologians seeking to correct the other-worldly biases of much Christian thinking: Social Gospel leader, Walter Rauschenbusch; Lutheran theologian, Joseph Sittler, Paul Tillich, Howard Thurman, and H. Richard Niebuhr, to name but a few.[129]

This early history laid the foundation for a more vocal, post-Earth Day, flowering forth of theological and institutional shifts. In 1975—around the same time that I was fighting my way on to an all-boy's little league team—Rosemary Radford Ruether published *New Woman, New Earth*, becoming the first American scholar to link the subjugation of nature with the subjugation of women—and to identify the complicity of Christianity in both.[130] Throughout her ensuing work, however, Ruether consistently identified the promise that lay within the Christian tradition for the story to be changed, articulating distinctly Christian ways of taking nature seriously, such as seeing the divine Logos as a force that creates and sustains all things such that "the whole of creation can be seen as sacramental."[131]

A sacramental, embodied, and feminist view of nature as divine incarnation was further elaborated roughly a decade later by the constructive theologian Sallie McFague. McFague took her life-long interest in the power of metaphor and deployed it as a means to think boldly in the face of the dual threats of ecological and nuclear destruction. Her extensive work in this vein began with the publication of *Models of God: Theology for an Ecological, Nuclear Age* (1987) and continued to evolve with the times, addressing climate change with her *A New Climate for Theology* (2008) and later confronting some of the root causes of the climate crisis in *Blessed Are the Consumers: Climate Change and the Practice of Restraint* (2013).[132] While Christian eco-theology leapt out of the post-Earth day starting gates fairly quickly (in large part to defend against critiques from secular or ex-Christian environmentalists), Jewish earth-based theologies were not far behind, with the path-breaking voices of Rabbi Arthur Waskow, Rabbi Arthur Green, and Ellen Bernstein still influencing the Jewish ecological conversation today.[133]

While theologians were breaking new ground—and newly addressing ground, soil, earth, and non-human beings as worthy of theological reflection—religious institutions were also raising their voices on behalf of nature and ecological health. For instance, as early as 1981, the US Conference of Catholic Bishops (UCCB) issued a declaration on the energy crisis that raised questions that, alas, we are still urgently asking today:

> Will the development of alternative sources of energy contribute to a just society in which access to the necessities of life is universal? Will it reduce the risk of self-destruction through war that competition for energy supplies now poses? Will it help balance the need for economic development with the need for environmental integrity? Can it be a creative force in shaping a more hopeful future than the world seems to face today? In the remaining years of this century, the human community will answer this question for better or for worse.[134]

It is fair to say that in terms of US policies and cultural norms writ large, we have answered these questions for the worse. Nevertheless, the interpretive lean of the USCCB is revealing.[135] While recognizably anthropocentric in some respects, the authors' moral call to justice and the "preferential option for the poor" is made without hesitation, reminding us that in the *religious* realm a commitment to environmental justice—along with the broader term "eco-justice"—was always deeply intertwined with the religious defense of nature.[136]

The justice emphasis from within religious organizations tellingly contrasts with the mainstream environmentalist discourse of the nineteen sixties and seventies which, at that time, centered largely on pollution (without much attention to the inequities of its distribution), the defense of wilderness and the protection of endangered species. Attending to environmental justice is now commonplace within environmental scholarship and activism, both global and local, but this was not always so. Very rarely does a student of mine take note that the landmark study *Toxic Wastes and Race* (1987) was commissioned by the United Church of Christ. What was once deemed "shallow environmentalism" (a focus only on the harm to humans caused by pollutants) has now come full circle, such that reflective environmentalists must now ask themselves searching questions about how to address justice at *all* levels, with equal concern for human and "more than human" communities of life.[137]

Beyond the realm of theology per se, the rise of explicitly "religious" forms of environmentalism began in the mid-1980s.[138] What started as a trickle of statements from religious authorities in the 1980s (such as the USCCB Energy Crisis declaration noted above) by the 1990s and early 2000s became a flood of declarations and resolutions, culminating in Pope Francis' 2015 path breaking encyclical on climate change *Laudato Si*, a visionary text rooted, in part, in Leonardo Boff's insistence that "the cry of the earth and the cry of the poor" are one in the same.[139]

Emerging hand in hand with these statements (and often the sources of them) were eco-religious organizations such as the National Partnership for Religion and the Environment (founded in 1993) with its original constituent members: the Evangelical Environmental Network, the Coalition on the Environment and Jewish Life (COJEL), the National Council of Churches of Christ and the social justice arm of the USCCB.[140] In more recent decades, organizations such as *Dayenu*, The BTS Center, Young Evangelicals for Climate Action (YECA) and the Jewish Youth Climate Movement have focused their attention on the climate crisis in particular, harnessing the energy of a new generation of religiously-oriented climate activists, while leaning into the wisdom of those who preceded them.

A comprehensive history of either eco-theology or religious environmentalist innovations is well beyond the scope of this essay. My purpose in sketching out some basic contours here, however, is to demonstrate that affirming the sacredness of the natural world (whether or not as "Creation" per se) is no longer the dangerous pursuit that it once was within a largely colonial Christian culture that was ever on the alert against "pagan" practices, such as the reverence for nature in and of itself.[141] Something *has* changed. In terms of environmental concern in the United States, the rivers of Western religious traditions have altered their course and are, indeed, "watering new territory" in just the ways that Diana Eck evoked in *Encountering God*.

Indeed, eco-religious expression has become common enough that even an otherwise staunch conservative Catholic thinker such as Pope Benedict could proclaim to a German audience in 2011: "Young people . . . realize that something is wrong in our relationship with nature, that matter is not just raw material for us to shape at will, but that the earth has a dignity of its own and we must follow its directives . . . We must listen to the language of nature and we must answer accordingly."[142] Of course, in recognizing that the "earth has a dignity of its own" Pope Benedict was not seeking fundamentally to collapse the distance between Creator and Creation. Nevertheless, following the ecological innovations of Pope John Paul II before him, Benedict did *shrink* that distance considerably, creating a papal precedent that Pope Francis could take up and run with in his considerably bolder *Laudato Si*.

As I mentioned early in this essay, one valuable aspect of the concept of sacred geography is that it can serve as a marker for what is and is not present within the context of religious environmentalism in the US. The story that I have briefly captured in this essay is a story that traces how religious expressions of "ecological intimacy" have steadily emerged—against considerable odds—within the American religious context. But outside of the most creative and edgy forms of eco-religious expression—Wild Church movements, the eco-Jewish innovations of Jewish Renewal, and ecologically oriented "Engaged Buddhist" practices—does US culture make space to recognize and honor the inherent sacredness of our lands and waters, a sacredness that has been honored without ambivalence by the indigenous tribes that have dwelt here for thousands of years? Are we there yet?

In his captivating study of tree worship in India, David Haberman encourages his readers to stretch beyond Western cultural norms, reminding us that while our worldviews may *appear* to be fixed, we are always making choices about the cultural worlds that we inhabit. In framing his study, Haberman reminds us that our *a priori* views of nature (what we assume to be "the way things are") are to a large extent culturally determined. The dominant Western view of nature, he notes, "rejects animistic and anthropomorphic views of the non-human as childish and primitive," thereby dismissing perspectives that are the majority view in other parts of the world, as well as within indigenous cultures that preceded colonial settlement.[143] By contrast, Haberman argues, a wide range of non-Western, non-colonial cultures offer a way of apprehending the natural world that "does not recognize an absolute boundary between the human and nonhuman and consequently, embraces animistic and anthropomorphic views of the non-human as being the inherent result of continuity between the human and non-human being and as being vital to abundance in human experience."[144] While being careful not to over-argue his case, Haberman clearly sets out to jolt his audience into the recognition that Western worldviews (resting on the assumption of human-nature dualism) do *not* represent "the way things are," but merely one interpretive choice among many.

Meanwhile, in his adventurous theological inquiry, *When God Was a Bird: Christianity, Animism, and the Re-enchantment of the World*, Mark Wallace asks (referencing the Apostle Paul and Acts 17:27–28): "Are not sun, water, earth and air the animating elements within which we all live and move even as our very being is daily sustained by their providential gifts? . . . God is the pulsing, driving life force within the wide expanse of the green world that brings all things together for their, and our, common sustenance."[145] In making this claim, however, Wallace recognizes that he has walked well out on the limb of normative Christian theology, no longer engaging in metaphorical experiments in the manner of Sallie McFague. "This animist vision of God and nature," Wallace admits, "is a bridge too far for many religious thinkers who seek to isolate God from the Earth."[146]

In the realm of sacred geography and its sister concept of religious animism, Haberman, Wallace, and a growing community of scholars and practitioners are declaring two things at once: 1) While we have come a long way in eco-religious thinking and institution-building, we religious people (in the colonized West), are mostly *not* "there yet" in terms of recognizing and honoring the presence of divine in the natural world and 2) With the right blend of creativity, imagination, cultural openness and a willingness to trust our own experiences, we *could be*. Indeed, some of us have already arrived.[147]

Diana Eck has so much to teach us in this realm of new possibilities. As mentioned above, when she brings her readers into the spectacularly varied religious worlds of India, she does so by first naming what she could not quite see when she began her work decades prior: that looking for a "sacred center" was not quite the right question. In reflecting on the limits of her own initial assumptions, she dares us to do likewise. As with India, so too with the American religious landscape. In this time of climate crisis, we can (and should) dare to look beyond the *almost* sacred geographies of our lands and water and toward a time when the "almost" could actually fall away, a time when animistic articulations of Western religious traditions will no longer be dismissed as a "bridge too far." But to get there, we first have to remember that religions are more like rivers than like stones and that the *actual* rivers we think we know well may have something yet to teach us, if we know where and how to look.

· Chapter 14 ·

DARSHANA:
LEARNING TO SEE FROM DIANA ECK[148]

Rahul Mehrotra

Diana Eck has been both my teacher and colleague. I first met Diana in 1986 when I enrolled for her class on religion at the Faculty of Arts and Sciences. While it focused on Hinduism, it never claimed to explain Hindu life but rather to explore the Hindu world of art and culture. I signed up for the class as an elective merely to be able to experience teaching outside the professional graduate program in which I was enrolled. Having grown up in a Hindu family, I had assumed Hinduism was a singular way of life or belief. And I had taken for granted the complexity and virtual imagination that is critical in understanding the pantheon of Hindu gods and their interrelationships, and the nesting of stories within stories that weave together a rather complex context through which to communicate the simplest ideas.

Diana's teaching style, passion, and insights opened a whole new world for me—a world where I understood the role of religion in objective terms and for the first time was able to place the religion I had grown up with into a broader landscape of religious thought and meaning. This was perhaps my first introduction to the idea of pluralism, an idea that would open up for me many subsequent research and writing projects to understand architecture and cities in contemporary India. In any case, this one class motivated me to ask Diana if she could advise me on an independent study on traditional Hindu cities, for which I would produce an annotated bibliography. It was a fantastic task that allowed me to rummage through a wealth of scholarship on the subject, but the truth was that the annotated bibliography was actually an excuse to engage in conversations with Professor Eck.

The exercise of carrying out an independent study with Diana was seminal in my own formation as an architect and urban designer. It introduced me to the idea of how crucial the purpose of the city is to its form. It made me see that cities have their underlying logics—sometimes tangible and often intangible—and understanding this principle is critical in sustaining change in robust ways. This exercise also introduced me to Diana's critical work on Banaras (now Varanasi). Through her book *Banaras: City of Light*,[149] as an urban designer I came to understand a completely different way to navigate and experience a city. It is a dramatically different understanding from the Eurocentric imagination of the city as an absolute idea. Diana's description of Banaras and its incremental growth, structured by a complex logic of movement and circumambulation at the urban scale, displays a pattern far removed from both the rationale and the clearly perceivable urban grid that emanate from modernity in Europe. This new understanding of the city—as an artifact that is made additively through privileging the experiential act of moving through space—is in fact an abstract representation of the city as sacred geography. Through Diana's eyes, the city became a place where architecture is not the only spectacle or instrument by which it is perceived or structured, but rather the very form through which the beliefs and the associative values that people hold in their relationship to urban space is molded. This exposure exponentially expanded my training as an urban designer. It prepared me to engage with my own city of Mumbai (formerly Bombay), where I went back to practice after graduating. The insight I had gained from Diana allowed me to discern the patterns I saw in Mumbai in completely different ways. It propelled me to write extensively about the city in which I lived and worked. It inspired an alternative formulation to describe the city in India—as the Kinetic City! This interpretation is the counterpoint to the Static City, which is familiar to most of us from conventional city maps. Instead, I argued that the city should instead be perceived, read, and mapped in terms of patterns of occupation and associative values attributed to space. Such a framework accommodates a better understanding of the blurred lines of contemporary urbanism and the changing roles of people and spaces in urban society. Clearly, this was the culmination of a process I had started in my conversations with professors at Harvard and specifically with Diana, whose insights enabled me to ground these thoughts in the context of India and its historic cultural continuum.

Jump to 2010, when I returned to Harvard University as a professor of urban design and planning at the Graduate School of Design. Naturally, one of the first professors I reached out to was Diana—now a colleague. Our paths then continued to cross as we both served on the steering committee of the South Asia Initiative at the university. I learned more about her Pluralism Project and was once again inspired to work with her. In 2011, after reading somewhere about the forthcoming Kumbha Mela occurring in January 2013, I sought an urgent audience with Diana and made the audacious proposition to her that we take a group of students and faculty to the Kumbha Mela to map this ephemeral megacity. I will never forget the way her face lit up and how she said it would be a dream come true! This encouragement and endorsement of the project gave it great traction and support around the university. I finally had a project that brought my association with Diana full circle, and I could re-engage with her to study what I had started in 1986: Indian urbanism, albeit in this case an ephemeral megacity!

The next year, leading up to the site exploration in 2013, we taught a seminar class together to prepare students for the visit to the site. The students came from the Faculties of Arts and Sciences, Divinity, Public Health, Engineering, Business, and the Graduate School of Design—a truly interdisciplinary group. After this intense preparation, we finally spent two weeks on the ground in mid-January 2013 at the start of the festival and the occupation of this ephemeral megacity that we were there to study. On arriving at the site, it was mind-blowing to see that in a matter of weeks, an entire temporary megacity had been constructed for the biggest public gathering in the world. This was a city that deploys its own roads, pontoon bridges, cotton tents serving as residences and venues for spiritual meetings, and a spectrum of social infrastructure—all replicating the functions of an actual city. It houses 5 to 7 million people who gather for fifty-five days and an additional flux of 10 to 20 million people who come for twenty-four-hour cycles on the five main bathing dates. Once the festival is over, the whole city is disassembled as quickly as it was deployed, reversing the constructive operation, disaggregating the settlement to its basic components, and recycling a majority of the material used. This is the biggest impermanent megacity in the world.

While we were on the ground, it was amazing to see how Diana moved easily between questions about religious practices and the implications of this gathering on the environment. She focused a great deal of her energy engaging with groups as well as religious leaders who were campaigning for sustainable practices on how this ground for the city was occupied and how waste was managed, and so on. What was remarkable was her interest in placing the practice of religion in the context of contemporary questions: she wanted to understand the challenges that societies in the world face today—problems that might somehow be addressed through religion as an instrument.

Working on mapping the Kumbha Mela with Diana Eck was the most profound experience in my career, as both an architect and an academic. It taught me a great deal about life. And in the same way that studying traditional Indian cities with Diana had made me expand my own view as a student of how cities are made and remade and perceived, the Kumbha Mela project opened up even more expansive questions. Fresh perspectives on the notions of attachment and reversibility raised the question, does permanence even matter? For an architect this is indeed a challenging lens insofar as we are taught to see permanence as a default condition. And it is for these new perspectives that I am indebted to Diana. The only way I can accurately express what I have learned from her is to borrow her own words:

> The pursuit of wisdom, *jnāna* has always been an important strand of the Hindu tradition. *Jnāna* is not conventional knowledge, but liberating insight, the deep-seeing that changes one's entire consciousness of

oneself and the world ... and the philosophies that emerged from them were called *darshanas*, "points of view" or "perspectives." *Darshana* comes from a verb meaning "to see," and it conveys the understanding that any philosophy is one way of seeing a truth that can be viewed from different angles."[150]

It is for this multiplicity of perspectives and ways of seeing that I will always be grateful to Professor Diana Eck.

· Chapter 15 ·

SHIFTING PATTERNS OF EPIPHANIES

Vijaya Nagarajan

Professor Diana Eck is a superb scholar and a wonderful human being, who stands tall and graceful with a rare elegance, and a gentle but firm heart and mind. For nearly four decades, as I slowly turned from being a full-time environmental activist into an academic, Diana Eck was someone I would go to for advice, consultation, and mentorship.

I first met Diana in Cape Cod at the Conference on Religion in South India (CRSI) in the summer of 1986. The theme that year was "Women's Lives and the Life of Women." It was my first academic conference in the field of religion. Diana and Mary McGee (then a Harvard graduate student who helped organize the conference) along with many other scholars, saw me, talked to me, and included me. They tucked me into their lives, as if I belonged to this tribe, even though I was outside the academy. There were few Indian scholars of Hinduism at that time in the United States (A.K. Ramanujan, Indira Peterson, Vasudha Narayanan, and a few others). The field of Hinduism, and the humanities in general, were not attractive to most Indian immigrants who, concerned with economic security, often looked to careers in engineering or computer science. I had left my own engineering program after a couple of years, in the late 1970s; I finished a degree in environmental science and economics at University of California, Berkeley in 1983, and when I met Diana at that gathering in 1986, I was still searching for my path forward.

Steeped in the world of cultural and environmental activism, I had co-founded two tiny non-profits in 1984: the Recovery of the Commons

Project and the Institute for the Study of Natural and Cultural Resources. I was also working part-time for Friends of the Ganges and the Swatcha Ganga Campaign with V.B. Mishra. I was investigating alternative sewage systems to help process the waste along the river Ganga in Varanasi/Banaras. I was also just beginning to pursue more intensely the fuller meaning of the *kolam*, a women's ritual art tradition in southern India that I had grown up experiencing in both India and the United States. These seeds of work grew over the next decades and Diana was one of my key conversation partners throughout.

Diana traveled with me in thought and practice, along with three other great scholars, Professor A. K. Ramanujan, Professor McKim Marriott at the University of Chicago, and Professor David Shulman at the Hebrew University. We shared an appreciation for Hinduism that can be, at its best, capacious, and hospitable to other religious traditions, whose literatures and places of worship contained multitudes of meanings, in many times and spaces; whose radical honesty revealed to me the deep paradoxes, contradictions, and unsettling, shifting paradigms of belief and practice, of non-violence as well as violence. Diana's love of my book, *Feeding a Thousand Souls: Women, Ritual, and Ecology in India–An Exploration of the Kolam*, moved me deeply. When she read one of the early drafts, she said, with a joyful glint in her eye, "Every Indian-American teenage girl should read this book!" I laughed, giddy at her enthusiasm and delight.

During 2001–02, I was selected as one of six research associates and fellows at the Women's Studies in Religion Program at Harvard Divinity School. We moved to Cambridge with our nine-month-old twins, and that was when Diana revealed, to me, her big heart and soul. She invited us to weekly tea on Thursdays at Lowell House, which she and her beloved partner and wife, Dorothy Austin presided over: they were both so gracious and introduced us to many fellow guests and students. Her genuine and deep affection, not only for me, but also for my family, was a rare experience for me as a scholar in the academy. Her eyes glowed as she looked at these two young souls, our twin babies. She was playful and delighted in them whenever she saw them. Dorothy Austin also invited me to do the Morning Prayer at Memorial Church. I was awed by the people who had done this Morning Prayer before me, and I was deeply honored to create that offering of a prayer in that beautiful space. These are all experiences I will never forget.

The range of Diana Eck's research combines personal, scholarly, and reflective ways of writing. She achieves a challenging but unwavering balance of being both accessible and poetic. This has been an inspiration for my own writing. She exhibits courage in her ability to traverse unique intellectual and emotional landscapes, each book requiring her to extensively puzzle through braided themes, twisting paradoxes, and revelatory shifts. Each book has also become a classic of its field.

For example, Eck's *Darśan: Seeing the Divine Image in India*, is a ground-breaking book, which still resonates with students, helping them understand both how Hinduism is perceived by those from western epistemological traditions and how it is seen from a variety of perspectives from within Hinduism. Also, Eck's *Encountering God: A Spiritual Journey from Bozeman to Banaras*, is a profound, mind-altering journey, shared with such radical honesty, that as soon as I finished it, I wanted to read it again. Above all, I wanted to write a book in response, to keep the conversation going. How *does* someone from one faith encounter another, as Diana does, a Christian from Montana who becomes a scholar of Hinduism? It was revelatory. How could I, as a Hindu coming to the US in the 1960s as a child, describe my experiences of being in a Southern Baptist Church where I went every Sunday with my best friend for nearly two years, from the ages of seven to nine?

Her book, *India: A Sacred Geography* is also an extraordinary accomplishment, almost an impossible one, given the scale of her ambitions. It took nearly half a lifetime to write, and it gives lyrical and detailed insights into how geography becomes sacred through myth, ritual, and pilgrimage in Hinduism. This is only a glimpse of Diana's work that has impressed me deeply. The body of work Professor Diana Eck has created stands tall in the field of religious studies. It is common parlance to say we stand on the shoulders of others. Indeed, Diana's wide range of intellectual interests in Hinduism and related fields such as sacred geography, pilgrimage, ritual, and waste inspire me. The following is the beginning of a chapter from a new book I am working on, *Hinduism and Climate: Waste, Fire, Death, and Love*. I cannot imagine working on such a book without having Diana Eck and her phenomenal body of work on which to stand.

CLIMATE CRISIS EPIPHANIES

In June 2003, on a rare vacation with friends on the island of Ischia near the coast of Naples, the abnormal heat was so intense you couldn't go to the beach until very late in the afternoon: If you put out your arm in the sun, you felt as if your skin was an eggplant on a skillet burning under a high flame. It was a terrifying experience.

In July 2011, I was on a river trip in the US with another group of friends to celebrate my 50th birthday. The snowmelt had been unusually high. The river was so swollen even highly experienced river guides could no longer read it. Our boat crashed against a gigantic stone that rose up eerily out of the water. I fell out of the boat, along with most of my friends. The rest were able to get out fairly rapidly, but I was knocked hard against large, partially submerged rocks. Once rescued, I realized with horror: I was paralyzed from the waist down. Twelve hours later, at one in the morning in the ER, it felt as if a real miracle happened: I could move my toes again. Until that moment, the doctors were uncertain what the outcome would be.

In October of 2017, in northern California, where I had lived for nearly forty years, I suddenly found it hard to breathe. The asthma that flared often when I was a child in New Delhi, and whenever I visited as an adult, started becoming commonplace in northern California. From then onwards, the air around me felt dried out, as if the air itself had been wrung tightly, twisted by our collective hands, a cloth that no longer had any moisture left. Smoke blanketed the San Francisco Bay Area, turning the sky a perennial gray color for days. Ashes dropped. The sky steeped to a strange orange pekoe color, as if the sun itself had burst its seams and leaked beyond its boundaries. We adopted new language to describe what was happening to the earth: Sky-high fires, fire whirls, and fire tornadoes. What had been speculative fiction now sounded like non-fiction. Our unbalanced use of fossil fuels and insatiable energy use was causing excessive heat and changes to oceans and atmosphere.

WASTE IN THE INDUS VALLEY

From 2017 onwards, as a scholar and professor of Hinduism, I started wondering: how could we think about the climate dilemmas from the multiple disciplines embedded in the sacred geography of the Indian subcontinent? Archeology, literature, mythology, philosophy, and poetry have developed over thousands of years. Were there clues in these disciplines that could spark innovation, redesign, and imagination in a collective response to pervasive climate chaos? With our modern life conveniences, with our nearly complete global devotion to the idea of unilinear progress, how is it possible to reconcile the fact that we need to reduce carbon output with both western epistemological traditions as well as those home-grown in India? These are preliminary notes from my reflections on these questions.

The Indus Valley civilization, one of the largest ancient civilizations, straddles present-day Pakistan and western India. It arose around 3300 BCE and fell apart around 1800 BCE. We don't really know how the ancient Indus Valley civilization ended. But we think that the river, what we now call the Indus River, may have dried up and forced the people there to migrate, over several centuries, to the Gangetic Plains. Or, the Indus River may have flooded and caused people to search for a more stable site for the continuation of their life and community.

I remembered that in the winter of 1988, two years after my first encounter with Diana Eck, I was contemplating whether to become an archeologist: I wanted to explore the archeology of waste. Dr. George Dales and Dr. Mark Kenoyer, both from UC Berkeley, were conducting archeological investigations and were kind enough to invite me to come and stay for a visit in Harappa. Harappa and Mohenjo-daro are two of the major sites of the Indus Valley civilization. With streets laid out on a grid they are the earliest examples we have of planned cities. I was dazzled when I first learned of their complex sewage systems connecting each household with a drain made of brick with clay covers.

In Mohenjo-daro, I had the strange experience of walking around the ancient perpendicular streets and feeling as if I were walking in a modern city. I was struck by the exquisite bathrooms, laid out nearly five thousand years ago with waterproof tiles that looked so contemporary. Many of the houses had private toilets and elaborate drainage systems using pipes made of fired clay. The waste stream of water moved from each of the houses to a drain on the side of each house, which, in turn, led to a slightly inclined plane, that moved the waste down the side of the street to a waste pit outside of the town, that would have been regularly cleaned. The brick drains were impressive, even with our modern gaze.

What struck me forcibly was the complex and thoughtful management of waste moving from each house to the municipal supply system: a system that was more advanced and thorough than in some of our contemporary South Asian cities, towns, and villages. There was, most of all, a transparency at the heart of this sewage system. Most of the sewage system was visible, unlike our contemporary modern underground sewage systems. They were covered with fired brick layers, which could easily be lifted and cleaned, if blocked. This ancient sewage system was beautiful as well: its covered drains, traced the path between the bathrooms and the kitchens to the outside of the building, and connected to channeled drains which ran alongside each house, one after the other.[151] I wondered how the municipal organization of sewage worked in this ancient culture. As the language of this civilization remains largely undeciphered, we can't fully answer this question yet.

In many ways, these sewage systems were more advanced than what was available in western Europe as late as the mid-nineteenth century. Cleanliness and waste management were clearly important to the Indus Valley culture. If nearly five thousand years ago we were able to organize our waste in such a systematic and exquisite manner, can't we do it now, even with all the obstacles? What would it take to re-imagine our present societies through the lens of how we manage waste of all kinds? How do we begin thinking of waste generated by industrial processes as part the design phase itself, rather than putting it off to a later time period for unknown humans or non-human animals, or mountains, forests, glaciers, ice sheets, rivers, lakes, or oceans to have to deal with? Right now, most waste is treated as "externalities" as economists would have us call it: that is, "external" to the engineering design. Why not make thinking about waste internal to the very design process, so fewer externalities arise in the short-term and the long-term?

In the fall of 2019, I interviewed Amitav Ghosh, the writer and thinker, live on stage, as part of the launch of his brilliant novel, *Gun Island*. This novel was his bold attempt to incorporate the climate problem into his fiction. When I asked him a question about the climate problem, he said, thoughtfully, something akin to: "The problem of climate is really a problem of waste." This sentiment has haunted me ever since.

When we pour out carbon from excessive fossil fuel use, as a consequence of many of our industrial processes, machines, and technologies—whether they are from the energy used in cars, trucks, and ships, or factories, offices, or homes—what do we exactly mean to do? Can we re-imagine industrial processes so that they do not create waste in the first place? How can we redesign the production systems of all that we use so that "waste" itself is only created if it can be used as food for another creature, as nature often models?

Can the Indus Valley civilization serve as a distant signpost of a culture that made waste visible to its people rather than hiding it away? Can we shift our paradigms to make waste transparent and visible in every step of the design process, so we can make careful decisions about whether creating surplus waste is *actually* worth the cost? The impact of our answers to these questions will be felt in every heated part of the entire planet, the land, the oceans, and the atmosphere.

· Chapter 16 ·

RESIDING ON THE HAIR OF ŚIVA, RISING FROM THE FOOT OF VIṢṆU: THE RIVER GAṄGĀ IN THE KHMER LANDSCAPE[152]

Vasudha Narayanan

"The Gaṅgā is the river of India—a single river flowing from the Himalayas, gathering tributaries, and streaming across the fertile plains of north India. At the same time, the Gaṅgā is the source of all sacred waters everywhere in India. The Gaṅgā is also a goddess— Gaṅgā Mātā, 'Mother Gaṅgā,' and Gaṅgā Devī, 'Goddess Gaṅgā.' Her true headwaters are not really in the highest Himalayas, but are said to be in the highest heaven, emerging from the very foot of Viṣṇu. She was carried in the water pot of Lord Brahmā, and when she plummeted from heaven to earth, her cascades fell first on the head of Lord Shiva."
—Diana Eck, *India: A Sacred Geography*, 131

Diana Eck's contribution to the study of sacred geography in India and her vision in the ambitious Pluralism Project have been seminal contributions to the study of religion. Inspired by her work on the sacred river Gaṅgā in India, I will look further east, and write about its importance in the Khmer landscape in the first millennium CE.[153] In the passage quoted above, Eck makes several points in talking about Gaṅgā; in inverse order, she resides on Lord Śiva's head, she emerges from the foot of Viṣṇu, and she is a river flowing across India. And finally, she is the source of all waters, she is Mother Gaṅgā. I will use these ideas as a frame to talk about Gaṅgā in Cambodia.

RESIDING ON THE HAIR OF ŚIVA, RISING FROM THE FOOT OF VIṢṆU

Most Hindus hold the river Gaṅgā to be the holiest of rivers. It is the archetype of all rivers, and some hold her to be present in every water body. On the festival day of Deepavali, she is said to be in all rivers of India. But what did the Gaṅgā, a river and a goddess in India, mean to the Khmer people who lived thousands of miles away? In everyday life, even today in Cambodia, rivers are called Kongea, the Khmer version of "Gaṅgā." Gaṅgā with the final 'a' elongated (pronounced 'e-a') is a literary form in Khmer which can mean 'water,' 'waterway,' or 'river.' The river Mekong means Ma Gaṅgā.[154] Looking back at how Gaṅgā—the goddess and the river—figured in the Khmer world view about 1,200 years ago, we see three interlocking strands. The first is her intimate connection with Śiva and the chagrin of Umā-Pārvatī, Śiva's consort. The second evokes the story of her coming from Viṣṇu's foot (*Viṣṇupada*). The third is her physical manifestation as a river, flowing through the countryside, fertilizing the crops and being a source of nourishment. In the final section of this paper, I note the difference in her status in Cambodia and suggest that her heightened importance there may be because of the state's strong involvement with an elaborate water management network. Kbal Spean, the river compared to the Ganga in Cambodia, fed into the Siem Reap River, and its course was altered for irrigation and water management through Angkorian history.

RIVER GAṄGĀ AS THE CONSORT OF ŚIVA

In a popular story in the Hindu Purāṇas, Gaṅgā comes from the heavens at the request of the king Bhagīratha. The force of her fall would be life threatening to the world; and so, Śiva breaks the speed by catching Gaṅgā, the river and goddess in his hair. Eventually, he lets a drop fall on the earth and that is the river that we know of today. The river Gaṅgā in Hindu stories is physically and romantically entangled with Śiva, and resides on his head, tucked into his long hair that is piled on his head.

In narrative, sculpture, and rituals in India, however, Śiva's primary consort is Pārvatī, also known as Umā. While in many portrayals, she stands or sits by Śiva's side, sometimes Śiva is portrayed as androgynous, half man, half-woman with Pārvatī physically being the left half of his body. Thus, Śiva has the goddess Gaṅgā in his head, and in some depictions Pārvatī is half his body; the male and female are fused in one. Although Gaṅgā and Pārvatī are occasionally portrayed as sisters,[155] in literature and in folk traditions the proximity to Śiva leads to tension between the two co-wives. Sanskrit literature,[156] and occasionally inscriptions in India, speak about their rivalry.

Several Sanskrit inscriptions in Cambodia offer salutations to the river Gaṅgā (K. 528, v. 7); many more (K. 528, K. 826, K. 829, K. 1222, etc.)[157] say that the goddesses Umā and Gaṅgā accompany Śiva. An inscription from 881 CE in Bakong (K. 829), for instance, says that the king, Indravarman, erected a deity named "Umāgaṅgāpatisvara," that is, the lord of Umā and Gaṅgā.[158] So often are the three mentioned together that Śiva, Gaṅgā, and Umā are said to form a triad in Cambodia.[159] This is remarkable, and we should note, different from India where, although Gaṅgā is said to be a consort of Śiva, in most of the subcontinent she is *not* considered equal to Parvati and part of a "triad," as she is in Cambodia.

There are several references to, and literary conceits used to describe Gaṅgā dwelling in Śiva's matted locks. In a ninth century CE inscription (K. 675), for instance, Śiva's head glistens with the waves of the Gaṅgā and is radiant like ten million young moons.[160] Many more, like this one from the tenth century (K. 250), found in Damnak Sdac, mention, in passing, the river's abode on Śiva's head: "May Bhava, whose body is adorned with ashes, who bears both the weight of the [crescent] moon and the fall of the Gaṅgā, be propitious to you."[161]

But often it is the jealousy generated by the physical proximity of Gaṅgā and Umā that dominates Sanskrit inscriptions in Cambodia. A seventh-century inscription (K. 81) found in Han Chey, about ninety miles northeast of Phnom Penh, and the earliest one to mention Gaṅgā, glorifies Śiva as the god who has her on his head. Śiva's well-known consort, Umā-Pārvatī, looks angrily at Gaṅgā, jealous of the river's close connection with Śiva. In the poet's soaring imagination, the waters of Gaṅgā, fearing Umā's wrathful gaze, move rapidly, as if to escape or to hide. In that process, the river seems to form a garland around Śiva.[162]

This theme is replicated many times in the inscriptions. The Prasat Beng inscription (K. 989, verse 4, dated to 1008 CE), for instance, is even more dramatic: "Victory to Umā," it says, beginning with the standard salutation; and then it continues, "whose lip trembles, teeth grind, eyes ignite, as if she had touched fire, when she sees Gaṅgā for a moment beside Śiva."[163]

There is even a verse with *nindā stuti*, a genre in which the devotee praises the deities by paradoxically reproaching or mocking them. In an eleventh century CE inscription from Tuol Ta Pec, Kompong Thom (K. 834, lines 7–8), the devotee says: "Sambhu is radiant; although he is endowed with great power and is master of the universe, he is frightened by the frown of Umā, who is furious to see him adorned with Gaṅgā!"[164] The Khmer people seem to delight in this human moment of anger displayed by one wife towards another woman with whom her husband is romantically involved, possibly as a reflection of life in the royal families.

GAṄGĀ'S CONNECTION WITH THE GOD VIṢṆU

While Gaṅgā the goddess is associated with Śiva, the river is associated with both Śiva and Viṣṇu in India and in Cambodia. As Diana Eck notes:

> In the many Vaiṣṇava versions of the myth, the river is called Viṣṇupadi, after its origin in Viṣṇupada ("the celestial realm of Viṣṇu" or "the foot of Viṣṇu").... In taking his famous three strides, Viṣṇu, the dwarf-turned-giant, stretched through and took possession of the threefold universe. With is third stride he is said to have pierced the vault of heaven with his toe and released the heavenly waters.[165]

Although the story is less well known than Gaṅgā's association with Śiva, the primeval cosmic waters are said to have come to earth because of Viṣṇu. When his left toe pierced through the membrane of the universe, it is said, the cosmic waters flowed through Viṣṇupada, the domain of Viṣṇu, then over his foot, down to earth, and was caught then in Śiva's head.[166]

In the tenth century, the powerful king Rajendravarman built a large temple (known today as Pre Rup) to Śiva near the Eastern Mebon, in modern Siem Reap, Cambodia. The Sanskrit inscription in Pre Rup (K. 806) is possibly the longest one of its kind in the world. In it, the Gaṅgā is called Viṣṇupadi, that is, the river that comes from Viṣṇu's foot. Rajendravarman, says this inscription (in verse 272), "defeated by force of his arm the king of Campa." He then "offered the fortune of this king to Hari Svayambhu [Viṣṇu] on the bank of the Viṣṇupadi (i.e., the Gaṅgā) as if to give meaning to his name Campesvara."[167] Here, Viṣṇu's local name "Campeśvara" is explained by saying he is the lord of the land of Campa that was conquered and appropriated by Rajendravarman. Coedès assumes that the river Mekong is probably called Viṣṇupadi or the Gaṅgā here.[168]

An inscription from c.1071 (K. 782) found in Prasat Sralao, not far from Angkor Thom's North Gate, also mentions Ganga's association with Viṣṇu with an interesting tweak: "I salute the foot of Viṣṇu which has spanned the earth and which the Gaṅgā raises, as if to lower the height of the king of the mountains, father of her rival [Umā Pārvatī who is said to be the daughter of the Himalayas]."[169] The idea of the Gaṅgā lifting up Viṣṇu's foot is unusual but as Coedès explains and we can also observe, it seems to articulated in art in several depictions of Trivikrama. Here, the waters being poured seem to elevate the feet of Viṣṇu.[170]

The Pre Rup inscription (K. 806) that we have encountered several times in this chapter has, as we have seen, referred to the Gaṅgā as a goddess (verse 7), the consort of Śiva, and as associated with Viṣṇu (verse 272). It also speaks about Gaṅgā as a physical river in India. Declaiming the grandeur of king Rajendravarman (verse 121) it says that when he "went on an expedition on the ocean, the tight file of his boats and the caravan of white sails appeared exactly like a garland of wild geese driven by the rapid current of the Gaṅgā."[171]

And although Gaṅgā is a goddess who is the beloved of Śiva, and also the cosmic waters flowing from Viṣṇu's foot on to this earth below, she is ultimately the life-giving river. She nourishes crops and irrigates fields, she hydrates our bodies and infuses them with life. We note that at least by the tenth century, the time of the Pre Rup inscription, local rivers in Cambodia came to be identified with the Gaṅgā in India.

KBAL SPEAN, THE RIVER GAṄGĀ THAT FLOWS THROUGH THE KHMER LANDS

Eleventh century inscriptions (K.1011, 1012, 1015, and 1016) near the Kbal Spean river identify it as the river Gaṅgā itself. The eponymous site is a wooded area in the hills, about thirty miles northeast of Siem Reap and nine miles from the famous temple in Banteay Srei. While this area is part of the extended sacred site of Phnom Kulen, it is quite distinct from it. After parking the car at the foothills, one has to climb for about an hour through wooded area, a trek that I have done many times. The hike is broken with waterfalls, and we come a spot where we begin to find multiple carved Śiva liṅgas as well Viṣṇu—Anantasayin, that is, Viṣṇu reclining on the serpent, Ananta. As IM Sokrithy of the APSARA authority of Cambodia notes, "flowing past and over the reliefs of O Thom and O Kbal Spean, the water [of this river] is sanctified before entering the Siem Reap and Pouk rivers, which continue south onto the plain and through the temple complexes of Angkor. Thus, the water is seen as the source of prosperity."[172]

The Kbal Spean is one of the waterways that feeds into the Siem Reap, and this "river is thought to have been deviated from an original watercourse by Angkor's "urban planners." This action is given as an example of how "specific geographical elements simultaneously shaped and were shaped by the Angkorian civilization."[173] According to the inscriptions there, in 1054, a minister of Suryavarman I (r. 1006 to 1050) had the site decorated with a thousand liṅgas (*sahasraliṅga;* inscription K.1011–1). Inscription K.1011–3 states that c.1059, King Udayadityavarman II (r.1050 to 1066) visited the river in which there are several carvings of Viṣṇu reclining on his serpent bed. The inscriptions also mention the raising of a gold liṅga.[174]

The mention of these royal names is significant in terms of the hydraulic management of Angkor; it was Suryavarman I who started a massive construction of a reservoir, the Western Baray, that, though a thousand years old now, is still considered to be the largest one in the world. When built, "this baray allowed for nearly complete agricultural occupation of the plain."[175] The large reservoirs also "formed the structure of the city and was the basis for its water management."[176] Its dimensions are 8 km x 2.1 km and one of the main rivers that fed this reservoir was the Siem Reap, the same one into which we saw, the Kbal Spean flowed. His successor, Udayadityavarman II completed the reservoir. It is therefore striking that apart from their major hydraulic enterprises, these kings ordered the carving of the liṅgas and set up the gold liṅga in the river.

Then we come to the dramatic inscription of the same eleventh century CE (K.1012-1) from Kbal Spean, one that identifies the Kbal Spean with the river Gaṅgā: "Thundering torrent of Rudra, River of Śiva," it says, and continues, "this Gaṅgā manifested itself visibly and loudly, she who completely destroys the faults of the world, like the heavenly river!"[177]

As we saw earlier, Gaṅgā, the goddess and the river, is connected to both Śiva and Viṣṇu. By carving these deities into the body of the flowing river, the Khmer people showed their understanding of both these narratives and held them as equally important. IM Sokrithy observes, "the Khmer carved liṅgas and representations of various gods deep into the bed of O Thom and O Kbal Spean. These two streams give birth to the Siem Reap River. The water flowing past and over these liṅgas is like the rain falling on the chignon of Shiva. Thus, the Siem Reap River is transformed into the Ganges."[178] And flowing over the bas-reliefs of the reclining Viṣṇu, the river also comes from his foot.

GAṄGĀ AND GONGEA: THE GODDESS AND THE RIVER IN INDIA AND CAMBODIA

The mighty river that flows through the heart of the north India is seen to flow through the Khmer territories. This does not necessarily mean that there were migrants from India who named the rivers or places after those they left behind; rather, we can say this identification indicates the familiarity that the Khmer people had with Indian *tīrtha*s or holy sites.

RESIDING ON THE HAIR OF ŚIVA, RISING FROM THE FOOT OF VIṢṆU

But will the Gaṅgā of India recognize the Kongea of Cambodia? We can say "yes," with some confidence, given the repetition of tropes and the narratives recalled in Cambodia, but as one can expect in a case where a culture selectively chooses and adopts ideas and practices from another country (like yoga becoming popular in America), there are subtle as well as explicitly expressed differences.

One of the main differences from India is that in Cambodia, as we saw earlier, she is evoked as an important and popular goddess. The Khmer people seem to have venerated Gaṅgā on par with other celestial deities. Rajendravarman in the Pre Rup inscription, for example, salutes Śiva—his primary deity of choice but immediately follows up with Viṣṇu, Gaṅgā, et al. There are invocations to her in the beginning of inscriptions, along with invocations to Viṣṇu, Śiva, Umā-Pārvatī, and so on, showing that she is the elite category of deities to be venerated. And, along with Śiva and Umā, she forms a triad in a way do not see in an obvious way in India.

Her importance in Cambodia seems far more marked, as perhaps one may expect in a country and a culture where management of water translated to royal power. When King Indravarman (reigned c. 877–890 CE) became king, "he first made a promise: in five days from today, I shall begin dig," indeed, he is said to have started digging for the large reservoir (*taṭāka*) very soon after his coronation.[179] His Indrataṭāka is one of hundreds of reservoirs (*baray*) constructed during the Angkorian period (ninth to fifteenth centuries CE). Rulers in the Angkorian empire consolidated their power through the creation of such large public work projects throughout the lands. Angkor covered about 3000 square km and LIDAR research shows a "landscape integrated by an elaborate water management network covering >1,000 km, the most extensive urban complex of the preindustrial world."[180] While it was commonly understood, that the kings lost this power when the water networks disintegrated over time, ongoing research is still exploring the extent to which "the water management network and the environmental effects of the urban expansion of Angkor were implicated in . . . [the] decline of that civilization."[181] The reliance on water management was high; the appreciation of Indian narratives and traditions also seems to have been high, at least, in elite circles. Gaṅgā, therefore, is evoked frequently in inscriptions, far more than I have seen in Indian ones, and given this civilization's involvement in water management, it is easy to see why she is valorized considerably.

While Gaṅgā's connection with Śiva and Viṣṇu are spoken about in India, it is the Śaiva story that is dominant there. In Cambodia, in the sculptures of Kbal Spean as well as in inscriptions, we see concerted effort to also reiterate her association with Viṣṇu. By carving Viṣṇu and emblems of Śiva into the Kbal Spean River, they could understand it as the Gaṅgā. IM Sokrithy observes, "Cambodia doesn't have an equivalent to the Ganges River. So, the ancient Khmer modified the existing rivers and consecrated them to form a kind of Ganges."[182] And the Khmer kings used the liquid *śakti* of the Gaṅgā to flow through their channels to irrigate lands as well as their own structures of power.

· Chapter 17 ·

MEDIA AND MEMORY:
FROM CAMBRIDGE TO MANZANAR

Susan Shumaker

I begin this entry with a confession: I am not a typical *festschrift* contributor. Then again, Diana Eck is not a typical academic.

From that first moment in her office, in the fall of 1988, it was clear to me—a newbie Harvard Divinity School (HDS) student and lucky Eck advisee—that Diana had "got it goin' on." The adventures emanating from her garret room atop Phillips Brooks House (PBH) included not only scholarly book projects and papers submitted to journals and anthologies, but a PBS documentary in the works (and a possible film series to follow) and a nascent project, focused on Boston, that had the potential to change the way the study of religion was taught.

Diana was in the process of writing a grant to explore the changing religious landscape of the greater Boston area, and to craft a course from her findings that would engage students in boots-on-the-ground learning: a mash-up of ethnographic site-visits, crash courses in each tradition's beliefs (and site-specific etiquette), and in-depth conversations with adherents that would allow students to learn first-hand what it meant to *experience* a tradition, in a way that lectures and assigned readings alone could not. Diana's enthusiasm was contagious, and—in what I soon learned was her typically generous style—she wrote me into the grant. I was hooked. That summer of site visits, interviews, and research reports resulted in the promised seminar and the first, self-published, comb-bound edition of the guidebook, *World Religions in Boston* (now in its fifth, and much fancier, edition).

In 1991, I moved into my own small corner of PBH's top floor, and the Pluralism Project was launched. It was an exciting, germinal time, with those first seasons of students fanning out across the country to engage in what Diana called "hometown research," and I was privileged to be at the heart of it with her, coordinating the project as Diana dreamt of bigger things that the project might—and ultimately would—become. Shortly thereafter, and much to her credit, Diana took a risk on my enthusiasm for "new media"—aka, the bleeding edge of interactive CD-ROMs and that new thing out of CERN, the World Wide Web. She innately saw the possibilities that multimedia storytelling could bring to teaching, and *On Common Ground*, in all its forms, was born—as was my love of filmmaking. The project moved from the "library" atop PBH to its new digs in Vanserg Hall, Harvard's decommissioned ROTC barracks, and the staff expanded to include in-house researchers, designers, photographers, sound editors, and—most crucially, for our mental wellness—office dog, Morgan. A few years later, the *On Common Ground* CD-ROM had won multiple educational and design awards, and the Pluralism Project had begun its full throttle love affair with media—a relationship that is still thriving today, thanks to the continued interests of Diana, Ellie Pierce, and others.

Along the way, I grew closer to Diana, considering her not just a mentor, or a boss, but my Cambridge family, and when Dorothy was the officiant at my wedding, it was only right that Diana took it upon herself to be our "unofficial officiant," wearing her robes and standing not far from Dorothy's side at the altar. On a beautiful autumn evening a few years later, as we sat together on the porch of their home on Trowbridge, I broke the news to Diana that my career lay not in academia, but in public media. She was beyond supportive, sharing (with her uncommon genius for engaged empathy) that—had she not chosen a career in the academy—she, too, might well have followed that path.

I have devoted the last twenty-five years to a career in documentary filmmaking, working almost exclusively with director Ken Burns. One of my projects, in particular, can be traced directly to Diana's influence: a series of short films entitled "Untold Stories in the National Parks," connected with our larger Emmy-winning film, *America's Best Idea*. With enthusiastic support from the larger film's writer, Dayton Duncan, the short films were written and produced by me and served to bring the story up to the present. Each explored a way in which people of color—typically underserved by the parks (and who, in fact, often don't feel welcomed or even safe in green spaces)—had contributed to the fabric of the park system, with the goal of encouraging these underserved communities to embrace the parks as their shared birthright. One of the films, *Manzanar—Never Again*, is a tale of cultural collision in America, showcasing a community working together to reclaim its history and force the United States to grapple with and tell that history—especially important today, as school districts across the US erase "prohibited topics" from their textbooks and libraries. The film is still being broadcast within the community, is used in classrooms nationwide as part of middle school social studies curricula, and is available on the PBS site. The editors of this publication have graciously allowed me to share its script here, as my contribution to our shared work celebrating Diana.

I learned more than I can put into words from Diana, lessons which have served me in my work, and in my life: how to enter any situation with grace and humility; how to appreciate and value ideas that seem foreign, at first, as new entries to understanding and insight; how to treat students and co-workers as colleagues; how to engage respectfully with others in the public square; how to put on a kick-hiney Christmas party (and somehow get everyone present to sing multiple verses of "O Little Town of Bethlehem"); how to speak truth to power; how to devote yourself to your work with all your heart, and still have room there for the people you love. I hope that some of these lessons are clear in the following.

MANZANAR—"NEVER AGAIN"

Title: Florentine Films
Footage of hawk circling, Taeko drummers calling participants to the pilgrimage, people seated
Title: Manzanar—"Never Again"

Bruce Embrey: You know, it was a very humiliating experience to be rounded up by your own Government. It was very painful because you not just were cast as enemies, um, you lost everything materially.

Historic footage of the bombing of Pearl Harbor.

Ken Burns (Narrator): After the Japanese bombed Pearl Harbor in December of 1941 the United States government decided Japanese Americans were enemies of the state. Within months, over 100,000 US citizens and legal residents were ordered to leave their homes and report to one of ten remote internment centers. Manzanar, in the high California desert, is one of those internment camps.

Footage of spam frying on portable grill; sushi-making table. A woman and a man stand together, looking at photos.

Man: Now this is Janice and— **Patty Sakamoto:** That's Janice and that's me. **Man:** That's you. **Patty:** Yeah, little fat kid. **Man:** Oh my goodness! (laughing) **Patty:** This was in Manzanar. And it looks like—what? Do you think maybe I was 12 months old? **Man:** Yes. **Patty:** And then, this is Janice and Mom with the barrack behind them. **Man:** Oh, yeah!

Footage of three people standing together, talking about Japanese Americans and interment.

Marjory Sperling: If you look at our pictures every group of folks that are being evacuated were all dressed up. Can you imagine being ordered to come into camp and like, like a— **Patty:** Wearing their best clothes. **Marjory:** Yes, wearing our best clothes and being— **Patty:** And coming early! (laughing) **Marjory:** Yes, and being on time! (laughing) **Bruce Embrey:** Showing up early to be evacuated. **Marjory Spellman:** And being on time. It was absolutely asinine when I look back on it. And if it were to happen today, oh, my—I would raise such hell! (laughing)

More footage of musubi-making at table. Footage of friendly-looking young man, early twenties. He shouts to someone off camera.

Young Man: Mom! Uh, we need more spam! **Woman** [off camera]: Here, I'll get it for you.

Patty shows photos.

Patty: My father never saw me. My mother was pregnant with me and he gave up his citizenship and left with his family to go back to Japan and my mother was not gonna give hers up.

Koo Sakamoto: Not me. I said, "I'll join the WAVs, the WACs, anything—but I sure am not leaving America." [laughs]

Bruce Embrey: Eight hundred volunteers from the Japanese-American community came up here, including my uncle, to build the barracks. So, they dressed in their finest, they showed up early, and they built (laughing)—AND they built the barracks where they were to be housed! The barracks were cobbled together out of scrap lumber and tarpaper. **Patty:** Tarpaper. **Bruce:** There was no insulation. There was no privacy, because they were just these 20-x-25-foot boxes.

Historic footage of Manzanar being built, scenics of landscape, historic photos.

Newsreel narrator [from original footage]: Pre-fabricated barracks spring up. It's in no sense a concentration camp, but a city with its front yard in the snow-peaked Sierra Nevadas. Here eventually 12,000 will live and work.

Sets Tomita: I came to the camp when I was almost ten years old. We left early in the morning; took us nine hours to drive here and when we got here it was really dusty, and it was nothing but just barracks there. So, it was very stark. It was like being abandoned, yeah.

Jenni Kuida: I think when you come out here and you feel the heat and you see the dust and some years it's very windy, the dust is going up your nose and your hair is just flying everywhere, you really can appreciate what the people went through.

Ranger Alisa Lynch: Where the Japanese-Americans lived was basically one square mile, and it was enclosed by a five-strand barbed-wire fence. There were also eight guard towers. Security was really high, uh, very tight.

Monica Embrey: One thing I'll never forget my grandmother telling me is that when they first got here my great-grandmother would sit under the apple orchards and cry and sob that she couldn't give her children a better life; that she couldn't provide them the opportunities that she wanted to.

Footage of fishing.

Sets Tomita: Here you go. Ok? And I'll help your line out. Camp was boring; there was nothing to do. We had to leave everything we had behind so you made whatever toys you could make out of the material you had on hand. We had no other options. We were stuck behind a barbed wire fence, so we made the best that we can out of it. My older brother, he heard one day about, uh, some of the guys said that they went fishing in the local creek. So we'd climb under the barbwire and leave camp. We never had permission to go, we just snuck out of camp by ourselves.

MEDIA AND MEMORY

Historic photos.

Alisa Lynch: The war, of course, ends in August, 1945, but the camp didn't close until November 21st of 1945 and that is because a lot of the people who were here had nowhere to go.

Footage of Tomita fishing.

Sets Tomita: Camp life was really bad because we were in captivity, we couldn't do what we wanted to do. But a rougher life, a more devastating part of our, my life history is when we came out of camp, uh, because in camp you were fed three times a day, you had the necessities of life.

Ken Burns (Narrator): Before the war, Sets Tomita's father had a thriving trucking business in southern California and the family lived comfortably. When they left Manzanar, they had no home, no money, and faced rampant prejudice. The only job Mr. Tomita could find was cleaning rabbit pens.

Sets Tomita: And the place to live was a two-car garage. All it had was one single light bulb; no water, no heat, no electricity, no gas. We had two beds and nine of us slept in that room there. So, you talk about harsh conditions! Camp was okay compared to that! (laughing)

Bruce Embrey: When the community emerges from camp with many people dispossessed of all of their, uh, possessions and livelihood and houses, they had to bury the pain and anger and frustration in order to survive.

Ken Burns (Narrator): For years, even mentioning the internment experience was taboo among Japanese Americans. Finally, in 1969, 250 students and activists returned to reclaim their history. Now thousands make the annual pilgrimage—to remember past injustices and raise awareness of other civil rights struggles.

Footage of Manzanar Pilgrimage program, speaker at podium.

Man: We're here to continue the legacy, bringing friends of our community together to remember what happened at Manzanar in the hopes of something like this never happening again.

Bruce Embrey: My mother became connected to these young students in this Asian pride movement and came back to Manzanar in '69. And Manzanar became bigger than life over the course of the next year or two.

Ranger Alisa Lynch: Sue Kunitomi Embrey was really the driving force behind the creation of Manzanar Historic Site. She began organizing the pilgrimages and, you know, for almost forty years was involved in preserving this site. She was very patriotic. Not someone whose patriotism was, sort of, mindless nationalism, but defending your country and making your country stand for what its constitution says it stands for.

Sue Embrey (*actor voiceover*): I want people fifty years from now to remember what was there. Although it was a negative place, we want to turn it around to be positive, so that people will always remember that America is a democracy.

Ken Burns (Narrator): After that first visit, Sue Embrey threw herself into the cause. The next year she brought her children.

Bruce Embrey: So here I am, 11 years old, 12 years old, and I get to come to Manzanar to the next pilgrimage. And we pull up and I look around and I said, "Where is Manzanar?" And I'm thinking, "What the heck? All this excitement, all this animated discussion, all this time, and there's nothing here; there's desert!"

Ken Burns (Narrator): After the war, the camp was quickly torn down.

If not for a small monument, built to honor Manzanar's dead, no one would know the camp had ever existed.

Bruce Embrey: No one ever dreamed we would have a park. No one ever dreamed we would have the national government take responsibility for this—and many people didn't want them to. There were large numbers of even former internees that felt that, "Why are you bringing this up now? It's in the past. It's going to call unnecessary negative attention to us. There's people out there that already hate us; don't give them more ammunition."

Ken Burns (Narrator): For two decades, Sue Embrey and others pushed the government to commemorate the site. Finally, in 1988, Congress issued a formal governmental apology and paid $20,000.00 in reparations to every surviving internee. Four years later, the Manzanar National Historic Site was established.

Footage of Manzanar At Dusk discussion groups.

Ken Burns (Narrator): At the end of every pilgrimage, former internees tell their heart-wrenching stories.

Woman: The infant mortality inside the camps was ten times higher than outside the camps, so—I mean, you know, that's incredible—to believe that children were dangerous to this country.

Jenni Kuida: My family lived this. I imagine my grandmother with five children—you know, teens on down to my mom who was three, which is the same age my daughter is now. This can't happen again ever.

Sam: My dad had tractors; he had trucks; we had two cars. He must have been doing fairly well, financially. And then of course the war started and everything came to an end. And that's how, I'm sure, many Japanese families were affected. It was just totally devastating.

Ken Burns (Narrator): Other civil rights activists share their stories, too.

Footage of South Asian man and others seated on grass.

Man: My wife, they always harass her, tell her to go, go back. This is still goes on.

Young Muslim woman talks with others at picnic table.

Woman: As a Muslim American, I've been discriminated against so many times because of stereotypes presented by the media. People telling me, "I saw it on MSNBC; I saw it on this TV"—you know? Literally. Literally.

Internee talking with young people, seated in circle on grass.

Man: You had to speak out because nobody spoke out for us. And it makes a difference.

Marjory Spellman: These kind of things are going on now. And I think we tell the story because we really feel our country—I don't think they've learned much about prejudice.

Footage of Manzanar NHS.

Ranger Alisa Lynch: A lot of people think of the national parks as the great natural areas and the great recreational areas. But I think one of the really neat things about the National Park system is that we also preserve our history—and not just the glowing parts of our history, but in some of the newer parks like Manzanar, like some of the civil rights sites, we are actually talking about some of the not so wonderful parts of our history.

Superintendent Tom Leatherman: Roots were pulled up; people's lives were altered forever. It was an important part of our history because we have a Constitution and it says that we have rights. And these people basically were told that, "It doesn't apply to you."

Alisa Lynch: Having Manzanar as a part of the National Park system allows people to come and learn about this chapter of history. And I think it gives people an opportunity to think about their own civic responsibilities and what we can each do to help America live up to its promises.

Tom Leatherman: How the Government treats the citizens: that's our story. So I think if we don't have that conversation, we're not doing what we should be doing here at Manzanar.

Sue Embrey *(actor voiceover):* We want to shout to the world that we are a great nation, willing to say that we are sorry about what we did.

And not only are we a democracy but we work at it—for all of us. The working at it is the important part.

· Chapter 18 ·

SOMANATH AND THE RHETORIC OF "THE SHRINE ETERNAL"

Neelima Shukla-Bhatt

On the seashore of the town of Prabhas Patan (Veraval) in Saurashtra, the peninsular part of the current Gujarat state in western India, stands a grand temple of Hindu deity Shiva, known here as Somanath, the Lord (*nāth*) of the moon god Soma. With the vast Arabian Sea enveloping its three sides and touching its base with incessant waves, the temple appears as if hanging on the edge of the earth, at once within and outside of time. In the view of worshipers of Somanath pilgrims from all over India and many local residents—the temple is an eternal abode of Shiva where he manifested as a shaft of light (*jyotirlinga*) at the beginning of time, being pleased by intense penance performed by Soma. Using an expression famously employed by the well-known Gujarati author K.M. Munshi, pilgrims often refer to the temple as Shiva's "Shrine Eternal" (*"anant/śāṣvat dhām"* in local Gujarati), even though its current structure, completed in phases since 1951, is not even a century old. As such, there is nothing unusual in this paradox since sacred sites are generally seen as beyond the constraints of linear time. Yet the paradoxical rhetoric about Somanath demands attention because of its complex history of destructions due to normal erosion and raids by Muslim invaders, and its recurrent reconstructions. It also demands attention because the temple was used symbolically for political mobilization by Hindu nationalists in a rally in 1990.

This essay examines the paradox of the epithet "the Shrine Eternal," arising from the temple's history on the one hand and the faith of the pilgrims on the other. It agrees with historian Romila Thapar that looking at multiple sources of history throws light on the variegated perceptions of the shrine among diverse groups of people. The monolithic narrative focusing exclusively on the temple's destructions by Muslim invaders, which emerged during the British colonial period in the nineteenth century, is misleading and obscures the long peaceful coexistence of communities. This narrative can be and has been manipulated for political advantage in recent times.[183] Such manipulation in the 1990 rally received considerable media and academic attention. The current shrine was discussed in some articles mainly as a visual symbol of an aspiration for making India a Hindu nation since the outset, threatening social harmony and democracy in the country. It is certainly important to recognize the political manipulation of the temple's history through symbolic use. Yet conversations with pilgrims, priests, and local residents (of whom I was one for three years in the 1980s), reveal that the political matters are far from their minds when on the shrine's premises. Visitors use the rhetoric of "the Shrine Eternal" not to express an aspiration for a Hindu nation but because of beliefs shaped by age-old sacred narratives, rituals, and Shaivite teachings. This essay unpacks the paradox of the rhetoric drawing on insights offered by Diana Eck, whose seminal work on India's sacred landscapes and whose depth of understanding of Hindu pilgrimage remain uniquely significant in Hindu studies. The essay is dedicated to her.

ANCIENT TEXTS AND MYTHS

The area around Somanath has a truly long history. Archeological evidence testifies to a thriving pre-Hindu civilization in the third millennium BCE. In the Hindu tradition too, the area (*kṣetra*) known as Prabhas appears to have been identified as sacred early on. An e-booklet by Sanskrit scholar Prof. J.D. Parmar on the website of Somanath temple refers to a verse in the *Rig Veda* (dated ca. 1500 BCE), which mentions Someśvara ("the Lord of Soma"), and "Prachi Saraswati" as marking a sacred spot.[184] While "Soma" here refers to a sacred drink known to the Vedic people and "Someśvara" does not mean Shiva, the mention of "Prachi Saraswati" is significant because the now-extinct sacred river Saraswati is traditionally thought to meet the ocean turning east ("*prā-chī*") in Prabhas. Even if we see this Vedic reference as tangential, by the early Common Era, several references to Prabhas as a major *tīrtha* (pilgrimage center, lit. "ford") are found in the epic *Mahābhārata*. A *tīrtha*, as Eck explains, is the "locative" strand in Hindu piety, where the place itself is an object of devotion, seen as a place where one may cross over from the mundane to the spiritual shore.[185] The salvific power of Prabhas is mentioned in two books of the epic *Vana Parva* (31.13.14, 33.80.77 etc.) and *Śalya Parva* (Chap. 34: 40–77). The latter contains the now popular myth about Soma, the moon deity.

As per the myth, Soma (the moon) was married to twenty-seven daughters of Daksha (representing various constellations). But he spent time only with the most beautiful Rohini. When the other daughters complained to their father, Daksha cursed Soma who started to become emaciated. This created havoc for vegetation and life on earth. A group of deities requested Daksha to remove the curse. Daksha agreed to bring Soma gradually back to his full glory in the first half of every month if Soma would mend his ways and perform penance on the shores of the western ocean. After Soma complied, he began waxing and waning every month. Since Soma regained his glow in this place, it came to be known as Prabhas (splendorous). It should be noted that the *Mahābhārata* does not mention Shiva or the *jyotirlinga* in relation to Soma. Rather, Prabhas is identified as the place of Krishna's death in its *Mausala Parva*. Prabhas's association with Shiva is established in the Puranas, texts composed from the early centuries CE well into the second millennium, which contain myths of popular Hindu deities and their various abodes scattered around India.

The Puranas focusing on Shiva—*Vāyu* (23. 201–202), *Linga* (24.122, 77.40), *Śiva* (*Koṭirudra* and *Śata Rudra* sections), *Skanda* (*Prabhas Khanda*)—refer to Prabhas as one of the holiest *tīrtha*s where Shiva resides in the form of a *linga*. The *Śiva* and *Skanda Purana*s, considered later compositions, also contain the narrative about Soma with modifications. Pleased by Soma's devotion, Shiva manifests as a *linga* (shaft) at Prabhasa, cures him, and decides to remain there eternally. The Śata-Rudra section of the Śiva Purana also lists twelve *jyotirlinga*s in India in which Somanath appears first. There is also a section on the installation ceremony for the self-manifest *jyotirlinga* by celestial beings (not humans) in the *Skanda Purana*. The significance of Somanath as Shiva's abode clearly evolved over many centuries. While most pilgrims to the current temple do not read the Puranas written in Sanskrit, the story of Shiva's decision to stay eternally in Prabhas and Somanath's status as the first of the *jyotirlinga*s are known to them. This knowledge provides a basis for referring to the current temple as "the Shrine Eternal."

CONSTRUCTION, DESTRUCTIONS, AND RECONSTRUCTIONS

The exact date of the earliest man-made temple remains a matter of debate. However, it is certain that Prabhas evolved as a major center of Shiva worship in the early first millennium, being a hub of an important Shaivite sect—Pashupat. Shiva worship was also supported under the powerful Maitraka dynasty in Gujarat (fifth to eighth centuries). J.D. Parmar states that a temple was constructed by a Maitraka king in the seventh century and later reconstructed, perhaps because of corrosion with time. Most scholars consider this likely. Clear archaeological evidence of a well-constructed temple is found from the late ninth to early tenth century. This temple appears to have attracted significant pilgrimage traffic and devotional offerings. Certainly, by the end of the first millennium it was known for its grandeur and richness even outside of India.

In 1026 the Somanath shrine was raided and destroyed by Sultan Mahmud of Ghazni, who led seventeen invasions to Indian cities with grand temples, perhaps for their wealth. His raid of Somanath, considered his crowning glory, was recorded by Alberuni, his scholar-companion. Alberuni's astute work on India contains the Somanath myth, stresses the temple's significance, and indicates that Mahmud broke the *linga* and took its pieces to Ghazni to be placed at the doorsteps of its mosque. Other poets of Mahmud's court also made references to the destruction of Somanath in their eulogies. The temple was reconstructed soon. But that its destruction by Mahmud acquired legendary status is evidenced in multiple texts written by central Asian authors in subsequent centuries, each making grander claims for the wealth captured and giving ever more fantastical descriptions of the temple.[186] Indeed, in presenting this event as legendary, the authors may have indirectly contributed to interest in its repetition among a few later Muslim rulers in India. Somanath was destroyed in 1298 by Delhi's Sultan Alauddin Khilji's army, in 1469 by Sultan Mahmud Begda of Gujarat, and by Mughal emperor Aurangzeb in 1706. Khilji's court chroniclers also praised their army's raid as an instance of iconoclasm. Yet one of them also took note of the beauty of Shiva's *linga*. Begda and Aurangzeb established mosques in the place of the temple, both of which remained functional only for short periods.

The question that arises from this sequence of events is: how was it that the temple would thrive again a couple of centuries after every instance of destruction? It is clear that the worship of and pilgrimage to Somanath was not stopped by the raids. Local patrons at this port town and rival Hindu kings repeatedly renovated the temple. In bardic poems and epigraphs written during the time, various patrons were praised excessively for valor, devotion, and generosity. Centuries later, during the British colonial period, the romanticized stories about Somanath's raids written at the courts of its invaders and those about its reconstructions composed by Hindu bards were used in a metanarrative of Islamic conquests and Hindu resistance. This helped buttress the theory of irreconcilable antagonism between Hindus and Muslims of the country, which formed the basis of the idea of the partition of British India in 1947. The installation of the *linga* in the current Somanath temple in 1951 came on the heels of that colossal tragedy in which millions lost their lives and homes.

K.M. Munshi, an eminent Gujarati lawyer, was one of the leaders for the new temple project, which stirred sharp debates at the time. Munshi was also a novelist, who, influenced by Walter Scott's historical romances, wrote popular novels about the Solanki dynasty of Gujarat (10th–12th centuries). On the occasion of the installation of the *linga* in the new temple, he published a booklet titled *Somanath: The Shrine Eternal*, where he employs his dramatic style in giving an overview of the temple's history and claims significance for it at the national level.[187] The booklet is historically inaccurate and mixes myth with facts, highlighting the sequence of its destruction by invaders. To his credit, Munshi admits in the preface that it is not a scholarly work based on research and advises the readers not to take it as such. However, since the work aligns with the narrative of conquest and resistance circulating in India since the nineteenth century, it offers an easy resource for Hindu nationalists. In 1990, the rally of Hindu nationalists who eventually demolished the Babri mosque in Ayodhya (alleged to be constructed after demolition of a temple of Hindu deity Rama) began from outside the new Somanath temple. The rally leaders symbolically claimed an ideological connection to Somanath. Violent Hindu-Muslim communal riots occurred in the years following the demolition of the mosque in 1992—the 1993 Bombay and the 2002 Gujarat riots (this, with a larger percentage of victims being Muslim). In many reports and writings about the rally and the riots, the Somanath temple was linked to Hindu nationalism. The views of pilgrims and visitors were not considered.

Yet as scholars have shown, a close review of multiple sources is important in understanding the complexity of a place like Somanath.[188] Looking closely at medieval Persian and Hindu texts reveals that there was no singular narrative about Somanath. There were significant differences in tone and detail. Some texts throw light on rivalries within communities. On the other hand, some other texts, inscriptions, and records reveal that during the entire second millennium, Muslims, Hindus, and Jains routinely interacted and collaborated in trade and everyday business in the town of Prabhas Patan. Mosques were built where Muslim residents prayed and Hindu pilgrims continued to visit Somanath even during the long periods when the territory was under the control of Muslim rulers, at times even with their support. After the Mughal Emperor Akbar took control of Gujarat in the sixteenth century, the temple was extensively renovated. Only by looking at multiple sources and contexts (religious, socio-political, business) can we begin to unpack its history and perceptions. A helpful contemporary source is offered by conversations with the temple's visitors.

VOICES OF VISITORS

I lived in Veraval (the town sharing the municipality with Prabhas) in the 1980s as a young ESL instructor. J.D. Parmar, cited above, was my senior colleague and a trustee of the Somanath temple. I had avidly read Munshi's novels, among which *Jai Somanath*, a novel about Muhamad's raid, was the first. Here, the chief villain is not Mahmud, but a disgruntled ascetic who helps the invading army to enter the town in an act of revenge. I had not even heard of the *Somanath* booklet, which is very different in tone and in the portrayal of Mahmud. No one at my institution (except perhaps Parmar), nor any of my acquaintances, knew about it. While I visited the temple weekly and had numerous conversations about Somanath, the raids were rarely mentioned. People generally spoke about the beauty of the site and told stories about the help they received from *dādā* ("grandfather" in Gujarati), as Somanath is lovingly called in the town.

Ten years later, after the demolition of the Babri mosque and after reading much about Somanath's link to the 1990 Hindu nationalist rally, I had trepidation returning to the temple, now as a US resident. Many things had changed—more people, more hotels, and a lot of noise. There were also security measures like metal detectors due to a reported threat. But once I entered the temple premises, the cool ocean breeze, the large beautifully adorned *linga*, the rhythms of the rituals, and the excited voices of the visitors soothed my spirit. It was still the same abode of Shiva. After bowing to the image, I proceeded to the balconies facing the sea where one can sit for hours. I stayed in town for a week, coming to the temple daily to speak with pilgrims (names changed here) from near and far. For a peasant woman from Rajasthan, Jethi, this was a dream-come-true and her first time seeing the ocean. She told me a great deal about rituals her family would perform here but knew nothing about the raids. Of the three young couples I spoke with, only one responded to my questions about the invasions and the 1990 rally, chastising me for bringing it up in a place where people come to find grace and peace.

All of them stressed that things that happened in the past (whether in 1026 or 1990) are irrelevant now and it is proper to focus on the temple's glory as Shiva's shrine eternal. "How is it eternal," I asked, "since it is so new?" With a smile on her face, a young mother, Smriti, responded: "It is all about His wish. The Lord leaves a material image when He finds His devotees slipping in faith. But He is always here as light. His *linga* of light subtly pervades all of Prabhas. And when a new *linga* is installed in a new temple with devotion, He becomes present in it again. There is no need to doubt it. People are not foolish to come here to worship Somanath." For her, Lord Shiva has been present here forever.

The local residents to whom I spoke—priests, Hindu worshippers, and Muslim vendors—all showed deep reverence for "*dādā*." Religious differences did not matter. Their responses reconfirmed that the ways of peaceful coexistence developed over many centuries may be disturbed temporarily; but they are not forgotten. The local residents were quite unhappy about the rally, partially because it impacted their businesses and partially because it led to an image of their town that starkly contrasted their own view of it. Speaking about Hindu-Muslim relations, a priest at the temple indicated that several Muslims in the town regularly come to the temple and even make offerings. He knows some personally and recognizes others by their way of expressing reverence. The Muslim horse-carriage driver whom I had hired for three days confirmed that he goes every week to see "*dādā*" with whose grace he feeds his family. A schoolteacher related how her students from diverse religious communities were united in expressing anger over the rally. These responses revealed that the old patterns continue in spite of temporary breaks. They echoed key insights about Somanath and Indian pilgrimage more broadly found in Diana Eck's works.

IMAGINATION, FAITH, AND THE RHETORIC OF THE "SHRINE ETERNAL"

Eck discusses Somanath as a place "heaped high with both myth and history, with episodes of destruction, periods of reclamation, with emotion, devotion, politics." And yet, "through all of this," she adds, "there is the enduring attraction of the place itself, in good times and bad. While temples may be *tīrtha*s, *tīrtha*s are not necessarily temples. *Tīrtha*s endure, while temples come and go."[189] Eck's remarks succinctly capture the understanding of Somanath as reflected in Smriti's comments without overlooking the aspect of politics associated with it. It also asserts the significance of Prabhas as a *tīrtha* that has reverberated in Hindu sacred texts since ancient times. Importantly, it confirms George Mitchell's observation that as "sacred images and symbols in the Hindu temple art represent only temporary receptacles for the gods and goddesses who intermittently inhabit their outer forms, so the temple as a whole is also understood as a temporary abode of gods in the world of man." At the same time Mitchell acknowledges that if transitory, it serves as a stage "in the journey from the temporal to the eternal."[190]

In Hindu understanding, an image is sacred only while the divine resides in it. What is eternal is the divine presence in a *tīrtha* and pilgrims' faith in it. This is why, for the pilgrims who knew the Somanath temple's history, the episodes of its destruction and its use as the starting point of a controversial rally were not relevant. What mattered to them was the presence of Shiva in the *linga* worshiped in the current temple in the Prabhas *tīrtha*. As Eck points out in *India: A Sacred Geography*, any sacred landscape is founded on an imagined relationship. In India, hundreds of *tīrtha*s have been long visited by pilgrims based on the understanding of such relationships. Yet sacred landscapes alone do not make *tīrtha*s. Pious persons (*sādhu*s) who can take one across to the spiritual shore are also seen as *tīrtha*s. And the most important ones are the *tīrtha*s in one's own heart—truth, charity, self-control, celibacy, and wisdom—recognized by philosophers and saints alike. A place, a person, inner search, anything that helps one to cross over from the phenomenal to the spiritual is a *tīrtha*.[191] Somanath temple is in a landscape perceived to be sacred since ancient times; one expects to meet *sādhu*s there; and importantly, pilgrims hope to purify their hearts with the viewing (*darśan*) of Shiva's *linga*. Many contemporary visitors are aware of its political manipulation but refuse to dwell on it. For them, referring to the current temple as "the Shrine Eternal" is not a matter of exclusivity, but of living faith.

· PART III ·

BEYOND COMMON GROUND:
CONSTRUCTING PLURALISM

· Chapter 19 ·

A LEGACY OF EMBODIED SCHOLARSHIP:
STORIES OF PLURALISM IN PRACTICE AT HARVARD

Halah Ahmad

I worked with Diana in various capacities during my time at Harvard College: I was a student in her last Religion 97 Seminar in the Comparative Study of Religion, I was her advisee on my senior thesis research in a refugee camp in Greece, and I was an employee of the Pluralism Project—the nonprofit extension of her interfaith work in the United States. I was also a regular guest at Lowell Tea and attended discussions in religious studies at the Center for the Study of World Religions and in the cozy private dining room at the back of Lowell House's grand dining hall.

 I came to know Diana well through all of the ways she supported students like me at Harvard. For some years, Professor Eck advised the Palestine Solidarity Committee—one of the first organizations I joined at Harvard—signing the paperwork that allowed us to be a student club, but also facilitating sensitive discussions relating to the Palestinian student experience. As a senior, Diana supported me in the unfamiliar territory of applying to post-grad fellowships—many of which I had never heard of prior to the frenzy of senior fall applications among my peers. Finally, Diana and I were both on the Office of the President's Selection Committee for Harvard's first paid Muslim chaplain, the culmination of a decade or more of Muslim alumni and students' organizing for more resources—which was made even more urgent with Donald Trump's election and "Muslim ban." She was there for students also when, in 2017, three young Muslims were murdered by their neighbor at UNC-Chapel Hill, jarring Muslim students across the country in reckoning with not only interpersonal Islamophobia, but structural anti-Muslim racism.

In the end, Diana shaped the best and most redeeming parts of my experience at Harvard, and I will never forget the lessons she imparted both through the content of her scholarship and her embodied pedagogy of pluralism. Below are some reflections on how Diana's scholarship in religious studies—and emphasis on pluralism—manifested in my time at Harvard. It is a legacy that continues to shape my thinking now in my public policy work.

"PLURALISM IS NOT DIVERSITY ALONE BUT THE ENERGETIC ENGAGEMENT WITH DIVERSITY."[192]

In 2014, a group of Palestinian Harvard students and peers noticed that the Harvard dining halls had begun to offer water carbonation machines built by SodaStream, a company that had factories on stolen Palestinian land in the occupied West Bank. Despite the settlements being considered illegal under international law, and despite SodaStream having faced criticism for its decision to place a factory there, the company maintained that it employed Palestinian labor and was otherwise impervious to the outcry of human rights organizations and Palestinian civil society. Members of the Palestine Solidarity Committee managed, with the facilitation of Professor Diana Eck—then the group's faculty supervisor—to arrange a meeting with Harvard University Dining Services (HUDS) leadership to discuss the ways this procurement decision alienated Palestinian students. Students signed a joint letter asking that the dining halls be supplied with a neutral vendor. In the end, HUDS agreed, and found a vendor for future years that would be less costly and avoid complicity with Palestinian displacement and occupation.[193] Palestinians are a very small minority at Harvard, and I was among them. Our voices were not often heard either within class curriculum on Palestine or amid other campus events that celebrated the Israeli military or aspects of the Israeli settler colonial project.

In the summer of 2014, this was especially severe as over 2,000

Palestinians were killed in Gaza, a third of them children, in the Israeli "Operation Cast Lead." During that time, Harvard's first-ever student from Gaza received little outreach or support, and was stuck on campus waiting anxiously for periodic updates about his family or friends. Palestinian diaspora students took on a heavy mental and emotional toll as international governments, universities, and peers largely ignored or moved on quickly from the devastating violence, supported by US military aid to Israel and by bipartisan legislators. Their experiences were often invisible or worse—vilified by virulent Islamaphobes and right-wing Zionists alike, the likes of Ayaan Hirsi Ali, a Fellow at the Kennedy School known to suggest students were "terrorists" or in-cells if they defended Islam or Muslims, or were critical of Israel.

When we came back in the Fall of 2015, an Israeli military commander was invited to speak at Harvard Hillel—an event widely advertised across campus—and Palestinian students struggled to place an op-ed about the conflict in the *Harvard Crimson*. The casual SodaStream machines in dining halls were just a cherry on top, but they were symbolic of a financial decision that already-marginalized students had to face regularly. Without the careful dialogue Professor Eck enabled, Palestinian students would have faced this additional erasure. Instead, a pluralistic approach that heard students' concerns won the day. When backlash erupted[194] on the dining services' change, dialogue had already prevailed.

"PLURALISM IS NOT RELATIVISM BUT RATHER THE ENCOUNTER OF COMMITMENTS."[195]

After decades of Muslim student and alumni advocacy, Harvard hired its first-ever paid Muslim chaplain in 2017. It was a moment of incredible triumph for Harvard's commitment to religious life and diversity, as Muslims grappled with the Trump presidency and the major rise in anti-Muslim violence that came with it. Professor Eck was among the two or three faculty members of the Selection Committee at the Office of the President, and I was among two student body members represented. After years of making space for Muslim students at Harvard both in religious studies and the intimacy of Lowell Tea, Professor Eck was committed to using her position to select a candidate that students would feel supported by. As the Harvard Islamic Society arranged student surveys and discussions to provide input to the committee, Professor Eck took seriously the diverse and deeply-felt needs of the student body.

This expression of commitment to the varying needs of Muslim students was deeply affirming for myself and others. In the process, Muslim students at Harvard observed an instance of being made part of the university's very structure and fabric. While I was a senior and, on my way out, I felt comfort that greater institutional support for Muslim students would be protected by this move—something I certainly couldn't take for granted in my time, nor could many Muslim alumni before me. In light of the Supreme Court's recent decision to reject affirmative action in admissions at Harvard, I am reminded that the legacy of decisions like this—to establish a source of pastoral care for minority students—may do much to preserve the university's commitment to pluralism and diversity regardless of the Supreme Court's position. I am reminded also of W.E.B. Dubois' quote[196] that he was "in Harvard, but not of it," speaking as the first African-American to receive a doctorate from the university, after having been at Harvard for both college and postgraduate education. By responding to students' calls for a Muslim chaplain, Professor Eck and the faculty and staff of the Office of the President made a choice to affirm a place for Muslim students *of* Harvard—not settling for the mere presence of diversity but enabling an institutional way to belong and be supported as well. The chaplain continues to serve in this role today.

"'PLURALISM' AND 'DIVERSITY' ARE SOMETIMES USED AS IF THEY WERE SYNONYMS, BUT DIVERSITY IS JUST PLURALITY, PLAIN AND SIMPLE—SPLENDID, COLORFUL, PERHAPS THREATENING. PLURALISM IS THE ENGAGEMENT THAT CREATES A COMMON SOCIETY FROM ALL THAT PLURALITY."[197]

In 2016, under the guidance of Professor Eck, I went to Greece to study refugee camp volunteerism in a participant-observational ethnography.

As a student of comparative religion and sociology, it was perhaps a somewhat unusual site of research because most of the volunteers I was to observe did not ascribe to a singular faith—or indeed, religion at all. But the encounter between largely non-religious volunteers and often visibly religious refugees surfaced competing convictions and notions of the "sacred" in much the same way as interfaith encounters between faith groups. It was my task to understand sources of empathy and moral imagination among the volunteers, to understand their compulsion to travel sometimes long distances to help in this crisis. In the process, I observed a generalized conviction to humanitarianism, environmentalism, open borders, and tolerance of diversity—if it affirmed normative European and American ways of dressing, acting, and thinking. Of course, no one could generalize or overly simplify a code or creed of normative Western values, but such a vague normative framework was observable in contrast to the religious "other" of refugees in the camps where I was also a volunteer. This religious "other" likely identified as Muslim, even if such an identity was primarily a cultural association with the Islamic antecedents of norms in majority-Muslim countries.

As I understood volunteers' sources of empathy through both observation and interviews, I also noted instances when volunteers struggled to understand or accept things they observed among the refugees. Some volunteers were deeply troubled by littering in the camp, the use of plastic bottles and containers for food, lack of cleanliness in a shared restroom, some residents of the camp stealing from others or speaking in derogatory or racist ways about various ethnic groups or religious sects in the camp. I remember a particular instance in which a few volunteers decided to end their time in the camp after some refugees rejected some clothing donations which were offered to them—the volunteers saw this as baffling ingratitude. In another instance, the volunteers organized a workshop and asked me to translate the materials into Arabic—hoping to "develop," in their words, the thinking of the refugees if they were to integrate into Europe. The subjects of discussion were the refugees' perceptions of difference, discussion of norms in the camp, and expectations for Europe. In preparation for this workshop, the volunteers brainstormed ways to change the camp residents' thinking because the ideologies and norms the volunteers observed were not well suited to integration in Europe, they thought. In other words, in many instances the refugees were not *enough* as they were, and their religious, ethnic, or cultural commitments were somehow lacking in the eyes of the volunteers. In those instances, as I expanded upon in my thesis at the time, the mental models or moral imaginations of the volunteers was met with some contradiction in their experiences of refugees in the camp. In my view, those differences were not purely rational or secular, but rather a meeting of varying convictions and pseudo-religious beliefs. Other scholars[198] have critiqued at length the catch-all category of the "secular" in Europe as a modern, rational opposition to religion and religious life. My own simplistic observation was that the secular ideological convictions of the volunteers were not purely rational within the context of the camp, and that some volunteers hoped to proselytize those convictions and normative behaviors as a precondition or pathway to tolerance. I call this a display of "pseudo-religious" difference. There were material impacts for such differences: more stringency from the volunteer organizations in distribution of food or resources, volunteers leaving the camp earlier than they intended at times, and a general distrust that worked against the instinct toward empathy that may have first motivated their arrival in Greece.

In this instance, I found that a general principle of respect for diversity was insufficient in the face of such religious difference. The form of diversity represented by Muslim refugees in Europe could be threatening, even to the most progressive and liberal volunteers in the refugee crisis. But I posit that it was also insufficient to see the volunteers' ideologies within a purely secular, and by extension, rational framework. Seeing the volunteer's convictions, priorities, and norms as similarly "religious" can enable us to utilize practices from interfaith dialogue to produce more humanitarian implementations of international aid, development, volunteerism and similar—the microcosm of which was the context of refugee camps all over Europe at the time.

Professor Eck's notions of pluralism—a principle not synonymous with the presence of diversity alone, or even tolerance, but requiring learning about and understanding difference—were apt for the interactions of refugee residents of the camp and the volunteers. My conclusions echoed these principles, though formed through a process of grounded theory within a single case study and ethnography, unlike Eck's many case studies of religious difference: those volunteers who could flexibly adapt their moral imaginations and pseudo-religious convictions to understand and allow for alternative beliefs and norms, however different, were more inclined to stay as volunteers in the camp, form lasting relationships with the refugees, and flexibly support the refugees according to their needs and input. In other words, achieving even a secular ideal of pluralism required "more than the mere tolerance of differences; it requires some knowledge of our differences," in the words of Diana Eck.[199]

A UBIQUITOUS AND ENDLESS LESSON AND PRAXIS

Professor Eck's scholarship will continue to influence the study of religion, but I also believe that it may be practiced as well as "preached." There were many examples of Professor Eck's own embodiment of her commitment to pluralism, and my own research and experience in public policy has only manifested more examples of the resonance of her work. I have observed that challenges of interfaith and multicultural democracy will continue to need such principles for pluralism. It was a privilege to learn from her directly in both theory and practice. Her legacy remains—and will be needed as Harvard navigates what is next in diversity and student life.

· Chapter 20 ·

DIANA ECK
PARTNER AND CO-PILGRIM IN MY INTERFAITH JOURNEY

S. Wesley Ariarajah

It is difficult to even imagine that Diana would retire. She brings so much passion, energy, enthusiasm, and endless commitment to hard work to whatever she does that one is hard-pressed to associate the word "retirement" with her. I know gifted teachers, speakers, and writers. However, I do not know of anyone who as a teacher, thinker, speaker, researcher, writer, and communicator, equally excels in all these dimensions of one's work, as Diana does. In this brief piece, however, I have been requested to reflect on what she and her work have meant to me personally.

Diana Eck and her spouse Dorothy Austin are among the closest of my friends. They played a major role in 1997 in bringing me to the Drew University School of Theology as professor of ecumenical theology, where I had the pleasure of working with Dorothy as my colleague and friend. My friendship with Diana, however, began in 1976 when she and I participated in the interfaith dialogue ministry of the World Council of Churches (WCC), Geneva. When I was appointed director of the dialogue sub-unit of the WCC, Diana was the moderator of the working group on dialogue that guided and oversaw the work of the dialogue program (1984–91). The passion and commitment she brought to her responsibility as moderator was an inspiration and example to everyone in the working group.

Diana has a special gift of building close relationships with people she comes to know, which often extends to members of their families. In my case, she drew close to my spouse, Shyamala, and our three daughters Dharshi, Niro, and Anu. The highlight of this relationship was when Diana and Dorothy flew all the way from Boston to London to participate in the *Arangetram* (graduation dance) where our daughters danced together and individually for about three hours before nearly a thousand people at the University of London's Logan Hall. Diana, as the chief guest, gave an address on Bharatanatyam, its rich artistic, cultural, and spiritual dimensions, and what excelling in this art meant for Dharshi, Niro, and Anu. Her speech held the large audience spellbound; she had done all the research needed to make her presentation the highlight of the occasion.

Originally from Sri Lanka, I studied in India for seven years and worked, as Diana did, on Hinduism as my main field of study up to the doctoral level. Although my work was more on the philosophical and theological dimensions of Hinduism, as part of my attempt to have a firmer grasp of the tradition, I visited many temples and attended numerous festivals, and had sat down to talk with a number of Hindu teachers. When I met Diana and got to know her work on Hinduism, I realized that here was someone who had visited temples, participated in festivals, and sat down with Hindu teachers, gurus, intellectuals, and worshippers a hundredfold more than what I had managed to do in seven years! Diana's books on Hinduism attest to the depth and breadth of research she does on the subjects she chooses to work on.

As part of her interest and involvement in interfaith relations, she came to know a number of men and women from a variety of different religious traditions. She always carried a thick, black handbook with her, where she recorded the names, contact details and interests of persons of other religious traditions she had met.

This rich resource became very handy on one special occasion. As part of our interest at the WCC in enhancing women's participation and addressing the concerns of women in interfaith discussions, Diana and I hatched the idea of organizing an all-women interfaith meeting. For this meeting, which took place in Toronto, Canada, in June 1988, we brought together fifty women from eight different religious traditions for two weeks. It turned out to be one of the best dialogue events that the Sub-Unit had organized. It was Diana who was able, with her address book as the starting point, to identify most of the appropriate persons from such a variety of religious traditions.

She also produced and edited the study booklet, *My Neighbour's Faith—and Mine: Theological Discoveries through Interfaith Dialogue*, which formed the basis of the dialogue sub-unit's groundbreaking work on theology of religions.

I deeply value her friendship and the inspiration and support Diana gave me in leading the work of the dialogue sub-unit for a number of years. She and Dorothy have a special place in our hearts.

Much more can and needs to be said, but I stop here, and join Shyamala in wishing her happy, productive, and refreshing years of retirement—if she ever manages to really retire!

· Chapter 21 ·

A TRANSFORMATIONAL CONFERENCE:
"WOMEN, RELIGION, AND SOCIAL CHANGE"

Sissela Bok

In June 1983 I noted in my diary that the week-long conference, "Women, Religion, and Social Change," at Harvard University was "perhaps the most interesting I have ever taken part in. What a superb conference Diana has organized, with spirited, forceful women from the entire world. The discussion of what religion can do for and against peace has led me to think more about violence and non-violence, about individualism and collectivism, and about how strongly people's different perspectives are influenced by experiences they have lived through."[200]

In an essay reporting on the conference, Diana Eck later described it as the result of nearly three years of thinking and planning. Among the participants, "twenty-four presented case-studies on some aspect of the relation of religious values or ethics to the kinds of social change issues with which they were most involved or concerned."[201] I was moved by the accounts of imaginative forms of non-violent action in those case-studies: by Gandhian activist Radha Bhatt, speaking of working with women in villages in the Himalayan foothills to prevent the demolition of trees and combat exploitative liquor shops; by Palestinian Quaker and pacifist Jean Zaru to promote dialogue between occupiers and occupied; and by physician Nawal el Saadawi, a former Egyptian minister of public health, released from prison just months before the conference, who had worked against the practices of genital mutilation that she herself had suffered as a young girl.

But I also noted how sharply speakers from Latin America and South Africa took issue with the stress on nonviolent methods of bringing about social change. It was too late, they argued, to rely simply on non-violent resistance; in order to overcome the brutal injustice and persecution they were facing, it might be necessary to join their comrades in combat. For example, exiled Guatemalan theologian, poet, and human rights activist Julia Esquivel spoke of the Indigenous people of her country suffering torture, rape, and massacres carried out by the military and argued that the response to non-violent methods had been death. And Brigalia Bam, exiled from South Africa, held that she would use all available means to own land in her country: "I would kill, finally, to get my land back."[202]

The term PTSD, for post-traumatic stress disorder, had not been fully diagnosed at the time; but the reports of trauma from rape, torture, mutilation, and every form of assault resonated in the debates about whether to take part in non-violent or other struggles. I could see how those present were moved by accounts of such experiences, yet how strongly many disagreed about going beyond nonviolent means of resistance.

As Diana Eck and Devaki Jain put it in *Speaking of Faith: Global Perspectives on Women, Religion, and Social Change*, "The session on violence and non-violence revealed fundamentally different presuppositions held by the Gandhian and pacifist women on the one hand and the women from Latin America and South Africa on the other. /.../ For many, they were discussions so difficult and painful that they had never been attempted."[203] Nevertheless, the most important outcome of the conference may have been, they concluded:

> Not only its contribution to the understanding of particular issues, but our affirmation and consensus that the process of dialogue is itself illuminating and crucially important—important enough to elicit the continued commitment of the participants to ongoing relationship and dialogue.[204]

Eck's unique talent for fostering genuine dialogue rather than mere posturing illuminated the issues under debate, including the most divisive ones. And it was clear that participants looked forward to continued dialogue. Many shared Nawal el Saadawi's hopes: "Out of conflict comes movement. This conference opened our eyes to many things, because conflict came into the open air, and we discussed it. We may disagree here, but at our next conference, we will agree."[205]

The personal accounts and the fierce debates about non-violence also resonated, for me, with memories from Oslo, Norway, where I had seen, only six months earlier, my mother Alva Myrdal receive the Nobel Peace Prize. It had been awarded to her along with Alfonso García Robles from Mexico, to honor their work for disarmament and nuclear-free zones to counter the nuclear balance of terror.

In her 1982 Nobel Lecture, "Disarmament, Technology, and the Growth of Violence," my mother spoke of how the arms race between East and West, with its excesses of armaments and its aggressive rhetoric, had contributed to an ominous cult of violence in contemporary societies. Our civilization, she suggested, was in the process of becoming both militarized and brutalized. Because of the proliferation of arms, sophisticated weapons were now exported the world over and available on the domestic markets as well. She pointed to the growth of terrorism and to the many governments disposing of means to persecute their own citizens and to intern them in prisons and concentration camps. She singled out the role of the mass media in promoting violence. In turn, Western exports of films and TV programs worked in tandem with the arms trade to satiate the Third World in patterns of brutality.[206]

My mother closed by referring to a passage from Alfred Nobel's will and testament that had long gone unnoticed: that the Fund was to support the holding and promotion of peace conferences. Future Nobel Peace Prizes could be awarded to support such meetings, she argued, that might "provide excellent occasions for submitting important questions to a dynamic, intellectually factual analysis and debate."[207]

That same year had seen a new edition of my mother's 1976 book, *The Game of Disarmament: How the United States and Russia Run the Arms Race*. It began with "An American Update—1982. So Much Worse."[208] In it, she speaks of the two superpowers being on a catastrophic collision course while avoiding genuine dialogue through empty rhetoric and gamesmanship; and of many Third World countries having "stepped up their own dangerous game of militarization, tyranny, and terrorism."[209]

I believe my mother would have been fascinated to listen to the testimony from the women at the conference about their experiences of such tyranny, such militarization, and such terrorism. And she would have found their dialogue about forms that resistance might take far more relevant for the dynamic analysis and debate she had called for in her Nobel Lecture than the stale, unproductive disarmament rhetoric at the UN.

My experience at the 1983 conference, following so closely upon those surrounding my mother's Nobel Prize, represented a turning point in my own work. I saw a way to combine my writing and teaching about practical ethics with reflections on my mother's work on disarmament and on the testimony at the conference, so as to explore dialogue between adversaries in conflicts large and small.

When asked to contribute an essay to the volume about the conference edited by Diana Eck and Devaki Jain, I entitled it, "Toward a Practical Ethic of Non-violence." In it, I drew on the eloquent debates at the conference against the background of my mother's decades of equally eloquent advocacy of disarmament. I went on to teach a course at Brandeis University entitled "Philosophies of War and Peace," about the nature and the morality of war and what would be needed to establish a lasting peace; and began preparing a foreword to the translation of Gandhi's *An Autobiography: The Story of My Experiments with Truth*.[210]

In 1985, I felt honored to deliver two Joan and Erik Erikson Lectures at Harvard University. I published an expanded version of these lectures in my book, *A Strategy for Peace: Human Values and the Threat of War*, addressing moral and strategic requirements to reverse nuclear and environmental threats to survival.[211] In dedicating the book to my mother's grandchildren and great-grandchildren, I pointed to my discussions with her about practical ways to reduce the threat of war, "beginning with efforts to combat the many practices of violence and corruption in personal, societal, and international life that help stifle cooperation."[212]

My mother did not live to see the fall of the Berlin Wall and the end of the Cold War—developments that inspired new hopes for peace the world over. In a *New York Times* op-ed, I was invited to contribute for Christmas Day 1989, I asked whether the hopes of peace on earth might be a little less utopian at the end of that year than it had seemed at the beginning.[213] Though the course of history gives little reason to be sanguine about the prospects for peace, I suggested, the past year had shown us one non-violent revolution after another. True, fighting dragged on with no end in sight in places such as Lebanon, Ethiopia, El Salvador, and Sri Lanka. But non-violent movements have a better chance of ultimately succeeding than if they had resorted to violent uprisings. We now have a rare opportunity, I argued, for arms reduction, settling regional conflicts by peaceful means, and coping with mounting social and environmental crises: "The vulnerability that now confronts us all may at last elicit the resolve, the enlarged perspective, and the joint efforts that lasting peace requires. But this will only happen if we do far more at every level—international, domestic, local, and personal—than merely hope for peace on earth and good will towards all."[214]

During the early 1990s, many efforts were made the world over to "do far more" along these lines. I had the opportunity to discuss some of them with Diana Eck, as she launched Harvard's Pluralism Project in 1991. We talked about her experiences at the World Parliament of Religion in August 1993 and about her work with colleagues there in formulating a declaration of fundamental moral values recognized in all religions, all cultures: "Toward a Global Ethic."[215] And I was delighted to learn about plans for a twenty-year follow-up to the 1983 conference, scheduled for April 30 through May 4, 2003.

Entitled "Women, Religion, and Social Change II," this second conference reunited some of the women who had taken part in the first conference, along with new participants from the Pluralism Project and the new Women's Networks. The fact that Brigalia Bam had been able to come from South Africa, now that apartheid had been ended, showed what a difference women's efforts to bring about social change could make; she had only been able to come to the first conference from her exile in Switzerland, unable to set foot in South Africa. But other invitees had decided not to come, given the US invasion of Iraq on March 20, just a month before the conference was to open.

The conference took place, as had the first one, at a time of soaring international tensions and of violent strife. True, the end of the Cold War had eliminated the immediate threat of East West nuclear war; but many of the regional conflicts in the Middle East and Asia had continued, at times intensified. The horror of the September 11, 2001 assaults on the Twin Towers in New York and the Pentagon had shocked the world. Religion was at the center of the resulting anger and grief, with all major religions condemning the taking of innocent human life, even as the perpetrators and their leaders claimed to have been divinely inspired.

Diana invited those present at the first dinner to begin by making "some informal assessments of what 9/11 and the invasion of Iraq and war on terrorism has had for all of us . . . and the ways in which it has reshaped and even displaced many of our agendas."[216] Two of the sessions were devoted to "Dialogue in the Midst of Conflict" and "Religious Violence, Extremism, and Fundamentalisms." Dialogue was clearly more important than ever, as was the vulnerability of women working for social change. And religion, as Diana had already indicated when introducing the 1983 conference, played a part in all the areas where social and political conflict had been relentless "both in buttressing long-held established interests and in providing the vision and commitment for radical change toward a better society."[217] Having seen Diana in action over the years, beginning with that first, transformational conference, I had admired her gift for inspiring such dialogue and all that she has done to further just such vision and commitment.

Alas, there would be no third conference in 2023, twenty years after the second conference and forty years after the first—no "Women, Religion, and Social Change III." It would have been hard enough to plan for it, given the daunting social, political, and technological changes since

2003, with numbers of refugees and migrants fleeing brutal regimes surpassing any since World War II; rising environmental threats to survival; and at least nine nations, now including China, North Korea, India, and Pakistan, possessing nuclear weapons.

Once the COVID pandemic struck, however, such plans had to be put on hold, both for the Pluralism Project, and for past and potential participants the world over. Had it been possible for such a conference to take place, it would surely have had to focus on the conflict between oppressive religious authorities in states such as Iran and on the courage of women struggling for social change.

In October, the Norwegian Nobel Committee announced that human rights activist Narges Mohammadi, serving a ten-year jail sentence in Tehran's Evin Prison, had received the 2023 Nobel Peace Prize, for "her fight against the oppression of women in Iran and her fight to promote human rights and freedom for all."[218] When reached for a comment, Mohammadi replied: "The global support and recognition of my human rights advocacy makes me more resolved, more responsible, more passionate, and more hopeful. I also hope this recognition makes Iranians protesting for change stronger and more organized. Victory is near."[219]

· Chapter 22 ·

BRAIDING EPISTEMOLOGICAL, THEORETICAL, AND METHODOLOGICAL CONTRIBUTIONS

Patrice Brodeur

It all started with a telephone call, back in 1989, for which I shall be ever grateful to Professor Diana L. Eck. She had taken the time to reach out to me, one of many young applicants to the doctoral program at the Harvard University GSAS Committee on the Study of Religion, in which she has played a central role for many decades. She convinced me to choose Harvard over the famous "Other" . . . The University of Chicago Divinity School. As I discovered twenty years later, during a symposium in honor of the legacy of Wilfred Cantwell Smith on the occasion of the 60th Anniversary of the Faculty of Religious Studies at McGill University,[220] Professor Eck's personal invitation demonstrated an exemplary trait of her proactive personality that sees how a person reflects and connects to broad structural dynamics within the life of academic institutions and networks. Unaware of it back then, by accepting her kind invitation, I continued my academic journey that had first started at McGill University with a BA in religious studies and an MA in Islamic studies, with the additional privilege of Professor Eck becoming my *Doktormutter* for the duration of my doctoral studies. Two years later, Professor William A. Graham kindly accepted to take me under his wing too, becoming my *Doktorvater*. The complementarity between these two outstanding professors became a rare gift in my own academic training, the depth of which I suddenly became conscious of in 2009 at

McGill, while listening to their respective reflections on their shared *Doktorvater*, Professor Wilfred Cantwell Smith.[221] Their presentations made me realize for the first time that I was part of an academic lineage, not only through the parenthood and grand fatherhood of these three extraordinary human beings, but by having gone through the particular learning trajectory of academic programs that were all directly shaped by Wilfred Cantwell Smith,[222] with significant subsequent interpretations, improvements, and applications, often way beyond the realm of academia per se, by both Professor Eck and Professor Graham, among others.

In 1991, Professor Eck reached out to me with a second significant invitation: this time, it was sent out to a few of her graduate students who gathered in her own home living room to brainstorm on an idea she had been pondering over for some time, which soon became known as the Pluralism Project. Within a few years, this rapidly expanding academic project turned program had ripple effects throughout the United States in particular, but also in many other countries that have been going through similar socio-demographic transformations due to new migration flows, the extent and numbers of which had been unprecedented historically. The definition of "pluralism" she put forth was simple enough to make this complex concept accessible to a broad public, an approach that ensured a transformative understanding for countless citizens struggling to make positive sense of rapid social changes full of intercultural and interreligious challenges. Professor Eck's involvement in both kinds of dialogue has been rooted in her personal experiences as a college student with deep Christian Methodist roots from her childhood spent in Bozeman, Montana, and in her doctoral research year in India. Later, she demonstrated deep commitment to ecumenical and interreligious dialogue in her leadership roles at the World Council of Churches and at the then World Conference on Religion and Peace (now known as Religions for Peace).

Much later, on February 6, 2018, the Université de Montréal awarded an honorary doctorate to Professor Eck on the occasion of an academic colloquium celebrating an historic transition. Its founding faculty of theology, dating back to 1878, was transformed into an institute of religious studies with a triple orientation: the scientific study of religions, theology, and spiritual studies. Few scholars could reflect in their academic journey all three areas, albeit to different degrees. Professor Eck's multifaceted contributions were recognized on that day as exemplary of how to bridge those overlapping academic disciplines and fields of study, opening up towards a bright future of interdisciplinarity. Below are the introductory remarks I delivered on behalf of all my colleagues in the minutes that preceded Professor Eck's solemn reception of her new honorary doctorate:

> Dearest Professor Eck, (etc.), Dear participants to this highly symbolic ceremony, the choice of Professor Diana L. Eck to receive a *Doctorate Honoris Causa* today makes sense in light of both the University of Montreal's 2016–2021 Plan of Action entitled "Transcending Borders," whose first objective is to increase its collaborations by way of interdisciplinarity, interconnections between knowledges, and innovation, as well as this year's integration of the new Institute of Religious Studies into the Faculty of Arts and Sciences, whose colloquium over these past two days marks an excellent example of this objective.
>
> We could not have found a more suitable scholar to mark the importance of interdisciplinarity in Religious Studies today, not only from all three of the angles included in the new Institute of Religious Studies (the scientific study of religions, theology, and spiritual studies), but also from her work interconnecting with numerous other disciplines, from South Asian studies, sociology of religions, and history to engineering, architecture, and health.
>
> One can summarize Professor Eck's career over the last forty years with the image of the double helix of a DNA molecule: The first helix is represented by her studies of Hinduism through a historical-critical and phenomenological approach influenced by the Canadian Wilfred Cantwell Smith, one of her doctorate studies mentors. Her dissertation was published as *Banaras: City of Light*, with both academic and popular acclaim, especially when judged by its five editions. With her

second book, *Darśan: Seeing the Divine Image in India*, a third book coedited with Dr. Mallison entitled *Devotion Divine: Bhakti Traditions from the Religions of India*, as well as her fourth in-depth book *India: A Sacred Geography*, which makes accessible a rich interconnected network of pilgrimage sites throughout India, Professor Eck consolidated her international fame as an expert in Hinduism.

The second helix is represented by her sociological studies of the new religious diversity of the United States of America since 1965. Professor Eck carved a second international reputation for the impact of her work and that of her team through the Pluralism Project at Harvard University, which celebrated just a few months ago its 25th anniversary. The Pluralism Project has produced numerous documents, reports, and analyses, as well as case studies and interactive maps, these last two being particularly useful for teaching about religious diversity in the US, at the intersection of politics, law, and religion. Moreover, her team produced the CD-ROM *On Common Ground: World Religions in America*, which helped her be nominated to serve two years on the Advisory Commission on Religious Freedom Abroad for the Secretary of State. Many of her publications are written in a style that is accessible to the public at large. Her "bestseller" since 2001 is probably *A New Religious America: How a "Christian Country" Has Become the World's Most Religiously Diverse Nation*.

Finally, in between these two helixes, we can find her unique autobiographical journey: *Encountering God: A Spiritual Journey from Bozeman to Banaras*. This double helix of academic productivity and its central spiritual piece with theological overtones, not to mention her remarkable international contributions in interreligious dialogue, especially between women of a wide range of religious and spiritual traditions, explains why she was elected President of the American Academy of Religion for the year 2006.

Over the flow of the last forty years, her brilliant career unfolded, as a researcher, a public intellectual, an exceptional pedagogue, and as the mentor of a whole new generation of younger scholars. Her quadruple engagement brings together theory and practice at once, at the intersection of the sciences of religions, interreligious theology, and engaged spirituality.

Professor Eck is an exemplary paradigm of an academic life devoted to the practice of a philosophy of pluralism that is both engaged (and engaging), innovative, and always dialogical.

Five years after giving this address, I have moved from the image of a double helix of a DNA module to that of a braid; however, the first image remains useful to describe the two main strands in Professor Eck's research. In retrospect, what started to trouble me is that I used the simplistic description of "in between these two helixes" to somehow include the important personal autobiographical component of her writing, albeit much smaller in quantitative output. As I reread many of Professor Eck's books and articles for this essay, I realized that the personal is woven into almost all of her writings, although at times discreetly and often hidden in the acknowledgement sections. There in particular, she generously writes in a way to be inclusive of all who participated, from near or far, in the research or activities related to the content of each one of her books in particular. It made me think about her exemplary efforts to be inclusive in a way that was a precursor to the now central academic efforts to promote diversity, equity, inclusion, and belonging (DEIB).

So instead of treating the subjective, personal dimensions affecting how we conduct scholarship as a secondary in-between category of thought, I would like to build on Professor Eck's academic lifetime of epistemological, theoretical, and methodological contributions to suggest that it is now time to add the realm of epistemology to the traditional "Theory and Method" introductory courses in the academic Study of Religion ("Study of Religion" including not only all religious traditions but also theologies of various religions, where applicable, as well as spiritualities, both of older indigenous cosmovisions and religions as well as of newer religious and/or spiritual movements). I would go as far as to argue that equal weight needs to be given to all three strands—epistemology, theory, and methodology—starting with "epistemology" as it is the grounding of our own subjectivity as students and scholars, not to mention any person we collaborate with academically, read about, or relate to in one form or another. In a way parallel to the increased importance given to DEIB in scholarly circles as well as society at large, and as a form of mirroring, the academic Study of Religion must transform its central "theory and method" course into the newly entitled "epistemology, theory, and method" course (i.e., ETM). This change will contribute to bringing greater self-critical reflection in the pursuit of our respective scholarly interdisciplinary endeavors, as exemplified in Professor Eck's lifetime journey.

Raising epistemological questions has become central to the triple task inherent to the scientific process in general, and within academia in particular: to conduct more inclusive and equitable research, write/lecture/speak more sensitively and dialogically, and broaden the modes of dissemination of our research results. These modes must also include options for receiving various kinds of reactions and criticisms that can enhance our comprehension and learning, further improve and/or expand any research project, as well as increase realms of application in order to make our interdisciplinary field of study and research ever more relevant to glocal dynamics of social transformations in an age of rapidly increasing anxieties of all sorts.

In particular, the exercise of centrally raising epistemological questions in new ETM courses will train us, professors and students alike, to be more critically self-reflective both personally and collectively in the classroom and within our institutional programs, as well as in our academic and social dynamics. It will also create a framework to think about ETM beyond the classroom and our specific universities into the societies within which our academic training and research productions are carried out, with all the structural and systemic influences that they may have on our modes of thinking, studying, researching, writing, and disseminating the kinds of knowledge we are so keen to advance. Decolonizing our interdisciplinary field of study in an age of transnational, borderless Internet-driven research technologies requires increased attention to epistemology as such, and not only as a component of some theories. Indeed, it is too easy to sidestep serious epistemological questioning when choosing theories that do not address epistemological challenges, thus failing to examine directly how our research choices carry implications in the larger purpose behind our investments as students and scholars.

In her 2009 brief article in the form of a memo to President Obama, Professor Eck wrote: "Our 'we' in America has become more complex over the past four decades, with all the new immigration. We are people of every faith, and none."[223] Fifteen years later, it is clear that "Our 'we'," not only in America but in the "we" of our common humanity worldwide, is exponentially more complex than one could have imagined back in 1969, when Diana started as a first-year doctoral student in the study of religion at Harvard University. There is no doubt that Professor Eck, with her large team of researchers and collaborators active in the Pluralism Project for more than thirty years, and her other important research projects, especially in India, has been a role model of compassionate academic leadership that has transformed our understanding of both "A New Religious America" and of India, using the hermeneutic lenses of pluralism, briefly defined as: "Pluralism is not diversity alone, but the energetic engagement with diversity."[224] Her unique leadership style has not only been exemplary of this energetic engagement with diversity; it has produced the active and ongoing legacy-in-the-making of numerous academic "children," whose passion for the study of pluralism in the US, and worldwide, are living examples of Professor Eck's immense contributions to both academia and engaged citizenship. Professor Eck has been a lifelong exemplar of walking the talk of an engaged and dialogical approach to pluralism, bridging academia and global citizenship.

· Chapter 23 ·

DIANA ECK:
SHE WHO CHANGED MY LIFE

Dhammananda

When I have written about my life, I always refer to one year: 1983. Something happened in that year that I can never forget when I reflect upon my journey along the river of my life.

For many years, I was happily married with three boys, and I was teaching at a prestigious Thai government university in the department of philosophy and religion, faculty of Liberal Arts. At that time, as a young lecturer, I was particularly eager to get out of my country and explore the larger world outside. One of the few ways offered to an academic was to attend international conferences. In the field of religion, during that time, international conferences were the world of men. This should not come as a surprise, as I was the first female scholar in my country with a PhD in Buddhist studies. I often found myself the only female participant at the so-called "international religious conferences." I had to get used to being a minority among these male—and often white male—academics in the field.

I was in international academic circles for about a decade before I got an invitation from Harvard University. The invitation did not come directly to me but to my university; the rector forwarded the invitation letter to the faculty and the dean forwarded the invitation letter to me. The invitation was from Professor Diana Eck at Harvard University: she was organizing an international conference on "Women, Religion, and Social Change." The participants were only invited academics, and mostly feminists, from around the world. Professor Eck was particularly looking for an academic from Thailand to write a paper on "The Future of Bhikkhunis in Thailand."

The letter was a God-sent invitation to me. In Thailand, in that decade, no one apart from myself had expressed an academic interest in the topic.

I received my education in India and Canada and considered an invitation to attend a conference at Harvard University as an asset for me as an academic. I did not realize that this particular conference would have a much deeper impact on me, far beyond my own imagination.

It was a closed conference, and this time, only women attended! This was a radically different academic atmosphere than I had previously experienced. At the opening ceremony, I must mention, State Senator Dorothy Eck was there to grace the occasion of this conference organized by her daughter. Looking back, why was I so struck by having Diana's mother among us? Perhaps because my father[225] was a member of parliament in Thailand.

"Women, Religion, and Social Change" was my first exposure to feminists, and those Diana Eck invited were the most prominent leaders from each country! They were strong, forceful—and at times angry. One, a medical doctor with white hair, particularly shocked me: she stood up and introduced her husband seated next to her: "This is my third husband." I came from a culture in which women seldom had public space; beyond this, to mention that he was her third husband in public was beyond me. But I learned a lot from her: I learned that to be frank and straightforward is also okay. Another participant from Latin America expressed her feminist concerns through poetry. It was so moving that most of us, if not all, were in tears. Together, we shared a common experience—the suffering of women.

Yet it was getting to be too much for me to take in all at once. I needed time and space to be on my own. I sneaked out one afternoon during the conference: I took the public train and ended up at a museum. What I saw in the museum, a seated Avalokitesvara—the bodhisattva of compassion, popularly known in its female form as Kwan-Yin—uplifted me and brought back my mental balance. He (or she) was seated in a very relaxed manner with the right arm resting on the knee, folded up to the side. The right foot was on the ground ready to get up, ready to reach out to those who might need assistance. The facial expression was serene. This helped me to be anchored and gain mental and spiritual balance.

I went back to the conference with a much more settled mind. I understood the suffering of women, and I wanted to be part of them, but recognized that I need not be angry: I can do it the Buddhist way.

The impact of the conference on me was profound. I had to re-shuffle my thoughts and my commitments. I was comfortable as an academic, even with my feminist understanding and a clearer sense of the issues around me. But I realized it was not enough. The message from the conference spoke to me loud and clear. I wondered: How can I bring about social changes if I sit comfortably in an ivory tower, as an academic? I had all of the necessary information about the ordination of Buddhist women in my hands, yet I was not doing anything about it.

After the 1983 conference, Diana Eck tried to connect the participants by bringing out a newsletter on their activities, but it would continue only for a few issues. After that, it seemed that nothing was happening: In each country, we must have been busy working in our own contexts. I recognized the importance of connecting among us, and—inspired by Diana Eck—started a newsletter on International Buddhist Women's Activities in 1984. Originally known as N.I.B.W.A., the newsletter was later named *Yasodhara* to honor the enlightened Princess Yasodhara, the Buddha's previous wife. *Yasodhara* created a space for Buddhist women who shared the same concerns—particularly on the ordination issue. This was a quarterly newsletter, sponsored from my own government salary. It started with only thirty copies and increased eventually to 1,000 copies; the mailing list covered more than thirty-seven countries. And, although I cannot believe it myself, it continued for thirty years, without one missing issue.

The newsletter successfully served the purpose of connecting Buddhist women who shared the same interest. Eventually, ordination for Buddhist women was no longer a dream but a reality, with the Theravada monks giving ordination to women in 1998.

I took the lower ordination in 2001, with full ordination 2003[226] when the line was clear; the lineage was from Sri Lanka.

My full ordination was exactly twenty years after the "Women, Religion, and Social Change" conference at Harvard in 1983. My question was, *How did Diana know at least twenty years ahead of time?* The title of the paper she asked me to present was "The Future of the Bhikkhuni Sangha in Thailand." We have to give credit not only to Diana as a person but also to Harvard for having a professor who has a clear understanding and can even predict the future of the Buddhist community.

In 2003, Diana Eck called for yet another conference. It was a meeting of the previous participants whom she invited in 1983. Not all of them attended, but I was there, with a changed hairstyle. With ordination, a Buddhist nun shaves her head and wears a saffron robe. A feminist whom I met twenty years ago sat across from the table at lunch time and asked if I was Dr. Kabilsingh: she could not recognize me from the way I looked but she said she remembered my hands!

I was the only participant who really confirmed the message from the theme of the conference in 1983, "Women, Religion and Social Change." Yes, I have changed as an individual, but more than that I have changed the circumstances of Buddhists in my country as well.

With the first ray of the morning sun, for the past 700 years, we could see only Buddhist monks coming out with bowls in their hands to receive alms from people—mostly women—waiting to offer food to them. Now, the scenario has changed with the rows of Buddhist nuns going out to receive food from the people, both men and women. The gender roles have shifted, and women who saw this for the first time were in tears. They never thought that they would see women ordained in their lifetime, but it has happened.

It all started with a change of the mind of one woman who came to attend the conference at Harvard University in 1983, and it all happened with the deep insight of Diana Eck when she planned and organized that historical conference.

Buddhist women, particularly in Theravada Buddhism, did not have access to full ordination in spite of the fact that the Buddha allowed them the ordination from his time, and the lineage continued for more than a thousand years at least in India and Sri Lanka. In Thailand, Buddhist women did not have access until I stepped out to receive ordination in 2001: It all started from that conference in 1983.

Words and writing are not sufficient to pay tribute to Diana Eck, but I am sure she will be happy that I have paid tribute to her with my life commitment. And this essay is to honor Diana Eck, who ignited that flame of responsibility in me to bring about social change in Thai Buddhism.

· Chapter 24 ·

BEYOND THE RULES OF INTERFAITH DIALOGUE

Blu Greenberg

Item: Although this will surely come as a surprise to Diana and may raise question of relevance for the reader (spoiler alert, see Conclusions), the fact is that I have thought of Diana on many mornings during these past two decades, winter and summer, as I open my "Diana Eck closet"—a few black skirts and slacks, some colorful blouses and jackets." I don't remember how or why she shared this advice with me. Perhaps I was fretting about my outfit. By now she may have even updated her fashion advice. But I still follow her program for quick decision-making on one's clothing for the day, essential information about the economy of time that enabled her to accomplish enough for two or three lives: "All you need is a few black skirts and slacks, some . . ."

Item: During my visit to Diana and Dorothy in 1999, they engaged in a side conversation about a young man living at Lowell House. The two women sounded like parents discussing a teenager's problem; curious, I pressed for details. Two brothers and two sisters, ages fifteen, seventeen, eighteen, and twenty, had recently become the foster children of Diana and Dorothy—not Lowell House dorm students but members of the household. The four young people had lost their mother a year earlier and were fully orphaned during the Kosovo war as they watched their father, an eminent physician, killed before their eyes. Diana and Dorothy became instant parents to them, nurturing them through their grief and helping them to build new lives in America as they grew into adulthood.

Anyone who has raised a teenager or adopted a child into their family knows how great is the pleasure and reward but also how time-consuming and emotionally draining such a task can be. I happen to have Diana's professional calendar of 2001–2002 saved in my bookmarks. When I look at it, the first thing that comes to mind is their children. How did she and Dorothy manage to accomplish so much as they nurtured four war orphans with such care and love, calm and grace?

Item: In 1988, Diana co-convened with Tarek Mitri of the World Council of Churches the International Consultation on Women in Interreligious Dialogue. The six-day meeting was held at Victoria University outside of Toronto. On day two, I was taking a pleasant stroll with an elderly nun along the beautiful grounds of the university when all of a sudden, this kindly woman commented in her gentle nun's voice, "Those soldiers over there [in Israel], they are acting like Nazis." I was thunderstruck; feelings of fury began to rise in me.

By 1988, with twenty-five years of dialogue behind me, I had already learned to not answer every slight or challenge every mistruth as I saw it. I had also become more sensitive to the suffering of innocent Palestinian families who paid the price of their poor leadership. But this was too much. The highly moral Israel Defense Forces (IDF), always asking of itself ethical questions in the field of operations, a citizens' army, my neighbors and my own gentle nephews and nieces, a civilized army defending its people against an enemy whose open agenda was to wipe Israel off the map and make the seas red with Jewish blood? Calling them Nazis? I knew it was useless to challenge the nun directly with Israel's right to exist in but a tiny segment of its ancient homeland, a state newly reaffirmed [1947] by the nations of the world; a state that had made multiple offers for coexistence with a Palestinian state side-by-side. Instead, I responded to the nun mildly with, "On the contrary, the Israeli army acts with great restraint under great provocation and threat." But I declared to myself the intention to run back to Diana later to report this assault.

To my shock, Diana brushed off the remark. She did not cancel the nun or the conference. She did not even plan to call the elderly nun on the carpet. I have to admit to bewilderment and disappointment at the moment. I knew that Diana had more sympathy for the Palestinian cause than for Israel; I knew that others like Diana saw Israel as Goliath, not the David defending its life. Yet, I also knew that she felt some positive feelings about Israel and its very right to exist.

It was a powerful lesson in dialogue behavior. The more I thought about it, had Diana done what I wanted, it might have wrecked the conference for the next five days, and that would have been a loss. The incident was a more extreme case of not rising to every challenge, but the principle holds: there would be no genuine dialogue if there was no restraint, sometimes on this side, sometimes on that.

Item: In 1991, Diana invited me to join a conference of the Pluralism Project, one of the many interfaith enterprises she created. The first meeting was a relatively short conference, one and a half days, held on the Harvard campus. The first session was to begin the morning after the twenty-five participants had settled into their accommodations. At such conferences I was accustomed to the first half hour of the first session, or at most, the first hour, devoted to introductions. But the program listed the entire first session as introductions. I thought this must be a mistake of sorts, Diana would be giving an opening address. Not so. Diana gave a very brief self-introduction as did other staff members. What remained to fill the next three-plus hours was so remarkable that it became a model for me in planning other conferences. Diana invited the participants one by one to speak spontaneously about their lives, backgrounds, identities, hopes, and more. The session created an intimacy unlikely for participants who represented such opposite views. It was also cost-effective in terms of the rest of the conference: when a woman spoke, she could be heard with her personal story in the background. The introductions accelerated a sense of cohesion necessary to speak the truth and listen well.

Item: In November 2001, Diana scheduled the Consultation on Women's Networks in Multireligious America. We met at the Harvard Club in New York City for a two-hour session. Many of us had been together in previous dialogues. But now, after 9/11, we had come with different emotions and agendas. Having participated in other post 9/11 dialogues, I was stung by the not infrequent references to Israel as the cause of 9/11; this included some of the participants here. As we went around the room introducing ourselves with one-liners, I chose my words, "I am an Orthodox American Jewish feminist and Zionist"—adding that I had the uncomfortable feeling that I was perceived as waving a red flag for proudly introducing myself as a Zionist. That I could speak my words and not shrink in the background swallowing feelings of hurt, I attributed to Diana's protocols and model, as well as the friendships that had been developed at earlier meetings.

More importantly, when the meeting ended, Diana quietly asked me if I'd be interested in engaging the subject of Israel in an open forum with another member of the group. She suggested a most likable and impressive Palestinian obstetrician-gynecologist (OBGYN) from Los Angeles—who was harsh on Israel's right to exist. I said yes and Diana scheduled a public lecture in one of Harvard's auditoriums. What is remarkable about this is that Diana and I continue to have very different views on Israel; she is not anti-Israel but has greater compassion for the Palestinian cause than concern for Israel's safety and security.

We had our dialogue, and I have to admit to not being in top form, not able to persuade anyone in the hall that Israel was a miracle sitting on top of a powder keg, a vulnerable, Jewish state whose neighbors continued to openly profess an agenda of destruction, a Jewish political entity that offered peaceful compromise solution after peaceful compromise solution; and the only real democracy in the region. Afterward, a few Jewish students in the hall who were afraid to speak up in the public setting (a harbinger of what was to come) approached to whisper appreciation in my ear. The Palestinian-American OBGYN was most impressive. To her credit, Diana did not say to each of us, "You did a great job." What she said was the essence of her philosophy of dialogue—that it was important to get these differing views out there. Classic Diana. Genuine Diana.

Item: As everyone in dialogue knows, one of the experiences of dialogue is that it not only makes you less inured to the pain of the other but also intensifies the connection to your own faith community. This happened to me many times during the dialogues that Diana created. Yet during the course of writing this tribute, I realized that she also brought me into other meaningful experiences that enlarged my life and feelings of pride as a Jew. She introduced me to the work of Wesley Ariarajah and Hans Ucko, consecutive directors of interfaith relations at the World Council of Churches (WCC). She did this behind the scenes, modestly and without ever claiming credit for her "matchmaking" efforts.

One particular experience was the WCC Women's Consultation. In preparation for the End of the Decade of Women meetings in Nairobi, 1985, the WCC assembled a group of eight women of different world religions. Our mandate was to prepare papers defining women's roles in our respective religions, model interreligious dialogue for the larger group, and be available each day of the conference to meet with its participants.

In the usual style of the WCC, extensive preparation was built into the project. Our group of eight met in Geneva for several days a year during the three years prior to Nairobi. It was at these advance meetings in Geneva that I came to know precious feminists of different faiths and cultures, including Marie Asaad, a gentle Egyptian Christian social pioneer of wide reputation, a social pioneer who fought against female genital mutilation in her country. At our second preparatory meeting in Geneva, in 1984, Marie said that she wanted me to meet her friend, a French Christian whom she had invited to dinner. That evening, I found myself sitting on a leather banquette next to Madeleine Barot, who—with a bit of probing—told me her wartime story. Every day, weather permitting, Madeleine ran a "summer camp." She would gather fifteen or twenty children and take them for a day of hiking in the mountains between France and Switzerland. She would cross into Switzerland with her charges and then return alone as her Swiss contacts would take the children onto the next part of "summer camp." Suddenly, I realized that I am hearing firsthand the story of a righteous Christian woman, a member of the noble French Resistance, who had made herself vulnerable in order to save Jewish children from certain deportation and death. I asked her if her story had been told to Yad Vashem, the National Holocaust Memorial Institute of the State of Israel. She did not think so. I wrote to

Yad Vashem whose researchers confirmed her story and subsequently, in 1988, honored her with the title Righteous Among the Nations, a most revered title for those who risked their lives to save Jews.

For thirty years, I had never thought to connect that moment with Diana, but suddenly, unbidden, another scene with Marie came to the fore and I realized that Diana had a friendship with Marie long before I did. And it was Diana who had recommended both Marie and me to Hans Ucko from the WCC, and that is how I happened to have this extraordinary experience in my life of sitting in a Geneva pub, meeting a heroine of my people, a woman whose quiet work saved hundreds of Jewish children whose descendants, seventy years later, probably number into the thousands and are replenishing the Jewish people.

To be sure, Diana follows all of the rules of interfaith dialogue—among them, open-mindedness to others' views, sensitivity to feelings and to language, active listening to the other, searching for common ground and potential areas of cooperation, compassion for the other's pain, and empathy for the other's suffering. But Diana has additional rules and traits of character that she brings to the enterprise and to every encounter—modesty and an unusual degree of selflessness, kindness of heart, genuine love of and concern for the other; also, patience and calm, a desire to be of help to humanity and to improve the world at large, and small ways to ease the burdens of everyone in her orbit. That is why Diana Eck can be a professor at a world-famous university, take four war orphans into her loving household with her life's partner Dorothy, know when to move forward and when to hold back a response that could either advance or inhibit progress, enlarge a conversation or derail it, and how to offer unsolicited but practical advice on clothing and the economy of time to a friend in need. Diana is a love, altogether a most extraordinary human being.

· Chapter 25 ·

POTENTIALS OF PLURALISM:
EID ON 9/11

Nancy A. Khalil

The question Diana Eck asked more than three decades ago rings truer today more than ever—"What does it mean to live in a pluralistic society?"[227] According to the Pluralism Project website, pluralism is "an ethic for living together in a diverse society: not mere tolerance or relativism, but the real encounter of commitments." Particularly, the Project's case study initiative seeks to document real life "encounter[s] of commitments." The cases, written by Pluralism Project research director Ellie Pierce, teach about religion and living religiously together through the difficulty, often (though not always), of mutually well-intentioned people trying to navigate opposing beliefs and practices. These commitments reflected in the case studies are not always friendly, and sometimes lack a true understanding of stakeholders' traditions and interests, yet it is in these negotiations, and all the tensions they may bring, that resides the objective of a shared society that defines the pluralism Diana Eck has been working towards for decades. Such pluralism exists with tensions between different faith groups, between religious groups and legal and social structures, and even internal to a singular faith group navigating a marginalized identity, as was the case with Eid-ul-adha in America 2016.

In 2016, Eid-ul-adha, or Eid of Sacrifice, Eid for short, would potentially fall on 9/11, and not just any 9/11, but the fifteenth anniversary of 9/11/2001. Eid-ul-adha is widely understood in Islamic scripture to commemorate the Qur'anic story of Prophet Abraham's devotion being tested by God through a command to slaughter his son, Prophet Ismail. After Prophet Ismail insisted his father follow God's command, God saved Prophet Ismail and sent a sheep to be slaughtered instead. This Eid of Sacrifice takes place every year on the 10th day of the last month of the Islamic calendar (Dhul-Hijjah). The Islamic calendar is a lunar calendar, a twelve-month calendar, each month beginning by the sighting of the crescent that emerges with the birth of the new moon. The lunar calendar is also about eleven days shorter than the dominantly used solar, or Gregorian, calendar, making the start of any Islamic calendar month fall ten to twelve days earlier than it began the year before it. Taking place at the same time as Eid-ul-adha, and also commemorating other stories from the Prophet Abraham's life, is the annual Hajj pilgrimage to the mountain of Arafat in Saudi Arabia. Muslims are called to complete Hajj once in a lifetime should they have the health and wealth to do so. Hajj is as diverse an activity as one can find on planet earth. People from all over the planet gather, and for the most part are even dressed the same, to perform the same rituals, within the same timeframe. That is not to say there is no xenophobia of groups from certain parts of the world and stereotypes propagated around how they may behave, etc. The Saudi government also remains the clear gatekeeper of who is allowed in to complete the pilgrimage, and who is not. Such gatekeeping was emboldened after the Covid pandemic when the Saudi government elected to no longer allow Hajj tour operators from a select few Muslim minority nations, including the US, to organize trips. In 2022 and 2023, pilgrims competed to attend through a Saudi-administered portal for Hajj visas and accommodations. Once on Hajj, however, in terms of the rituals themselves, everyone is on a level playing field—potential 5-star transportation and accommodations aside.

Outside of performing Hajj in Makkah and being deeply immersed in worship and rituals, Eid for Muslims around the rest of the world is a very festive time. Traditions vary but they almost always center around joy, community, and food. For Eid-ul-adha, slaughtering, particularly of sheep, is common practice. The meat is in part eaten and in part distributed to those near and dear and those in need. In many Muslim majority societies, where the sheep are overflowing in the markets, slaughtering can take place in the streets with children and adults witnessing it. For some, the thought of a child watching the slaughter of an animal might seem jarring. But for many children, it is a quite natural sight. Children, even here in the US, raised on farms are privy to this part of the circle of life well beyond the celebratory slaughter on Eid. In addition to the live sheep, there is the rising commercialization of the holiday including stuffed sheep that abound in many market stalls, sheep-shaped cakes, and sheep-themed cupcakes. In 2016, the sheep toys were a predicator signaling the marketization targeting holiday décor that would globally surge across urban markets in the years since: It would move well beyond cute and edible sheep to a plethora of beautiful and elaborate Eid signage.

Commercialization is a tricky thing in this globally capitalist society. One equally does not want a sacred holiday and tradition to be so commodified, and at the same time, many find it harder and further "othering" to kindle a sense of festivity without such material goods and decorations. When one already feels like an othered community owing to their religious identity, the path to reducing otherization becomes a strong objective. For some minorities, that can mean not overtly celebrating holidays at all to keep a discreet profile, hiding or minimizing the identity that otherizes them: For others, it can mean having comparable, embellished ways to commemorate and celebrate their own holidays as does the majority group celebrating their traditions in the nation they live.

For the 2016 Eid-ul-Adha, there was a very good chance that the 10th day of the last month of the Islamic calendar would fall on 9/11. Muslims across the US were anxious. Some say that on 9/11 Islam was hijacked, and in 2016 on that same day, Eid came very close to being hijacked. Some Muslim leaders were calling for all festivities to be canceled and celebrations delayed. They wanted leaders to spend the day attending 9/11 vigils and memorials. Other Muslims were calling for the day to be spent in service to neighbors or those in need. The calls were pragmatically unimaginable. What would a solemn Eid look like in practice? How could one stop millions of Muslims gathered, adorned to impress in their most festive attire, from feeling glee when seeing and greeting old and new friends at their community Eid morning prayer? Would laughter be shunned? Bright colors discouraged? Donuts not provided? Goodie bags for kids not passed out? Of course, it would mean delays in any Eid fairs. No bouncy houses or petting zoos. No jugglers, balloons, or cotton candy. Even if mosques around the country could agree to this, how would one stop people from celebrating in their homes? Or renting private spaces? That would not be possible, nor would it be possible for all, or even most, mosques to agree to defer Eid. Muslims have difficulty agreeing on how to determine when the new moon is born and Eid even begins, never mind agreeing on how to (not) celebrate it. Why then propose the idea of a solemn Eid? What is being signaled?

A striking element of this incident is that 9/11, like other days of our nation's historic tragedies, is not a day of mourning. We do not halt scheduled activities. Theme parks do not close gates. Sports games are not canceled. Weddings and birthday parties are still scheduled. Gatherings take place all around the country—yet many leaders in the Muslim community still felt a strong fear. One must ask, why? Responding to such fears becomes a tool of inclusion. Something some Muslims, when and if needed in front of media or other allies, can point to as an indication of loyal nationalism. It does not matter much if it can be implemented on the ground, it can still be discursively mobilized to mitigate backlash.

Scholars of Islamophobia and Muslim activists have consistently emphasized that false associations and stereotypes are a distraction for Muslims. They consume so much time and community resources trying to defend against external detractors that the proactive work many Muslims want to do to serve and develop their communities becomes collateral damage. Eid-ul-adha in 2016 emerged as an instance of just how extensive that collateral damage can be when the false associations and stereotypes become internalized by Muslims on behalf of detractors— before detractors can even launch an attack. In other words, Muslims were being so sensitive and cautious that many wanted to cancel or defer a major ritual celebration lest it trigger people fueled by bigotry. What might it mean in the long run for US Muslim children's identities to have their holiday celebrations hijacked and turned into a day of solemness? There was such a collective sigh of relief when the crescent moon was sighted and the new moon determined that Eid would be on September 12, that memes started surfacing on social media making light of the relief Muslims felt when Eid was determined to not conflict with 9/11.

Diversity and inclusion are tricky concepts. We have colloquially built them up as desirable ideals but often lose the influence of power dynamics in their pursuit. In her book *Regulating Aversion*, Wendy Brown[228] offers an analysis of tolerance through the lens of power and says that tolerance is almost self-contradictory because it is used as a concept to distinguish the better from the worse. Those who have space for tolerance, i.e., freedom, are the better, and those who do not, i.e., the threatening boogeyman of the moment (in this moment: Muslims) are the worse. Also, built into its understanding is the idea that there is a group, or people, or situation that needs tolerating and another group that will offer that toleration, empowering the latter and disempowering the former. This produces an empowered gatekeeper and a disempowered minority waiting at the door.

It can be the same with diversity and inclusion if we are not careful. To actively pursue a notion of inclusion, or to seek to diversify an institution in a society is to say that there is a gatekeeper, an empowered group that needs to permit others in, and a marginalized group that is otherwise left on the outside. The tricky part is, if the marginalized group is welcomed in, how can that occur, if at all, so that they now share that inner space in an equally empowered manner? Is there a benefit to being "inside" if the only way in is to be allowed in by some other entity that is de facto the more powerful one, and the only way to stay in is on their terms? Pluralism, in the ways it came alive through Diana Eck's work, is not a pursuit of inclusion, and it does not attempt to offer itself as a type of solution to this dilemma; instead, it must be a reality that recognizes the tensions the ideas of diversity and equity can bring and wants to see those ideas collectively acknowledged and engaged. Unlike tolerance and inclusion, pluralism is not a call for the dominant group to unilaterally intercede with attempts to resolve issues of inequity and discrimination. It is a call to acknowledge them and to collectively recognize they need to be addressed—how that happens cannot be a singular response, concept, or action.

This is the struggle I'm witness to; this is the struggle Muslims around the country face. It is what we can call living a *terrorfied* life. Wanting to hijack our own Eid festivities. Hosting "Meet the Muslim" events, speaking at events titled "Are all Muslims Terrorists?," insisting in the media, at interfaith events, to their friends and neighbors that Islam means peace, which in one way is technically true, but is also falsely pacifying the faith. Anyone who studies Islamic jurisprudence knows it is not pacifist by any stretch of the means—even if the vast majority of Muslims today live a pacifist life. These tactics are all knocks on the door by the outsider, by a marginalized minority. They are attempts to shatter imaginations of threat and fear to be allowed inside. They are a pursuit of inclusion. In inclusion's attempt to break open the gates of exclusion, it reinforces the gate itself as the structure of the society we live in. So long as that gate is there to begin with, so long as some need to knock on its door to enter and others are empowered to permit them in, or not, so long do diversity and inclusion work against themselves.

It is the week of Eid-ul-adha in 2023 as I write this, reflecting on the same Eid from 2016 and the words it inspired me to deliver at the Pluralism Project's twenty-fifth anniversary celebration. That would mean the Pluralism Project today is moving towards its thirty-third year. We are currently living through culture wars that have in part been reflecting the parallel rise in right-wing extremism against marginalized communities with the uptick in diversity, equity, and inclusion programming expanding in recent years from educational institutions to corporate America. Amplified discourse on varying lifestyles is increasingly polemical and vitriolic, sadly making even Wendy Brown's rightly critiqued argument on tolerance seem appealing and viable. When I spoke at the twenty-fifth anniversary conference, my focus was on the idea of inclusion. I borrowed from Wendy Brown's intervention and theory on tolerance in her book *Regulating Aversion* to ask, how does inclusion pursue equity when it inherently needs a gatekeeper that does the including and a marginalized group that gets to [or not to] be included? I asked whether inclusion really could be the gold standard activists and scholars were treating it as by institutionalizing it and promoting it in so many arenas. Wondering then, and today, I continue to ask how these initiatives sustain momentum and funding, especially as we seem to be regressing in the causes they champion. In the summer of 2023, the Supreme Court ruled against affirmative action, following legislation passing the year before in several states forbidding teaching critical race theory in their curricula. Pursuing inclusion is not enough.

What makes the idea of pluralism and "encounters of commitment" more appealing is the premise that those involved come knowing they will be uncomfortable, knowing they will sit with feelings that come from acknowledgment of and contributions to inequity, and recognizing our different identity-endowed privileges. If we can come willing to think deeply enough to dismantle assumptions upon which our minds have constructed so many layers of value, layers that define a person, and layers that bound our worldviews, if we can allow ourselves to rupture those values, to question those worldviews, and to allow for the equal existence and autonomy of other worldviews, to me, that would be brilliance. Much like a brilliant light that illuminates, so too does the brilliant encounter shine a guiding light. I'm not trying to suggest that pluralism is brilliance, but I do think that unlike inorganic inclusive efforts to address our hierarchies of power, pluralism creates an environment that can allow for brilliance to potentially emerge—and for Eid to be celebrated on any day of the year with no shame or guilt.

· Chapter 26 ·

DIANA ECK AS TEACHER

Pranati Parikh

I.

Diana Eck was the first professor I met as a first-year student at Harvard University in 2017. It was a hot day towards the end of August. I was walking into a first-year barbecue beside my new roommate, Caroline, with the tentative confidence of someone recently oriented to campus. It was easy to get caught in conversations poking out this way and that from students clumped together in various nodes across the quad, their normally intensely academic guards down, wiping ketchup from their fingers, looking forward to their first weekend of college parties. It was so easy, in fact, that I lost track momentarily of Caroline, the two of us snagging on different branches of chatter. When we reunited a few paces later, she was out of breath and seemed reenergized. "I just met Diana Eck," she told me. "She studies Hinduism! You should introduce yourself!"

Of course, I knew the name Diana Eck. I had applied to colleges with professors with an expertise in Hindu studies and Sanskrit in mind. I wasn't sure whether I was going to study religion or not, but as someone deeply steeped in the Swaminarayan community since childhood, Diana Eck's focus on diasporic Hinduism and the American religious landscape made her work and teaching especially appealing to me. Steeling myself rapidly to interact with an esteemed faculty member I admired, I asked Caroline where Professor Eck was, surprised that she might be somewhere just around the corner. Without warning, a cluster of students scattered to reveal Diana Eck, sitting on the steps of Widener Library.

Those who know Diana's inclination to visual analysis of Hindu art and architecture will not be surprised to know that my memory imagines Diana at an ascending entrance to what would become my college education, like an auspicious deity at the doorway of a temple. There she was, conversing with students, addressing me before I could mentally rehearse anything at all. When I told her my name, she responded by saying that it sounded familiar. "I think I read your application essay," she said. "Was it about studying Sanskrit?" It had, in fact, been about Sanskrit. I don't quite remember what I told her after that—she remembered a startling number of details about my essay, and was curious about some tidbits from my childhood—and soon enough she was busy inviting the next student into the conversation, making me feel seen but not singled out, special but not scrutinized.

My first encounter with Diana Eck is important to me not because it was the first time I was acknowledged by a faculty member by name, but because it collapsed the distances between various poles that had until then structured my expectations of college. There was the obvious distance between professor and student. I had arrived at the barbecue certain that I would see no professors and instead walked right into Diana at home amongst my peers, holding a napkin just the way everybody else was. Then, there was the distance between the application reader and the admittee. Diana had openly acknowledged my application essay, violating some unspoken rule that I would never really know why I was admitted to Harvard. Diana named things she liked about my essay and also posed questions freely and without pretense. There was also a distance I had become accustomed to attributing to myself. I was, having grown up in a whitewashed rural Missouri, "other": brown-skinned, a child of immigrants, Hindu. A short conversation with Diana Eck gave me a glimpse into the way my background and culturally particular interests were not only worth studying and conversing about, but legible facets of my identity that harnessed me into a constellation of histories and ideas as opposed to cutting me out of one. And, finally, there was the distance between what I thought was the cold, detached academic inquirer and the genuine, invested person. By asking questions that were just as casual and warm as they were sharp, Diana Eck was both all at once.

These dualities were not just abstract concepts that lay over the surface of my experience, or theory I applied to it in retrospect. They were real forces in my life. I was Indian and American. I was a person of faith and a person intellectually interested in religion. I was entering a predominantly white, Christian academia. Each pole viewed the other with suspicion; there was something martial about the push and pull between them. The idea of collapsing those distances—of building, conversely, a unity more accurate to the reality of being a student of religion—defined my college experience, and Diana Eck's courses were one of the most important mediums for this reflection.

II.

In my first year, Diana taught a course called "Case Studies in Religious Pluralism." The course was taught in the Center for Government and International Studies. Encircled by tiers of chairs, an individual microphone attached to each seat, Diana usually stood at the front of the room, shuffling through the materials for the day. The course materials were drawn from the Pluralism Project, an initiative that Diana herself had founded as a way of encouraging people to both increase their literacy of other faiths but also deepen the quality of their engagement with them from mere tolerance to real dialogue. The eponymous "case studies," were miniature briefs on pluralistic encounters across the United States. Who were the parties involved? What was the context in which they encountered one another? How did they react and respond to one another? The written material only cursorily summarized these events; it was our job, as students in class, to discuss the case's nuances, to consider the assumptions and implications at play. Diana was at the helm of the discussion.

The second day of class, we were assigned a case about a Wiccan invocation at a county's board of supervisors in Chesterfield, Virginia in

2002. Cyndi Simpson, who identified as both a Wiccan and as a member of the Unitarian Universalist church, had asked to be added to the list of religious leaders allowed to perform the invocation at legislative meetings. When she was refused, on the grounds that Wicca, considered "neo-pagan" and invoking "polytheistic" and "pre-Christian deities," did not fit the Judeo-Christian paradigm of traditions permitted to offer invocations in legislative offices, she eventually filed a lawsuit. Upon first read, I thought the questions, though insidious, were relatively simple. The hegemony of Christianity prevailed despite protections in the US Constitution for the free exercise of religion. It was unfortunate but unsurprising.

However, Diana opened class that day with a video of a Hindu priest, Rajan Zed, giving an invocation at the Nevada State Senate in 2007. It was a video that raised similar issues—it was a prayer from a religious tradition considered, like Wicca, pagan, polytheistic, and as far away from the paradigm for worship and articulation of Christianity as one could get. But it struck a nerve in me in a way the five brief pages about Simpson's lawsuit did not. Maybe it was because the video recorded not only the prayer that Zed tried to give—a gentle, inclusive one about peace, health, and happiness for all—but also the ugly protest mounted by right-wing Christians in the balcony of the chamber. Maybe it was because the frame gave us a view of Zed from a slightly elevated angle, showing the way he looked over at someone out of frame when the shouting got particularly loud, the way his face showed apprehension, hurt, even fear. Maybe it was because the sight of him in his orange robes and *rudraksha* beads was so familiar that it felt like the assault was directed not just toward Zed, but me, too. When the lights came back on in the classroom only a minute or so later, I was almost in tears.

To have had this feeling in only the second meeting of our class transformed my experience of subsequent ones. Diana's move to put us in the sensorial midst of a pluralistic encounter that went particularly badly was strategic, I think, in two ways. For one, we confronted that day the acute feeling of suffering on behalf of someone. To see that others in the class who were not Hindu or even South Asian were outraged, too, gave me that same sense of collapsing distance that meeting Diana on the steps of the library had all those weeks ago. If we could feel—really *feel*—injustice, then perhaps we could become advocates for change. The fact that we were not all from the same community did not have to mean that we were, in our silos, left to fight for ourselves. Second, this experience primed us to read the rest of the case studies in the course attuned to the way pluralistic encounters are not (only) theoretical arguments about religion. They involve strong affective currents. After this meeting, the case studies became gnarly, even harrowing. There was, for example, the case of the Islamic community center near Ground Zero, which sparked a controversy about whether a mosque should be built over the site of Ground Zero. Here, it was not only an interfaith encounter at stake. It was as much about political symbolism, the meaning of majority and minority in tension with each other, about raw grief and stubborn hope. This was the first important insight into unity under Diana's instruction: that academic study had to be situated in the world, since religiously diverse citizens are civically and affectively interlocked with one another.

III.

In the spring semester of my first year, I took another class with Diana Eck called "Hindu Worlds of Art and Culture." This time, the course was a little more traditional in its structure. It met in a musty classroom in Harvard Hall, a building near the entrance of the Yard. There were no microphones, no tiered rows. There were, instead, chairs facing a large projection screen where Diana would routinely show art and photos of temples, manuscripts, and other objects. Again, the class was sensory. We listened to music and pored over paintings as much as we read from books.

Many of my peers were surprised that I was taking the course in the first place, since I had gained a sort of reputation for being—and knowing a lot about being—Hindu. I had already been a regular member of Harvard Dharma, the Hindu students' association; by the spring semester, I was planning to run for the position of "Worship Chair," in which I would coordinate and lead regular gatherings for ritual worship, chanting, and devotional music. Peers came to me with their questions about the Ramayana, Mahabharata, and other texts, expecting that I'd remember the details of a story about a niche figure. I had continued my study of Sanskrit, deciding to take the placement exam that would allow me to join MA and PhD students in higher-level courses. If my other courses like "The Ethics of Atheism" and "Ethnographies of Religion" were still new to me, this one I expected to be a dip into waters familiar and welcoming.

I was proven wrong. Diana had a way, as was her specialty, of using well-known vocabulary to coax entirely new articulations. Our primary assignments in the course were to respond to a series of discussion prompts. When fellow students asked me questions like, "How does Shiva, who is a *yogi*, also have a family?" I might have responded with something like, "He has a family life, but remains unattached in the way that ascetics are." But in "Hindu Worlds of Art and Culture," Diana pushed us a step further, pointing out the contradictions in that statement. How so? What does it really mean to be attached or detached from a reality? What is the relationship between asceticism and sexuality? It was in response to Diana's questions that I thought more critically about the gods, figures, and concepts I thought I knew so well. What *is* the *linga*, anyway? How can Kali be both terrifying and benevolent? Are *dharma* and *bhakti* in tension in religious life? If one was not told that love poems to Krishna were religious, how would one know? What concept of time and reality do the myths of sages like Markandeya and others suggest? Now, rereading the responses I wrote those many years ago, I see convolution and resort to buzzwords like "embodiment," "consciousness," and "universality"; by no means did I achieve, in the few hundred words required of us every week, any groundbreaking answer. But in Diana's class, I learned not only to think in the space beyond obvious contradictions but also that the thinking was worthwhile.

One figure especially complicated by the art and text that Diana showed us was Sita. In traditional Hindu discourse, I had thought, Sita was the archetypical wife, steadfastly loyal and self-sacrificing in deference to Rama. But by that point in class, I knew there was no such thing as "traditional Hindu discourse," that my thinking so was a product of specific set of influences, and that while my background had certainly prepared me to recognize context in this class, it was not yet capacious enough to encompass the diversity of readings and retellings of the stories I knew. One homework assignment, then, involved watching Nina Paley's *Sita Sings the Blues*, a musical rendition of the episode at the end of the Ramayana when Rama abandons a pregnant Sita in the forest to protect his honor. In the film, Paley intertwines her own experience being dumped by a partner with songs narrated from the perspective of Sita, who, contrary to the demure interpretations by well-known Ramayana retellers, curses Rama and wallows in her grief. The protagonist of the film is unmistakably Sita. Rama is depicted in the film as a dull, overly masculine character, absorbed entirely in himself and his image, while those who worship him are characterized as indoctrinated robots who can't quite see the illogic of their beliefs.

Sita Sings the Blues disrupted many of my truths. There was, most obviously, the figure of Sita herself. If, at first, I found Paley's Sita overly sexualized, melodramatic, and stripped of the characteristics that made her so revered, soon I began to find power in her sadness and anger. Why shouldn't Sita have just as deep an interior as other characters in the Ramayana experiencing explicit moral dilemmas and strong emotion? I was also put off by Paley herself, a white woman advocating for free culture, appropriating and caricaturing a story that is sacred to so many thousands of Hindus. But slowly I began to realize, through discussion and reading in Diana's class, that the practice of retelling these stories was built into the tradition itself, and that for centuries people had been molding them into circumstances that more closely resemble their lives and interests in order to test hypotheticals and moral principles on a literary plane. Nina Paley, her ethnicity notwithstanding, had done just that. It was through *Sita Sings the Blues* that I began to see Hinduism defined not by a set of principles, but by a dazzling and complicated multiplicity of questions and answers. Recognizing unity, in this case, was seeing it all as hanging together despite divergences, that in addition to extra-traditional diversity I had seen in the pluralism course, there was an intra-traditional diversity that was just as critical.

IV.

As if full circle, Diana Eck was one of two readers of my senior undergraduate thesis, the culminating achievement not only of my college career but also my personal journey of thinking and feeling. It was about *dharma* in moments of ethical crises across three texts of different genres and historical periods. In many ways, my thesis grew out of the insights first encountered under Diana and then strengthened and nuanced by insights from other classes across the Religion, South Asian Studies, and other departments. Methodologically, too, my thesis explored the situatedness and internal complexity that I now knew characterized Hinduism. Diana's evaluation of it actively acknowledged this. "It is precisely because of the narrative situatedness of the protagonists that you write as a student of both Religion and Literature. . . . The texts you have chosen place us 'on the ground' with Praneshacharya, Yudhishthira, and Rama, and enable the reader to begin to appreciate the emotional texture of their experience," she wrote. Here, I can't help but recall the pluralism course, one of the first academic spaces in which we, as students, were compelled to take abstract interfaith or civic issues to the ground, understanding the "emotional texture of experience" as a primary facet of pluralistic encounters. Later in the evaluation, too, Diana writes, "*Dharma* is not single or simple, but multiple and often confusing . . . it becomes confused, and expands, changes. It is more fluid than one ever imagined." Here, I think of Paley's Sita, and the way she represented to me one of the first truly fluid figures in Hindu text and imagery. I couldn't have seen it then, but Diana's reflections on my thesis were pointing out the resonances across my college coursework—playing out over a foundation she helped build in my first year.

Even when I was not taking courses with Diana, I saw her often. She was consistently at afternoon teas in Lowell House or chatting with students in and around the Inn. She came to South Asian classical music ensemble events, at which I often sang. She came to Ghungroo, the largest student-run cultural show on campus; she even came to Dharma's Diwali pujas. On one occasion she offered to meet for office hours at her home on Prescott Street, where I met her kittens and got to see the unity of her many identities—scholar, spiritual seeker, teacher, art enthusiast—embodied on her bookshelves and on her walls. Her presence and investment in students were yet another testament to the unity—external, internal, and every other—she symbolizes to me.

At the end of her comments on my thesis, Diana wrote, "My word at the beginning of this reflection was Congratulations. And now, in conclusion, I say simply, Thank You. I have learned a great deal from this thesis and will think about it often in the years to come." I went on after college to do an MA in Divinity at the University of Chicago, graduating in 2023, and started law school back at Harvard in the fall. I hope to continue reading and writing about religion in civic spaces and its cultural, philosophical, and psychological relevance for people anywhere but especially in the United States. I echo her sentiment now: Thank you, Diana. I have learned a great deal from your teaching, scholarship, and persona, a learning which continues to buoy and challenge me even today.

· Chapter 27 ·

DIANA ECK:
THE SINGLE LARGEST INFLUENCE ON INTERFAITH AMERICA

Eboo Patel

It was the summer of 2000. I was in Cambridge, Massachusetts talking strategy with Jenny Peace for the organization that we had started two years earlier, Interfaith Youth Core. The goal of the organization was to bring more young people into interfaith work, and to focus interfaith work more on social action. Interfaith as a field had grown rapidly in the 1990s, but it was dominated by older religious leaders and theologians who favored a dialogue-based approach. A group of twenty-somethings—inspired by the promise of connecting faith, diversity, and social action—had started going to interfaith conferences, but found ourselves bored by the endless panel discussions. A critical mass of us were present at the United Religions Initiative Global Summit in June of 1998, and we organized ourselves into a fledgling nonprofit organization that sought to connect young people across faiths through social action. We called it Interfaith Youth Core.

Diana Eck was perhaps the single most influential figure in American interfaith work in the 1990s. She was a professor of comparative religions and Indian studies at Harvard University, and the director of the Pluralism Project, which was mapping the growing religious diversity in the United States. She played a central role in the interfaith unit of the World Council of Churches in the 1980s and 1990s, and also helped shape the seminal document "Towards A Global Ethic" at the 1993 Parliament of the World's Religions. Her book *Encountering God* was a major inspiration to many of us. It told Diana's story of growing up as a Methodist in Bozeman, Montana, finding her way to an elite college on the east coast in the 1960s, and then heading off to India for study abroad, where she found herself inspired by the diverse religions of the country of my birth.

Clearly, she was way too busy and important to meet with us about our fledgling nonprofit.

Not only did Diana meet with us, she invited Jenny and me to a long and lovely tea in the garden of Harvard University's Lowell House with her partner (now wife) Dorothy Austin. She listened closely to our vision, offered counsel and encouragement, and ended by saying something like, "Before long, you guys will be leading this movement."

For years, I found myself returning to Diana's words in my mind; they kept me going through all the trials and tribulations of organization building.

Diana has been a friend and partner throughout our journey at Interfaith Youth Core, now Interfaith America. She helped us get our first grant from the Ford Foundation. She invited me to give a major address sketching out the vision of Interfaith Youth Core at Harvard Divinity School in March of 2004.[229] She commented numerous times on the organization in her media appearances and public talks, including her presidential address at the American Academy of Religion in 2006.[230] And she was kind enough to be a guest on the first season of my podcast, "Interfaith America with Eboo Patel."[231]

Truth be told, I could not have imagined the podcast without her voice, because that voice has done so much to inspire and shape the organization I am privileged to lead. Interfaith America is now the leading interfaith organization in the United States—giving out more in grant dollars each year than the next largest interfaith entity—and Diana Eck has been the most influential intellectual in our journey.

Below are just a few of the ways that Diana has influenced the organization that I lead.

A PERSONAL, ACCESSIBLE, YET SCHOLARLY NARRATIVE STYLE

I marveled at Diana's first book about interfaith work, *Encountering God*. I could not put it down. It was spiritual memoir, comparative religions textbook, Christian theology, travelogue, and map to America's growing religious diversity all in one.

A quarter century later, so many stories from *Encountering God* are still vivid in my mind. I remember how Diana described being amazed that Hindus poured yogurt on their gods, and then in turn described the amazement of her Hindu friends when she casually remarked that American Christians typically do not remove their shoes in houses of worship. It was the perfect detail to describe cultural differences, and it resonated especially strongly for me, having grown up in an Indian immigrant household in the American Midwest.

Encountering God was the book that had the most influence on Interfaith Youth Core in those formative years. Diana, in describing her own spiritual journey, had created a kind of archetype that many members of Gen X could relate to. Born into a particular culture, as Diana had been into Mountain West Methodism, they found themselves enamored by a different faith, in Diana's case it was the Hinduism of Banaras (now Varanasi). At first their interest in the other religion caused them to be dismissive of their own roots, but over time they learned to appreciate each tradition on its own terms, find the resonances between them, and even deepen into their own faith. I would go through a similar process with Buddhism.

And then Diana wrote a second book that shaped my organization: *A New Religious America*. It was inspiring and accessible just like *Encountering God*, but if the earlier book was organized around Diana's individual's spiritual journey, this one could be described as being organized around a nation's spiritual journey. It traced the high ideals of the European Founder's with respect to religious diversity and interfaith cooperation through the ugly exclusion of too much of American history to our hopeful and precarious present moment where interfaith cooperation is a real possibility. If *Encountering God* felt like it was calling me as an individual to devote myself to interfaith work, *A New Religious America* felt like it was calling me to be the best interfaith leader that I could be: the nation was counting on us.

My own five books can easily be described as adopting the "Diana Eck style" of interfaith narrative. The fact that most of them were published through Beacon Press, which published *Encountering God* is a personal act of homage to Diana. And that my first book, *Acts of Faith* (which very much resembles *Encountering God* in structure and style) won the Louisville Grawemeyer Award in Religion, like Diana's book, is one of the great honors of my life.

MAKING THE CASE FOR THE IMPORTANCE OF RELIGIOUS DIVERSITY

Diana was one of the few academics in the 1990s making the case for the importance of religious diversity as a positive force, and a major contribution to American life. One of her contemporaries at Harvard, Samuel Huntington, was writing about religious diversity as a dangerous force in *The Clash of Civilizations*. And Robert Putnam highlighted in *Bowling Alone* that religion—by which he mostly meant Christianity—was a positive force in American civic life. But Diana was amongst the few major scholars to point out the importance of the growing religious diversity of American society. She did this in ways that were personally important to me.

The first was in reference to the religious diversity of India, the country of my birth, and the country of Diana's scholarship. India had been born in 1947 as a religiously diverse country, and the father of the nation, Mahatma Gandhi, had made it clear that interfaith cooperation was one of his highest ideals. Diana pointed out that India needed to work hard at this because religious diversity could be an explosive force, and then emphasized that as the United States got more religiously diverse, we would need to work hard at this as well. She underscored that Martin

Luther King, Jr., taking his lead from Gandhi, wrote often about interfaith cooperation, and that we should take this challenge as seriously as we take the challenge of racial equity and reconciliation.

Finally, Diana believed that the diversity movement within higher education was a powerful and positive national force, but that it needed to pay attention to religious diversity. We were deeply influenced by this view at Interfaith Youth Core, and basically took it as our marching orders, focusing most of the organization's energies on higher education.

DIANA'S DEFINITIONS

So many religious studies scholars focus on scripture and worship. But Diana's understanding of religion included the variety of manifestations that religion inspired. She built the Pluralism Project around this idea. She sent researchers out to find religious diversity in everything from the nation's architecture (like the mosques and temples that now dotted the American landscape, to the nation's civic institutions (the growing number of Hindu summer campus and Sikh youth groups), to the debates about zoning (in village boards and city councils).

I had grown up as an Ismaili Muslim in the western suburbs of Chicago, living the story that Diana was telling. My faith community had founded numerous houses of worship and also a range of community institutions like Ismaili sports leagues, service organizations, and religious education programs. And indeed, one of our houses of worship, a Jamatkhana, was having a hard time getting approval for zoning in a Chicago suburb called Glenview. I thought that this was all my little secret, but Diana was saying that this was a macro-level story of great national import. Religiously diverse groups like my own Ismaili Muslims of the suburbs of Chicago, many who had come to the United States after the 1965 Immigration and Naturalization Act (as my parents had), were literally reshaping the nation. We simply needed to understand that all of these things counted as "religion."

A second key concept that Diana advanced was the difference between diversity and pluralism. To Diana, diversity was simply the fact of people of different identities living in close quarters with one another.

The term said nothing about how we lived together. It might be peaceful coexistence, inspiring cooperation, or an ugly civil war. Pluralism was a manner of living with diversity that was characterized by positive, proactive engagement across difference. Interfaith Youth Core adopted this not just as a definition, but integrated it into the DNA of the organization. We expanded on Diana's understanding slightly by giving it a three-part framework: Respect for different identities; Relationships across lines of difference; and Cooperation on common projects for the common good. Respect/Relate/Cooperate. This is still our guiding framework today.

CASE STUDIES METHODOLOGY

Finally, Diana, along with scholars like Laurie Patton[232] of Middlebury, pioneered the use of the case method in interfaith work. The big idea was to generate an understanding of the interfaith dynamics of our religiously diverse nation by looking at the various tension points emerging when different religious understandings collided. Diana, in collaboration with the Pluralism Project's research director, Ellie Pierce, adapted the approach from the Harvard Business School. Ellie wrote dozens of decision-based case studies that the Pluralism Project shared widely. Diana became an expert teacher of case studies inspiring countless scholars, activists, and educators to use case studies to explore religious pluralism.

At Interfaith America, we love this methodology, and adopted it across our programs. First of all, it allows us to capture the "bottom up" nature of interfaith dynamics in the United States. What happens when doctors of different faiths differ on how to treat a patient? Or when a military veteran and a Muslim who disagree on the politics of the Iraq War find themselves coaching a baseball team? Second, cases center civic life rather than legal issues. So often religious diversity matters are reduced to religious freedom case law, but through Diana's influence we wrote more about the goings on at the Park District than we did at the Supreme Court. And finally, it helped us develop our theory around interfaith leadership. Interfaith leaders, we posit, have the vision, knowledge, and skill set to build pluralism (another reference to Diana's work) when religious diversity threatens to turn into conflict. And just as Harvard

Business School case studies prepare future CEOs to make hard business decisions, the case studies that the Pluralism Project and Interfaith America are developing do the same for future interfaith leaders.

We now use case studies in virtually every program we run and for every level of professional, from incoming first year college students to the CEOs of hospital systems.

CONCLUSION

People often say that the Pluralism Project was the mothership of the American interfaith movement of the early part of the twenty-first century. There's no doubt that that is true. So many of the books, courses, and leaders of interfaith work in the early 2000s can be traced back to the Pluralism Project in some form or another.

The relationship of my own organization, Interfaith America, to Diana is more intimate than that. In so many ways, she is our mother. Her ideas helped give birth to us, her encouragement kept us going through those topsy-turvy toddler years, and her counsel shaped our principles and our focus. We would not exist without Diana. I hope that what we are building makes her proud. I for one am grateful beyond words.

· Chapter 28 ·

AN ADVAITA VEDĀNTA THEOLOGY OF RELIGIONS:
A SKETCH

Anantanand Rambachan

In *Encountering God: A Spiritual Journey from Bozeman to Banaras*, Diana Eck describes how her "encounters with people of other faiths have challenged, changed and deepened" her own faith.[233] Although she describes her engagement with a variety of communities that include Buddhists, Jews, Muslims, Native Americans, and Sikhs, she gives significant attention to her dialogue with Hindu traditions through the study of sacred texts, conversations with practitioners and teachers, and visits to sacred places.

Eck's deep encounters with religious traditions other than her own led to challenging questions about the normative theological claims of her own tradition in relation to other traditions. In chapter seven, Eck summarized these responses under the labels of exclusivism, inclusivism, and pluralism. Eck, who identifies with the Methodist Christian tradition, does not explicitly describe herself as a Christian pluralist. Her exposition of the meaning of pluralism, however, leaves her reader with little doubt about her stance. "From a Christian pluralist position," Eck writes, "the multiplicity of religious ways is a concomitant of the ultimacy and many-sidedness of God, the one who cannot be limited or encircled by any one tradition. Therefore, the boundaries of our various traditions need not be places where we halt and contend over our differences but might well be the places where we meet and catch a glimpse of glory as seen by another."[234]

Eck's work challenges us all to think critically about our own theological responses to religious diversity and the task of developing distinctive theologies of religion grounded in the teachings of our own tradition. Francis Clooney defines the theology of religions as "a theological discipline that discerns and evaluates the religious significance of other religious traditions in accord with the truths and goals defining one's own religion."[235] I am guided in this essay by Clooney's definition and, like Diana Eck, working from a Christian place of meaning and commitment, I do so from my commitment as a scholar and practitioner of the Hindu Advaita Vedānta tradition.

First, a word about Advaita Vedānta. Advaita (Not-two) is an exegetical tradition that regards the teachings of the Vedas as revealed and authoritative. For Advaita, the highest teachings of the Vedas are to be found in end (*anta*) sections of the texts known as the Upaniṣads. For this reason, the word Vedānta (end of the Vedas) is appended to Advaita. Advaita looks also to the Bhagavadgītā, and to the Brahmasūtra, an aphoristic summary of the teachings of the Upaniṣads attributed to the ancient teacher Bādarāyaṇa. These sources are regarded as the three pillars of the Advaita tradition. Advaita is indebted to a lineage of teachers for the interpretation and transmission of its teachings. The foremost among them is Śaṅkara (ca.788–820) who wrote influential commentaries on the Upaniṣads, the Bhagavadgītā and the Brahmasūtra.

The meaning of Advaita has been unfolded variously by teachers and commentators at different historical periods. At the heart of the tradition, however, are two consistent and core claims. The first is that all is *brahman* (*sarvam khalvidam brahma*–Chāndogya Upaniṣad 3.14.1); the second is that the self (ātmā) is *brahman* (*ayam ātmā brahma*-Māṇḍukya Upaniṣad 2). The Advaita understanding of *brahman* as both ground and intelligent cause of the universe leads to the important claim that the relationship between *brahman* and the universe is best described as not-two. *Brahman* alone is the source of the universe, and the universe does not have a separate or independent ontological existence from its source.

At the same time, *brahman* has not transformed itself into the universe (pantheism). The teaching that *brahman* is the single ontological reality, the fundamental truth of all that exists, leads to the second Advaita core teaching: the self (ātmā) is *brahman*. *Brahman* exists as the ultimate subject, the non-objectifiable awareness that is the ground of all mental and cognitive processes.

These core claims have been professed by Advaitins in both exclusive and inclusive ways. Śaṅkara, for example, treats Buddhism and the Buddha with animosity. For him there is no truth in Buddhism, and it is not conducive to human wellbeing. It is illogical and "breaks down like a well sunk in sand."[236] The Buddha, according to Śaṅkara, "exposed his own incoherence in talk when he instructed the three mutually contradictory theories of the existence of external objects, existence of consciousness, and absolute nihilism; or the showed his malevolence towards all creatures acting under the delusion that these creatures would get confused by imbibing contradictory views. The ideal is that the Buddhist view should be abjured in every way by all who desire the highest good."[237] In a similar way, Jain teachings are illogical and deserve to be ignored.[238] In relation to Buddhism and Jainism, Śaṅkara's approach is exclusive; Advaita is true, and these traditions are entirely false.[239]

In the case of other Indian traditions, Śaṅkara adopts a more inclusive attitude. He is sympathetic to the Sāṅkhya-Yoga emphasis on right knowledge, on renunciation, and liberation from worldly existence. At the same time, he is clear that liberation, in the highest sense, is not attainable through Sāṅkhya-Yoga independently from the teachings of the Upaniṣads. The teachings of Sāṅkhya and the practices of Yoga are not dismissed completely. They are, according to Śaṅkara, accepted by good people and have some support in the Vedas. These can help a seeker to gain mental control, and physical well-being conducive to listening, reflecting, and assimilating the teachings of the Upaniṣads. These are not an alternative and independent path to liberation (*mokṣa*).[240] For Śaṅkara, the truth of Advaita is superior to all others and is the culmination of the religious search.

Scholars have noted the influence of Buddhist thought on Śaṅkara, even as he labored to argue against that tradition.[241] Śaṅkara, however, does not acknowledge this influence. The purpose of traditional debate was not mutual learning and enrichment, but victory over one's opponent. Śaṅkara did not read the Buddhist traditions with empathy or examine the underlying reasons why a particular position was advanced. There is no good reason, however, why contemporary Advaitins should not do so and extend such engagement to traditions like Judaism, Christianity, and Islam.

In her explanation of the meaning of pluralism, Eck gives special emphasis to the fact that the pluralist approach to religious diversity does not mean the relinquishing of commitments but "opening up those commitments to the give-and-take of mutual discovery, understanding, and, indeed, transformation."[242] Eck is careful to differentiate pluralism from relativism. "Relativism assumes a stance of openness; pluralism assumes both openness *and* commitment."[243]

Writing about commitment, Paul Griffiths, underlines the obligation of faithful intellectuals in any tradition. "If representative intellectuals belonging to some specific community come to judge at a particular time that some or all of their doctrine-expressing sentences are incompatible with some alien religious claim(s), then they should feel obliged to engage in both positive and negative apologetics vis-à-vis these alien religious claims and their promulgators."[244] It is obvious that Śaṅkara's commitment to core Advaita teachings leads him to apologetic engagement with other traditions. He is well aware that challenges to non-dualism must be addressed. What is missing, however, is the dimension of openness to these traditions. Where, in the tradition of Advaita, may we find grounds for openness and learning from other traditions? In this brief essay, I only sketch these grounds.

First, I begin with the tradition's understanding of what is an Upaniṣad. In the introduction to his commentary on the Kaṭha Upaniṣad, Śaṅkara expounds on the meaning of the word "Upaniṣad." His comments must be seen in the context of the fact that he regards the Upaniṣads as the authoritative source of Advaita teachings. In Śaṅkara's view, however, the primary meaning of Upaniṣad is not a book. The primary meaning is the knowledge of *brahman* that destroys ignorance and results in the gain of liberation.[245] For Śaṅkara, the Upaniṣad teachings are true, not because they are a sacred book, but because they are liberative. An Advaitin cannot be content with the argument that a claim is true because it is found in one of the Upaniṣads. Since the Upaniṣads point to a body of teachings, they must satisfy the criteria of valid knowledge that is applicable to all knowledge. The primary criterion is non-contradiction. Religious teachings should not contradict facts established by valid sources of knowledge. If such a contradiction exists, the religious teaching cannot be considered authoritative. As Śaṅkara stated in his commentary on the Bhagavadgītā (18:66), "A hundred śrutis may declare that fire is cold or that it is dark; still, they possess no authority in this matter."[246]

I describe the criteria of valid knowledge in Advaita to make the point that this tradition cannot but be engaged with religious diversity and other fields of knowledge. It cannot exist in isolation and indifference, arrogantly disregarding other claims and professing the truth of its own. It is required to understand and positively engage other traditions. Such engagement and search for understanding, as Eck reminds us, are some of the fundamentals of pluralism. Advaita, by nature, has to be a dialogical tradition.

Second, while admitting that there are diverse understandings of the meaning of non-dualism, Advaita, unlike traditions of exclusivism, cannot claim that the teaching of non-dualism is exclusive to the Upaniṣads. The claim for ontological singularity (*sarvam khalvidam brahma–all is Brahman*) that is at the heart of the Advaita teaching is certainly present in other traditions. There may be unique ways of imparting this knowledge and explaining its significance, but the fundamental insight of non-duality is not limited to Advaita. The Roman Catholic theologian, Daniel Soars, in his recent book with the intriguing title, *The World and God are Not-Two*, highlights a range of Christian theologians, across the centuries, who, like Advaitins, argue that God and the world, "should not be understood *non*-contrastively, such that being a creature does not exclude, but entails, in a certain limited and partial sense, also sharing in the being of the Creator."[247] Christian non-dualism or, by extension, Buddhist, Jewish or Islamic non-dualism, will not be identical to Upaniṣad non-dualism. However, non-exclusive, multiple expressions of non-dualism offer rich possibilities for mutual learning and enrichment. Such possibilities ought to be embraced. The famous Ṛg Veda verse (I.164.45) reminds us that wise persons speak differently about a singular truth. This is an invitation to engage religious difference respectfully and to avoid the inclination to denounce a teaching merely because it is different from our own.

Third, and perhaps most importantly, Advaita, more than any other Hindu tradition, cautions us about the limits of language and other symbols in relation to the sacred infinite. The Taittirīya Upaniṣad (2.9.1) speaks of the infinite as that from which all words, with the mind return, having failed to grasp. The Kena Upaniṣad reminds that *brahman* is not the object of any word; it is the reality that makes all words known. The limits of language are also made obvious in the numerous apophatic Upaniṣad verses that tell us what *brahman* is not. Kaṭha Upaniṣad (1.3.15) is a typical example:

> One becomes freed from the jaws of death by knowing That which is wordless, untouched, formless, without taste, eternal, without scent, without beginning without end, undecaying, and greater than the great.

Śaṅkara, in his commentary on the Bṛhadāraṇyaka Upaniṣad, warns that even widely used words in the Upaniṣads, like ātman and *brahman*, are inadequate. The words of sacred texts are also finite and are not exempt from the challenges of describing an infinite reality. Our languages are rich, precious, and necessary but will always only be pointers to a reality that transcends all symbols. When speaking of this reality we can only do so, as Bhagavadgītā 2:29 tells us, with a sense of wonder (āścaryavat), marvel, and awe.

What this means, as Eck reminds us, is that we must avoid claiming ultimacy for our human symbols and language. To do so is to be truly idolatrous.[248]

Positively, what the Upaniṣad caution about the limits of language means is that while our commitments are important, we must profess these with humility and openness to learning from others. This humility must extend across both inter and intra religious boundaries. Advaita must engage respectfully with other views, theistic and non-theistic, learning, sharing, clarifying, and critically reflecting on its claims.

Not-two (*advaita*) is an apophatic way of describing the relation between the infinite *brahman* and the world. It does not describe the relation as "one," since such a description denies the existence of the many and even comes close to pantheism. The Upaniṣads emphasize *brahman* as a transcendent reality that must not be equated with the world. At the same time, the relation is not "two," since this suggests ontological dualism in which the world exists as a separate and parallel reality side by side with *brahman*. Advaita avoids these extremes by characterizing the relation as not-two. What is not said often enough by Advaita commentators is that "not-two" tells us much more about what the relation is not and less about how it may be positively characterized. This has led to different ways of explicating the meaning of not-two. In some interpretations, the significance of the world is minimized by describing its existence as illusory. In other interpretations, Advaitins acknowledge the ontologically dependent status of the world but refrain from designating it as an illusion. There are also differences in understanding the implications of Advaita for life in our world between those who value renunciation and those who argue for engagement and activism.

Ontological non-dualism is a core Advaita claim, but all the analogies and words that we use to speak about the relation between *brahman* and the world are metaphorical and informed also by historical and other circumstances. As our knowledge of the world increases, especially with the insights of science, and as we engage other religious and philosophical traditions, also searching for faithful ways to describe the relation between the one infinite and the many, Advaitins will discover new questions to be addressed, more helpful metaphors, and fresh wisdom about what it means live in the world with a commitment to non-duality.

Finally, I offer the evidence of personal experience (*anubhava*) as

Śaṅkara himself does for the claims of Advaita, and as Eck demonstrates throughout her writings on interreligious encounters. My own life as a scholar and practitioner has been deeply enriched and challenged by encounters and engagement with other traditions. I see the claims of my own tradition with greater clarity and discern better my own core commitments. I continue to examine and critically interrogate these claims in ways that I would not do but for these deep encounters and friendships over the many decades. I am grateful to count Eck among such friends.

· Chapter 29 ·

BUDDHISM, RELIGIOUS PLURALISM, AND LABOR STRIKES IN HAWAI'I

Duncan Ryūken Williams

In my first year as a master of theological studies student at Harvard Divinity School, I heard of a new course on world religions in New England being offered by Professor Diana Eck. Although I missed the opportunity to enroll in that course, by the following summer I had the privilege of joining the Pluralism Project as a summer researcher to document the diverse lineages of Buddhism in Portland, Oregon. Professor Eck's scholarly profile, with expertise in the study of Asian (Indic) religions as well as in the increasing pluralism of America's religious landscape, was an inspiration during my time as a masters and doctoral student at Harvard. Training in the classical languages and histories of Asian (Japanese) religions alongside the study of American Buddhism during my graduate studies, I have tried to emulate Professor Eck's approach to scholarship by exploring the ways in which religious teachings, practices, and communities cross the boundaries of national borders. In this essay, I hope to honor Professor Eck's career by telling the story of a little-known, yet instructive, case study from the world of Asian American Buddhism that reveals how religion, race, and American belonging was negotiated by the earliest of Japanese American immigrants who crossed the Pacific to settle in the Hawaiian Islands.

In the first part of the twentieth century, the enduring debate about whether America was essentially a white and Christian nation or a multiethnic and religiously plural nation was put into sharp relief as Japanese immigrant Buddhists became a major demographic on the newly acquired territory of Hawai'i. By 1920, the Japanese immigrant population constituted the largest ethnic group on the Hawaiian Islands (at 47% of the total population). With the vast majority of the Japanese migrant laborers identifying as Buddhists, their efforts at gaining equal pay through labor activism and the growing political power based at their temples made for one of the earliest examples of Buddhist engagement in the questions of religious freedom and pluralism about who belonged and who had rights in the United States.

Their claims of equal wages, freedoms, and rights took place in a context of religio-racial hierarchy specific to the Hawaiian Islands in the early twentieth century. With presumptions by the government, media, and the general public of Anglo-Protestant normativity, status and wage differentials between different ethnic groups were tracked by closeness and distance to whiteness and Protestantism. On the sugar plantations, the Portuguese were considered the closest to the white Protestant Euro-American plantation owners and thus given the status of "luna" (or plantation overseers) while the large number of Filipino labor migrants were place on the next rung down. Whilst Filipinos were Asian in national origin, their Catholicism and mixed-race Spanish backgrounds meant that they had higher wages than the Japanese, who were primarily Buddhist and thus considered racially unassimilable and religious unacceptable.

The need for cheap immigrant labor from Japan to work on the sugar plantations was framed by those governing the islands as an existential threat to an Anglo Protestant identity of an American territory—not just because of the notion of racialized difference, but due to religious difference given that over 97% of the Japanese migrant laborers were Buddhist. The balance between economic necessity and identity politics played out in how the Japanese Buddhist migrants were treated on the plantations. Some plantation owners and managers would only support Christian institutions and evangelists on their plantations. For example, George Renton Sr. of the Ewa Plantation in Hawai'i firmly refused any space for building a Buddhist institution. Similarly strong disdain for the religion of the overwhelming majority of the workers was made clear at one of Maui's largest plantations, founded by the planter Henry Baldwin, who was known for funding Christian missions to the Japanese "heathens" (his father was the Rev. Dwight Baldwin, one of the first Christian missionaries to the Hawaiian Islands).

Despite a considerable number of anti-Buddhist plantations, some plantation officials across the islands believed that Buddhist institutions helped the laborers find something constructive to do in their free time and thought that Buddhist teachings, practices, and institutions might make the labor force more compliant.[249] Motivated by pragmatism, these individuals, implicitly supportive of religious pluralism, provided support in the form of land and subsidies for Buddhist temples on Oahu, Kauai, and the Big Island.

Over time, it became clear that Buddhist priests commanded considerable sway amongst the laborers that could be helpful in resolving labor disputes. This was because Buddhist priests had earned the respect of the overwhelmingly Buddhist population of laborers by serving their spiritual and material needs despite a range of obstacles from anti-Buddhist planter sentiment. For example, Bishop Yemyo Imamura of the largest Buddhist denomination in Hawai'i, the Nishi Hongwanji, played a critical role in helping alleviate tensions during one of the early strikes in 1904 at Waipahu that involved 1,600 workers striking against the Oahu Sugar Company. He recalled:

> The cause of the strike was, as expected, complaints about the cruel and insidious acts of the *lunas* (foremen) toward the plantation laborers, the pitiful labor pay, and improvements needed in the living conditions in the camps. . . . I stood before the emotional crowd, and spoke from a religious point of view. Whatever they decided to do, first of all, they should calm down in order to think clearly, I said. To my utter surprise, everyone calmed down and decided at least to return to work. . . . Through this turn of events, the plantation owners recognized the influence of Buddhism among the laborers.[250]

As Imamura noted, most strikes had goals of improving living conditions such as access to water or housing, removing vicious overseers, and other policies seen as unfair, like the race-based wage discrimination or the pay-withholding system implemented in 1898 to prevent desertion.[251] Although Buddhist leadership was helpful in reducing some of the tensions, these basic issues of equity and sanitary living conditions had not been addressed in any systematic way. Thus, it is not surprising that five years later the so-called "Great Japanese Strike of 1909" began when "1,500 frustrated laborers at the Aiea Plantation yelled 'Banzai!' three times after an all-night rally where the laborers discussed the need to do something."[252]

Buddhist priests and Young Buddhist Association (YBA) members served on the executive community of the Honolulu-based Higher Wage Association (*Zōkyū Kiseikai*) from its inception in 1908. Buddhist temples also responded by housing the suddenly homeless workers and feeding them. At one cookout kitchen in the Palama district of Honolulu, for instance, nearly 2,200 adults were served three meals a day during the strike.[253]

As with the strike of 1904, in the weeks after the start of the 1909 strike, Yemyo Imamura, the Buddhist bishop of Hongwanji in Hawai'i, and Takie Okumura, an outspoken Japanese Christian leader, were brought in at the request of Japanese businessmen in Honolulu to assist in efforts to alleviate tension between the owners and workers and avert a major strike.[254] The two religious leaders were only able to forestall the work stoppage briefly. After it became clear that the owners were going to do whatever necessary to break the strike without addressing the underlying concerns, the strike was resumed, with the demands to both remove specific overseers and to end the race-based wage discrimination. Calling for "equal pay for equal work," the Japanese strikers pointed not only to the fact that Portuguese and Puerto Rican laborers received $22.50 per month while the Japanese received $18 per month for the same work, but that their housing situations were so different (the Portuguese and Puerto Ricans were each given a stand-alone cottage while the Japanese were housed in crowded, filthy barracks).

The Buddhist Imamura sided with the strikers while the Christian Okumura sided with the planters. This was a striking juxtaposition of a Buddhist religious leader claiming equal belonging and religious freedom as promised in the Constitution while a Christian religious leader asserted the white Christian foundational identity of America. In both this strike and a later 1920 strike, Okumura viewed the work stoppage as an affront to American plantation owners and he thought it undignified for Japanese laborers to make demands of their American hosts. Several years later, he equated acceptance of labor conditions, even if unfair, to acculturating into American society by using the following metaphor:

> I think that we are like food in the stomach of the Americans. Of course, the food digested must nourish the body. What is not digestible or profitable for the body should be quickly expelled with a laxative. But are they deporting us back to Japan? We should be thankful for the tolerance and patience of the Americans.[255]

Indeed, Okumura believed that becoming American meant the acceptance not only of national social and economic norms, but religious norms; namely, adopting Christianity as one's faith. Okumura was not the only member of the Japanese American community to advocate against the strike. Sometarō Sheba, a self-described devout Methodist and the editor of the *Hawaii Shimpo* and *Kauai Shuho* newspapers, had a close relationship with the plantation owners, and had taken bribes from the planters to print articles opposing the strike not only in his newspapers, but also to convince other newspapers to do the same.[256]

Supporting the laborers in their desire to better their living conditions and attain equal pay for the same work, rather than simply bowing to the interests of the Japanese government or American plantation owners, were the Buddhist establishment in Hawai'i, the Higher Wage Association (*Zōkyū Kiseikai*), and the editors of a number of Japanese ethnic newspapers including the *Nippu Jiji* and the *Hawaii Hochi*. These groups noted that the strike was necessary in part because the plantation owners did not factor in savings to meet all the costs the majority

Buddhist laborers had to assume to practice their religion, as opposed to the Christians who had their worship spaces provided for them. In a pamphlet titled "The Higher Wages Question" put out by the Association, the strike leaders argued:

> Buddhists bear all expenses themselves. . . . These items of labor's expenditures were not included in the determination of [the] original wages schedule . . . needs of adequate and decent places of worship for the plantation's labor are something which should be provided for in determining the wages of laborers.[257]

Bishop Imamura justified his support of the strike from a religious perspective, noting that his sect of Buddhism, the Hongwanji Jōdo Shin tradition, had historically been known as a "heiminkyō" or a "religion of and for the ordinary people" and "laborers are the first ones to be saved by Amida Buddha."[258] The strikers also evoked a vision of America as a land of fair-mindedness and democracy that should not tolerate "the present undemocratic, un-American condition of Hawaii, that of plutocrats and coolies."[259] The use of rhetoric from certain strains of both Buddhism and Americanism to support the equal wages for Japanese laborers punctuated the discussion not only during this strike but in the decades that followed. The strike formally ended without remedies, though three months after the end of the strike, the Japanese wage scale was adjusted to match the wages of the Puerto Rican and Portuguese workers.

The dynamic of Buddhist support for migrant laborers and Christian support for the plantation owners would continue in the next major strike—the largest in the history of Hawai'i—the 1920 strike spearheaded by Filipino and Japanese workers. In 1918, several Young Men's Associations sponsored by Buddhist temples on the plantations began organizing conferences to petition the HSPA (Hawaiian Sugar Planters' Association) for higher wages. The young Buddhists were joined by several militant, labor-movement leaders on October 19, 1919, at a meeting held at the Hilo Japanese Language School calling for improvements in working conditions including an increase in wages and an eight-hour day. Meanwhile, on the island of Oahu, the Waialua Young Buddhists Association held a mass rally on October 25, 1919, to urge all Japanese Young Men's Associations throughout the islands to join this movement for higher wages and better working conditions.[260] And then in December 1919, Japanese plantation workers' organizations formed the Japanese Federation of Labor in Honolulu to coordinate a strike in 1920 with the Filipino Labor Union.

By January 1920, Bishop Yemyo Imamura wrote an opinion piece in the *Hawaii Hochi* newspaper sympathizing with the union and claiming that these calls for equal treatment were in the American tradition. He asserted that unlike the radical unions on the mainland, the Japanese labor movement in Hawai'i was simply trying to improve their working conditions to a bearable standard. On January 19, 1920, several thousand members of the Filipino Labor Union went on strike despite being urged to wait by their leader Pablo Manlapit, a well-known plantation worker turned labor lawyer. Buddhist leaders, including Bishops Yemyo Imamura (Nishi Hongwanji), Hōsen Isobe (Sōtō Zen), Chōsei Nunome (Nichiren), Ryōzen Yamada (Jōdo), Eikaku Seki (Shingon), Kankai Izuhara (Higashi Honganji) and two Shinto priests, but no Japanese Christian clergy, submitted a cosigned letter urging the plantation owners to increase wages, guarantee the laborers' freedom of religion, and allow Japanese language schools.[261] By the end of the month, roughly 10,000 Japanese joined the Filipinos, leaving many of the plantations deserted as the two groups represented 77% of the laborers on Oahu.[262]

While Christian churches closed their doors to the locked-out and homeless Japanese laborers, the Fujinkai (Buddhist women's auxiliaries) fed the thousands of men, women, and children, and Buddhist temples like the Hongwanji Mission housed them when the Hawaiian Sugar Planters' Association tried to break the strike. Buddhist priests raised money from all of their members to support the strikers and several YMBAs on Kauai sponsored talent shows to raise money for the now-homeless families.

The call for better working conditions crystallized in a push for a higher wage (from 77 cents per 10-hour work day to $1.25). The "77-cent flag parade" was a massive public protest held on April 3, 1920, a day the city had set aside to commemorate the centennial anniversary of the arrival of Christian missionaries to Hawai'i. The protest had the feeling of an American parade, with the Sōtō Zen Buddhist Mission contributing a large portrait of Abraham Lincoln inscribed with the words "We Believe in Lincoln's Ideas" and a group of 3,000 strikers marching through the streets of Honolulu to Aala Park.[263]

The local white-owned newspapers viewed this strike as a fundamental clash of religion and civilization, with headlines like "Buddhist Priests Interfere to Aid Strikers." They attacked the "pagan priests" for abusing America's religious freedoms to create social unrest.[264] John Waterhouse of the planter's association claimed on February 6, 1920, "The action . . . is an anti-American movement designed to obtain control of the sugar business of the Hawaiian Islands."[265]

The alignment of the strike with the "pagan" Buddhists and anti-Americanism was not only sounded by the white press and plantation owners, but leaders of the Japanese Christian community as well. Concerned that such a massive strike would inflame anti-Japanese sentiment among the ruling white political and economic powers, Christian leaders like Rev. Takie Okumura encouraged a more cooperative and conciliatory approach, marked with efforts such as conversion to Christianity, to demonstrate an assimilation to mainstream America. Another well-known Japanese Christian leader, Rev. Shirō Sokabe, urged his congregation to oppose the strike because, as he put it, the plantation owners had been "so good to the church." In his years working to convert the Japanese in Hawai'i, the Rev. Sokabe had often quoted from the Biblical passage, "Servants be obedient unto them that according to the flesh are your masters with fear and trembling in singleness of your heart as unto Christ" believing that "Christianizing the Japanese also made them more agreeable workers for the planters."[266]

In the end, the 1920 strike was resolved in a similar fashion to the strike of 1904 with behind-the-scenes negotiations by a Buddhist priest to stop the strike with promises of future improvement of working conditions and without any formal accession to demands by the plantation owners. Bishop Hōsen Isobe of the Sōtō Zen Buddhist Mission took the initiative to serve as an interlocutor between labor and the plantation owners and secured assurances from HSPA Chairman John Waterhouse to increase wages.[267] The strike thus formally ended after six months of turmoil when the Oahu Labor federation declared it over. Later that fall, plantation owners implemented various reforms including a 50% increase in wages, expanded social programs on the plantations, and at least in theory, the abolishing of race-based wage scale. The strike had cost the planters $12 million, and cost the Japanese immigrant community at least $200,000 as well.[268]

This event, for the Japanese Buddhist advocates of better working conditions, was inextricably linked to a slogan repeated often during the strike and in the months that followed: "We are demanding a wage increase because we are determined to live here permanently." With an increased investment in settling as permanent residents, rather than sojourning, the majority Buddhists of the Japanese community were clearly trying to find a way to assert equality in both religious freedom and in economic opportunity. And in so doing, served as one of the early examples of Asian American Buddhists providing a tangible contribution to the ideal of America as a multiethnic and religiously plural nation.

AFTERWORD

James Carroll

This book of tributes to Diana Eck is pluralism itself. Far from a mere exercise in diversity or tolerance, the essays gathered here, even while drawing on many points of view, amount to a profoundly moving display of mutuality; of, in Professor Eck's terms, energetic engagement. Out of many voices, one strong declaration: Diana Eck is a magnificent teacher, scholar, colleague, and creator of new possibilities not only for religion and pedagogy, but for civic society and politics.

In Karen Armstrong's words, Diana is the "Apostle of Pluralism," and she has set in motion the transfiguring apostolic succession embodied in this volume. She is the sort of teacher who inspires students to say, as Laurie L. Patton reports here, "Everyone wanted to be Diana Eck, but no one thought they could ever accomplish it." Instead, of course, what their professor encouraged them—enabled them—to accomplish was becoming their best selves, in all their intellectual brilliance and spiritual depth. Those achievements are on full display in these essays.

Across half a century, the driving purpose of Diana Eck's career, underlying high academic distinction, religious leadership, community organizing, and prophetic writing—has been nothing less than to change the way people live in the world—change it very much for the better.

And what a half century it has been! Historians will surely identify the era's key markers as including the end of the Cold War, defined by the dissolution of the Soviet Union in 1991, and the terrorist attacks on the United States in 2001. In America, those two critical junctures posed monumental challenges: How to recover from the Manichaean mindset that had, after World War II, rigidly shaped the contest between "the Free World" and "the Evil Empire;" and how to fend off the post-9/11 impulse to slide "Islamic terrorism" into the enemy-slot formerly occupied by "atheistic Communism?" Both challenges involved profound religious questions which few in academia, much less in public life, were equipped to handle.

As if commissioned by some benevolent goddess of history, Diana Eck stepped forward at both moments, putting on offer spacious new understandings of religion and society, changing the one and transforming the other. Recall that her milestone works—the 1991 launch of the Pluralism Project, and the 2001 publication of *A New Religious America: How a "Christian Country" Became the Most Religiously Diverse Nation*—responded exactly to those world-historic provocations, the consequences of which reverberate still. Unlike many others, Diana never broke faith with the commitment to hopeful transformation called forth by each of those threshold moments.

"The question Diana Eck asked more than three decades ago," as Nancy A. Khalil says here, "rings truer today more than ever: What does it mean to live in a pluralist society?" How are other people allowed the freedom simply to be other people—without, in Khalil's word, the "otherization" that reduces them to being an antagonist? The question became pointed in the United States after the Immigration and Nationality Act of 1965 led to significant changes in the ethnic make-up of the American population, changes that were readily apparent in an unprecedented multiplicity of religious practices and identities. "The religious other," as Francis X. Clooney puts it here, "has become our neighbor, co-worker, friend." Formerly well-defined boundaries between groups gave way to blurred and porous margins—part of what William Graham calls an "all-too-human messiness"—that challenged the most fundamental assumptions that a formerly univocal national collective could make about itself. The needed adjustments to America's self-understanding soon became apparent, as a once self-satisfied "Christian" nation was faced with the complicated new reality of being the "most religiously diverse nation" in the world.

Once Diana began her "mapping of the religious landscape," starting in Greater Boston, dozens of formerly unnoticed Buddhist communities, Islamic centers, and Hindu temples, as well as lively groups of Jains and Afro-Caribbean and Native religions, were found to exist side by side with the long familiar synagogues and churches. With the work of Diana and her colleagues, a magnificent new vision came sharply into focus. That's what maps do, transforming unfamiliar terrain into a possible landscape for new homes. What Diana's ingenious cartography enabled Americans to see was the simple truth, as succinctly put here by Chloe Breyer, that "The religious imaginations of immigrant traditions strengthen democracy."

Or, to express it the way Diana herself did in *Encountering God,* "The boundaries of our various traditions need not be places where we halt and contend over our differences, but might well be the places where we meet and catch a glimpse of glory as seen by another." Once Diana had invited this clear-eyed reckoning with America's new religious plurality as the occasion for a profound instance of what Francis X. Clooney calls "crossing over," the virtue of this complexity as an enrichment of commonwealth, instead of a threat to cohesive national identity, could be seen. The nation, indeed, could come more fully into its own. "Pluralism," Diana says, "is the engagement that creates a common society from all that plurality." Common society. Commonwealth.

But not everyone experienced the arrival of new neighbors with their varied worldviews, rituals, and customs in such benign ways—especially as the dislocations of a post-Cold War multipolar world and reactions to the traumas of 9/11 took hold. A shocking insecurity threw the nation off balance. Religion found itself at the center of American misadventures both abroad and at home, with, for example, President George W. Bush claiming God as a sponsoring ally in the Global War on Terror, and President Donald Trump demonizing newcomers with a Muslim ban as a way of rallying his supporters. The politics of culture war in an ever more divided America wielded religion as a weapon, with a fervent Christian nationalism even undercutting the separation of Church and State, threatening to tip a gloriously multi-faceted American democracy into a univocal—and white supremacist—theocracy.

But as all of that unfolded, Diana Eck herself, and the powerful movement she initiated and faithfully enabled, continued to serve not only as examples of a humane alternative to such chauvinism, but as practical sources of a reinforced democratic liberalism. "Bridging academia and global citizenship," in Patrice Brodeur's phrase, Diana—and the community of scholars and activists she inspired—helped Americans recognize and claim their own ongoing reinvention, which was, after all, nothing but a fulfillment of the nation's founding vision of *e pluribus unum*. Pluralism, as promoted by Diana Eck, amounts to a great American self-surpassing.

And in a wired world remade by technological innovation, economic interdependence, and crises of mass migration driven by war, climate catastrophe, and savage inequality, the global implications of that hopeful vision could not be clearer. If in the United States, where diversity is producing this pluralism, we are all now neighbors, one to another—how much truer is that across the globe, where a mutation in the meaning of our species is occurring, with boundaries broken, populations on the move, differences laid bare. When mass suffering is manifest on hand-held screens, the root meaning of "compassion" reasserts itself, as humans are called to "suffer with" their fellow humans both near and far away.

Today as never before every human being is the neighbor of every other human being in the world, and identities shaped by religion, or by the lack of religion, are determining whether that neighborliness is to be fulfilled or denied. Only an America fully at home with the new pluralism celebrated by Diana Eck can be genuinely at the service of such staggering demands for justice and peace. "Love Thy Neighbor..."—this Quaker line could be the Eck bumper sticker—"...No Exceptions."

The late Catholic theologian Hans Küng's famous mantra reveals what has been at stake all along in Diana's Eck's visionary scholarship:

AFTERWORD

"No peace among the nations without peace among the religions. No peace among the religions without dialogue between the religions. No dialogue between the religions without investigation of the foundation of the religions." And for religious people, that investigation is a matter of the careful re-assessment, above all, of the idea of God.

In univocal societies, where one worldview prevails, it is possible to imagine the Divine in small and tidy ways, God as hemmed in by doctrine, theology, cult, image, and language—all of which is understood to be "God-given." (*No salvation outside—you name the cult!*). But when worldviews overlap and religious assumptions contend—which are essential consequences of any pluralism project—notions of God erupt, and believers of every stripe come face to face with what Paul Tillich called the God beyond God. The radical transcendence of the Holy One can at last be—if not "grasped"—sensed, hallowed, honored. God can at last be God.

Diana's life story shows how that religious awakening comes about, defining as it does her own pilgrimage from Bozeman to Banaras, "city of all the gods," in Lawrence Cohen's phrase. Tellingly, Diana defined the inner meaning of that journey with the title she gave her account of it: *Encountering God*. When the well-known God of American Protestantism met the exotic deities of Hinduism in the crucible of a devout woman's well-formed conscience, the result was a life-changing insight that demanded a life-commitment. All at once, "the passion," in Preeta Bansal's words, "for encounter with the Divine in all their many forms," gave Diana her vocation, even while revealing for her, and for all who would learn from her, the true meaning of every religious impulse.

Or, as Diana herself put it in response to her encounter with Islam, "God is at the center of our very being, and the heart of the believer, so Muslims say, is the throne of the compassionate God. If we glimpse God in this way, there is no reason we cannot stand together, all of us, in prayer." To declare that God is great, as Ali Asani says here, is to honor the Holy One as greater than religion itself, greater therefore than every attempt to express God. Rabbi Abraham Joshua Heschel once said it, too: "God is greater than religion." But Heschel added, "Faith is greater than dogma."

No religion, no believer, no Word comes close to expressing the ineffable mystery of the Divine. Indeed, everything about religion—scriptures, rituals, creation myths, doctrines—is an invention of the imagination, which, however inspired is always human. It is "God-given" only in the sense that all of creation is. Faith, therefore, must be modest in its claims, which makes it hospitable to other claims. Otherwise, faith becomes idolatry—and, as every generation must learn, idolatry is dangerous.

Here at last is the profound revelation that comes with pluralism: not only human rights are protected, but Divine prerogatives are too. So of course, in Diana Eck's great phrase, we can stand together, all of us, in prayer. To such humane and holy worship this good woman has made her work and life the invitation.

ABOUT THE CONTRIBUTORS

Halah Ahmad received her master's degree in public policy from the University of Cambridge and an honors degree in the comparative study of religion and sociology from Harvard. Formerly vice president and lead researcher for policy at the Jain Family Institute, Ahmad has worked on issues of inequality and social protection in the US, Albania, Germany, Palestine, and beyond. Ahmad also served as US Policy Fellow for Al-Shabaka and as a Coro Fellow in San Francisco.

S. Wesley Ariarajah is professor emeritus of ecumenical theology at Drew University School of Theology, Madison, New Jersey, and now lives in retirement in Geneva, Switzerland. Before teaching at Drew for seventeen years, Ariarajah served at the World Council of Churches, Geneva, for sixteen years as director of the interfaith dialogue program and as deputy general secretary of the Council. His deep interest in exploring the challenges interfaith relations bring to the Christian faith resulted in his book, *Your God, My God, Our God: Rethinking Christian Theology for Religious Plurality*.

Karen Armstrong is the author of numerous books on religion, including *Sacred Nature*, *A History of God*, *Islam: A Short History*, *Buddha*, and *The Great Transformation*, as well as a memoir, *The Spiral Staircase*. Her work has been translated into forty-five languages. A former Roman Catholic religious sister, Armstrong received the TED Prize in February 2008 and used the occasion to call for the creation of a Charter for Compassion.

Ali S. Asani is Murray A. Albertson Professor of Middle Eastern Studies and professor of Indo-Muslim and Islamic religion and cultures at Harvard University.

A specialist of Islam in South Asia, Asani's research focuses on Shia and Sufi devotional traditions in the region. In addition, he studies popular or folk forms of Muslim devotional life, and Muslim communities in the West. The recipient of several awards for outstanding teaching, he was recently named the Harvard Foundation's Faculty of the Year.

Preeta D. Bansal is global council chair of the United Religions Initiative, a global grassroots interfaith peacebuilding network. A constitutional lawyer by background, she served for more than twenty-five years in some of the most senior posts in the public and private sectors. She currently sits on many corporate and community boards, teaches at universities, is an investor and philanthropist, and is experimenting with several innovative, spirit-based global and community service initiatives.

Whittney Barth is executive director of the Center for the Study of Law and Religion at Emory University and Charlotte McDaniel Scholar and teaches at Emory Law School. Barth holds a JD from the University of Chicago Law School, MDiv from Harvard Divinity School, and BA from Miami University. She was a student of Diana Eck during divinity school had the privilege of working with her for several years while serving as assistant director of the Pluralism Project.

Sissela Bok is a philosopher and ethicist. Formerly a professor of philosophy at Brandeis University, she has written extensively on topics in the fields of bioethics, practical ethics, biography, and public affairs. A former member of the Pulitzer Prize board, she is on the editorial boards of a number of journals, including the *Bulletin of the World Health Organization*, *Criminal Justice Ethics*, and *Common Knowledge*.

Chloe Breyer has served as director of the Interfaith Center of New York (ICNY) since 2007. An Episcopal priest in the Diocese of New York, Breyer has served at Harlem churches for more than two decades. In addition to local religious peacemaking work, Breyer has also participated in interfaith dialogues and humanitarian aid initiatives in Afghanistan and Iran and is a member of the Council on Foreign Relations.

Patrice Brodeur is an associate professor in the Institute of Religious Studies at the University of Montreal, as well as senior consultant at the International

Dialogue Centre in Lisbon, Portugal. He has over thirty years of experience in interreligious and intercultural dialogue.

James Carroll is an author, historian, and journalist. A critical Catholic, he has written extensively about the contemporary effort to reform the Roman Catholic Church, and has published not only novels, but also books on religion and history. He has received nine honorary doctorates and is a fellow of the American Academy of Arts & Sciences.

Francis X. Clooney, SJ is Parkman Professor of Divinity and professor of comparative theology at Harvard Divinity School. After earning his doctorate in South Asian languages and civilizations at the University of Chicago he taught at Boston College for twenty-one years before coming to Harvard. From 2010 to 2017, he was director of the Center for the Study of World Religions at Harvard. He is a Roman Catholic priest and has been a member of the Society of Jesus for more than half a century.

Lawrence Cohen is a professor in the departments of anthropology and of south and southeast Asian studies at the University of California, Berkeley, where he is co-director of the medical anthropology program. His long-term research has included work on aging and dementia, on sexuality and the political life of Banaras, on the regulation of the exchange of organs for transplantation, and on emergent rationalities of information technology in projects of government and surveillance.

Dhammananda is a Thai *bhikkhuni* (Buddhist nun). Venerable taught for twenty-seven years at Thammasat University in Bangkok, Thailand, in the department of philosophy and religion. She is author of many books on contemporary issues in Asian Buddhism including *Thai Women in Buddhism* (1991).

Rebecca Kneale Gould is associate professor of environmental studies at Middlebury College where she co-directs the religion, philosophy and environment focus. She is the author of *At Home in Nature: Modern Homesteading and Spiritual Practice in America*, a study of spirituality and back-to-the-land practices from the mid-nineteenth century to the 1990s. She has a longstanding interest in Thoreau, while also researching and writing about contemporary religious environmentalism.

William A. Graham is Murray A. Albertson Professor of Middle Eastern Studies and University Distinguished Service Professor, emeritus, in the Faculty of Arts and Sciences at Harvard University. During his forty-five active years (1973–2018) on the FAS faculty he also served as dean of Harvard Divinity School from 2002–2012. His scholarship has focused on topics in early Islamic religious history and the global history of religion.

Blu Greenberg is a writer specializing in modern Judaism and women's issues. Founder of the Jewish Orthodox Feminist Alliance (JOFA), she carved out the path for Orthodox women to become rabbis and explore greater participation in ritual. Greenberg, who holds an MA in clinical psychology from City University of New York, and an MS in Jewish history from Yeshiva University, has been passionately involved in both religious and political dialogue for the past fifty years.

John Stratton Hawley (informally, Jack) is Claire Tow Professor of Religion at Barnard College, Columbia University. He has taught at Barnard and Columbia since 1986. Hawley has directed Columbia University's South Asia Institute and has received awards from the NEH, Smithsonian, and American Institute of Indian Studies. He has been a Guggenheim fellow and a Fulbright-Nehru fellow and has been elected to the American Academy of Arts and Sciences.

Nancy A. Khalil is assistant professor of American culture at the University of Michigan, appointed in Arab and Muslim American studies. Her forthcoming ethnography with Stanford University Press analyzes the limits of a profession for US imams. She completed her PhD in anthropology at Harvard University and a fellowship at Yale University's Center on Race, Indigeneity, and Transnational Migration. Before academia, she was Muslim chaplain and advisor of the multifaith living and learning community at Wellesley College.

Rahul Mehrotra is the founding principal of RMA Architects. He divides his time between working in Mumbai and Boston and teaching at the Graduate School of Design at Harvard University where he is professor of urban design and planning and the John T. Dunlop Professor in Housing and Urbanization.

Lucinda Mosher, a theologian in the Episcopal tradition, is director of the master of arts in interreligious studies program and senior scholar for continuing and professional education at Hartford International University for Religion and

ABOUT THE CONTRIBUTORS

Peace. Concurrently, she is senior editor of the *Journal of Interreligious Studies* and the rapporteur of the Building Bridges Seminar—an international Christian-Muslim dialogue. The author of seven books, she is the award-winning editor of fifteen more, including the *Georgetown Companion to Interreligious Studies*.

Vijaya Nagarajan is associate professor in the department of theology/religious studies, and environmental studies at University of San Francisco. Her interests span the fields of Hinduism, environment/climate, gender, ritual, engineering ethics, and the commons. Author of *Feeding a Thousand Souls: Women, Ritual, and Ecology in India, An Exploration of the Kolam*, she has also been an environmental activist for forty years.

Vasudha Narayanan is distinguished professor, department of religion, at the University of Florida and a past president of the American Academy of Religion. She was elected to the American Academy of Arts and Sciences in 2023. Educated at universities in India and at Harvard University, her fields of interest are the Hindu traditions in India, Cambodia, and America; visual and expressive cultures in the study of the Hindu traditions; and gender issues.

Pranati Parikh is currently a first-year student at Harvard Law School. As a recent MA graduate from the University of Chicago Divinity School, she works in the intersection between philosophy, Hindu literature and literary theory, and psychology, and is also interested in the relationship between religion and the public sphere. She graduated from Harvard in 2021 with a joint religion and comparative literature concentration, where she worked with Diana Eck.

Eboo Patel is founder and president of Interfaith America, the nation's largest interfaith organization. Patel was a member of President Barack Obama's Advisory Council on Faith-Based and Neighborhood Partnerships. He has written five books on interfaith cooperation, including *Acts of Faith*, which won the Louisville Grawemeyer Award in Religion. Patel earned a doctorate in the sociology of religion from Oxford University and has received over fifteen honorary degrees in recognition of his civic leadership.

Laurie L. Patton is the seventeenth president of Middlebury College, and the first woman to lead the institution in its 222-year history. An authority on South Asian history, culture, and religion, and religion in the public square,

Patton served on the faculty and administration at Emory University and Duke University. She is also author of three books of poems and has translated the Bhagavad Gita for Penguin Classics. She served as president of the AAR in 2019, and was elected to the American Academy of Arts and Sciences in 2018 in two categories: philosophy/religion, and educational leadership.

Anantanand Rambachan is emeritus professor of religion at St. Olaf College. Rambachan has been involved in interreligious relations and dialogue for over forty years, as a Hindu contributor and analyst. He is active in the dialogue programs of the World Council of Churches and was a Hindu guest and presenter in four general assemblies of the World Council of Churches. His most recent book is *Pathways to Hindu-Christian Dialogue*.

Neelima Shukla-Bhatt is professor of religion and South Asia studies at Wellesley College. She received her PhD in the study of religion from Harvard University in 2003. She teaches courses on mysticism, sacred arts, women's practices, narrative traditions, religious pluralism, and films in South Asia. Her research focuses on Hindu devotional poetry and popular rituals as well as Gandhian thought. She works with interfaith organizations in India, the US, and other parts of the world.

Susan Shumaker is a producer and story researcher with Ken Burns, Florentine Films and Ewers Brothers Productions, collaborating on films exploring World War II, the Dust Bowl, the national parks, and country music, among others. She is currently at work on a film biography of Henry David Thoreau and *Hiding in Plain Sight*, a multi-film series exploring our mental health crisis. Susan received a master of theological studies degree from Harvard Divinity School.

Simran Jeet Singh is executive director of the religion and society program at the Aspen Institute and author of *The Light We Give: How Sikh Wisdom Can Transform Your Life*. He is an Atlantic fellow for racial equity with the Nelson Mandela Foundation and Columbia University, and a Soros equality fellow with the Open Society Foundations.

Duncan Ryūken Williams is a scholar, writer, and *Sōtō* Zen Buddhist priest who is professor of religion and East Asian languages and cultures at the University of Southern California. He also serves as the director of the USC Shinso Ito Center for Japanese Religions and Culture. He is the author of *American Sutra: A Story of Faith and Freedom in the Second World War*. His research focuses on Zen Buddhism, Buddhism in America, and the mixed-race AAPI (*hapa*) experience.

SELECT BIBLIOGRAPHY
FOR DIANA L. ECK

Eck, Diana L. *Banaras, City of Light*. New York: Alfred A. Knopf, 1982.

Eck, Diana L. and Devaki Jain, eds. *Speaking of Faith: Global Perspectives on Women, Religion, and Social Change*. Gabriola Island: New Society Publisher, 1985.

Eck Diana L. and Françoise Mallison, eds. *Devotion Divine: Bhakti Traditions from the Regions of India. Studies in Honour of Charlotte Vaudeville*. Groningen and Paris: Egbert Forsten and Ecole Française d'Extreme-Orient, 1991.

Eck, Diana L. *Encountering God: A Spiritual Journey from Bozeman to Banaras*. Boston: Beacon Press, 1993.

Eck, Diana L., et al. CD-ROM: *On Common Ground: World Religions in America*. New York: Columbia University Press; 1997, 2002, 2008.

Eck, Diana L. *Darśan: Seeing the Divine Image in India*. Columbia University Press, 1998.

———. "Honest to God: God and the Universe of Faiths." In *God at 2000*, edited by Marcus Borg and Ross Mackenzie. Harrisburg, PA: Morehouse Press, 2000.

Eck, Diana L. and Ellie Pierce. *World Religions in Boston: A Guide to Communities and Resources*. Cambridge: The Pluralism Project, 2000.

Eck, Diana L. "Dialogue and Method: Reconstructing the Study of Religion." In *A Magic Still Dwells: Comparative Religion in the Postmodern Age*, edited by Kimberly C. Patton and Benjamin C. Ray. Berkeley: University of California Press, 2000.

———. *A New Religious America: How a "Christian Country" Became the World's Most Religious Diverse Nation*. New York: Harper San Francisco, 2001.

———. "Dialogue and the Echo-boom of Terror: Religious Women's Voices After 9/11." In *After Terror: Promoting Dialogue Among Civilizations*, edited by Akbar Ahmed and Brian Forst. Cambridge, UK: Polity, 2005.

———. "What is Pluralism." The Pluralism Project at Harvard University. Last modified 2006. *https://pluralism.org/about*.

———. "The New Americans: Religious and Cultural Institutions." In *The New Americans: A Guide to Immigration Since 1965*, edited by Mary C. Waters and Reid Ueda. Cambridge, MA: Harvard University Press, 2007.

———. "Prospects for Pluralism: Voice and Vision in the Study of Religion." *Journal of the American Academy of Religion* 75, no. 4 (2007): 743–76.

———. "American Religious Pluralism: Civic and Theological Discourse." In *Democracy and the New Religious Pluralism*, edited by Thomas Banchoff. New York: Oxford University Press, 2007.

———. "The Deity: The Image of God." In *The Life of Hinduism*, edited by John Stratton. Hawley and Vasudha Narayanan. Berkeley: University of California Press, 2007.

———. "Diana L. Eck on Becoming a More Complex 'We.'" *Tikkun* 24, no. 1 (2009): 49–50.

———. "Interfaith at Ground Zero." *The Harvard Crimson*, September 17, 2010. https://www.thecrimson.com/article/2010/9/17/interfaith-muslim-rauf-cordoba/

———. "In Whom...." *Tikkun* 22, no. 2 (2010): 44.

———. "9/11 and These Ten Years: A Faculty Reflection." *The Harvard Crimson*, September 19, 2011. https://www.thecrimson.com/article/2011/9/19/muslim-communities-even-here/

———. "Gandhi in Egypt." *The Harvard Crimson*. March 2, 2011. https://www.thecrimson.com/article/2011/3/2/nonviolent-sharp-gandhi-people/

———. *India: A Sacred Geography*. New York: Harmony, Random House; 2012.

ENDNOTES

1 | DIANA ECK: APOSTLE OF PLURALISM | KAREN ARMSTRONG

1. Wilfred Cantwell Smith, *Towards a World Theology: Faith and the Comparative History of Religion* (Philadelphia: Palgrave Macmillan, 1981), 102.
2. Ibid., 123.
3. Christopher Boehm, "Egalitarian Society and Reverse Dominance Hierarchy," *Current Anthropology* 34, (1993).
4. Richard Lee, *The !Kung San: Men, Women and Work in a Foraging Society* (New York: Cambridge University Press, 1979), 457.
5. Elman R. Service, *Origin of the State and Civilization: The Process of Cultural Evolution* (New York: W. W. Norton & Co., 1975); A. R. Radcliffe Brown, *The Andaman Islanders: A Study in Social Anthropology* (Cambridge: The University Press, 1922); Elizabeth Marshall Thomas, *The Harmless People* (New York: Alfred A. Knopf, 1959).
6. Bhikkhu Bodhi, *The Suttanipata: An Ancient Collection of the Buddha's Discourses Together with Its Commentaries (The Teachings of the Buddha)* (Somerville, MA: Wisdom Publications, 2017), 118.

2 | WHEN RELIGION TURNS TOXIC | ALI S. ASANI

7. Diana Eck, *Encountering God: A Spiritual Journey from Bozeman to Banaras* (Boston: Beacon Press, 1993), 49.
8. Ibid., 50.
9. See chapters two and three of Wilfred Cantwell Smith, *The Meaning and End of Religion* (San Francisco: Harper and Row, 1978).

10 Ziauddin Sardar, "That Question Mark," *The Critical Muslim* 4 (2012): 3–17.

11 Nosheen Ali, "From Hallaj to Heer: Poetic Knowledge and the Muslim Tradition," *Journal of Narrative Politics* 3, no. 1 (2016): 5.

12 Anand Vivek Taneja, "The Critical Edge of Tradition: Understanding Ghalib as *Vali* in Contemporary Delhi," *Journal of Urdu Studies* 1 (2020): 234.

13 Ibid., 235.

14 The discussion on Salman Ahmad and Sufi Rock draws upon my article, "Transmitting and Transforming Traditions: Salman Ahmad and Sufi Rock," in *Sufism East and West: Mystical Islam and Cross-Cultural Exchange in the Modern World* ed. Jamal Malik and Saeed Zarrabi-Zadeh (Leiden and Boston: Brill, 2009), 259–72.

15 Salman Ahmad, "Nusrat as I Knew Him," *Blue Chip* 41, no.4 (Oct-Nov 2007): 51.

16 Ibid.

17 Diana Eck, "Honest to God," *God at 2000*, ed. Marcus Borg and Ross Mackenzie (Harrisburg, PA: Morehouse Publishing, 2000), 29.

3 | ENCOUNTERING OURSELVES | PREETA D. BANSAL

18 September 11, of course, is a significant day also for the interfaith movement and for Hinduism and its vision of pluralism as well. It was on September 11, 1893 that Swami Vivekananda gave his stirring speech to the World Parliament of Religions, and introduced the West to the notion of universal truths and anti-sectarianism. September 11, 1906—more than a decade later—was the day that a young lawyer, Mohandas Gandhi, introduced the concept of nonviolent resistance to an assembly that had gathered to consider how to defeat the Transvaal government's attempt to pass legislation disenfranchising colored people. On that day, September 11, 1906, in South Africa, the Indian nonviolent movement was born. Gandhi later called his Indian movement: "Satyagraha" or "the Force which is born of Truth and Love or non-violence." This movement went on to free 300 million people from the power of the British Empire and gave the twentieth century a most remarkable demonstration of the power of nonviolent struggle, inspiring MLK Jr. and Nelson Mandela.

19 Located near the Hindu Temple now in Omaha is the TriFaith Initiative—the

first interfaith campus in the world in which a church, synagogue and mosque are co-located over 38 acres.

4 | AT HOME WHERE WE LIVE | FRANCIS X. CLOONEY

20 Francis X. Clooney, "In Ten Thousand Places, in Every Blade of Grass Uneventful but True Confessions about Finding God in India, and Here Too," *Studies in the Spirituality of Jesuits* 28.3 (May 1996): 1–45.
21 Diana L. Eck, "Autobiographical Reflections on Anthropology and Religion," *Religion and Society: Advances in Research* 12 (2021): 1–20.
22 Forthcoming from T&T Clark, possibly with a revised title.

5 | CONCLUDING LECTURE FROM AN INTRODUCTORY COURSE IN COMPARATIVE HISTORY OF RELIGION | WILLIAM A. GRAHAM

23 It was Diana Eck who, having attended my "last lecture" (a collegial custom at Harvard) on April 24, 2018, urged me to publish my remarks somewhere. As we know, "no good deed goes unpunished," so here it is, in black and white, if slightly abridged, in her honor.
24 This course, like other introductory college religion courses, also enrolled master's students, primarily from Harvard Divinity School.
25 In his *Summa totius haeresis saracenorum*, cited in James Kritzeck, *Peter the Venerable and Islam*, (Princeton, NJ: Princeton University Press, 1964), 206.
26 James W. Watts, "The Three Dimensions of Scriptures," in James W. Watts, ed., *Iconic Books and Texts* (Sheffield, UK: Equinox, 2013), 9–32.
27 Johannes Leipoldt, *Heilige Schriften: Betrachtungen zur Religionsgeschichte der antiken Mittelmeerwelt* (Leipzig: Harrassowitz, 1953).
28 Rudolf Otto, *The Idea of the Holy*, trans. John W. Harvey of *Das Heilige* (1917), (London: Oxford University Press, 1923).
29 Mircea Eliade, *The Sacred and the Profane*, trans. by Willard R. Trask of *Le Sacré et le Profane* (1965), (New York: Harcourt, Brace, 1959); Émile Durkheim, *The Elementary Forms of Religious Life*, trans. by Karen Fields of *Formes élémentaires de la vie religieuse* (1912), (New York: Free Press, 1995).
30 Max Weber, esp. ch. VI in *The Sociology of Religion*, trans. by Ephraim Fischoff of "Religionssoziologie," ch. VI of Weber's *Wirtschaft und Gesellschaft* (1922), (Boston: Beacon Press, 1963).
31 On his ideas about binary oppositions, see esp. the 1955 article by

Lévi-Strauss, "The Structural Study of Myth," *Journal of American Folklore* 68 (270): 428-44.

32 Isaiah Berlin, *The Hedgehog and the Fox* (London: Weidenfeld & Nicolson, 1953).

33 Franklin Edgerton, "Dominant Ideas in the Formation of Indian Culture," *Journal of the American Oriental Society* 62, no. 3 (Sept. 1942): 151–156.

34 William James, Lectures XVI, XVII in *The Varieties of Religious Experience* (New York: Longman, Green, 1902).

35 Who, I have since discovered, was at the time (1963) likely drawing on a similar heuristic use of the poem by Donald K. Adams, *The Anatomy of Personality* (New York: Doubleday, 1954), 30–33.

36 First published in *The Saturday Evening Post* 207, no. 15, October 13, 1934.

37 I cited the entire poem in the lecture, but editorial constraints on length in the present volume do not allow for this.

38 Friedrich Schleiermacher, Über die Religion (1799); Eng. trans. John Oman, *On Religion* (New York: Harper, 1958).

39 Robert Frost, *A Witness Tree* (New York: Henry Holt & Co., 1942), 69.

6 | ONE WITHOUT A SECOND | JOHN STRATTON HAWLEY

40 This essay, originally titled "Diana-ana," is reprinted with permission from *Religion and Society* 12, no. 1 (Sep 2021): 12–14.

41 Diana L. Eck, *Darśan: Seeing the Divine Image in India* (New York: Columbia University Press, 1998), 22, 28.

42 Eck, *Encountering God: A Spiritual Journey from Bozeman to Banaras* (Boston: Beacon Press, 1993).

43 Eck, *India: A Sacred Geography* (New York: Harmony Books, 2012), 452.

44 Eck, *Banaras: City of Light* (Princeton, NJ: Princeton University Press, 1982), 22, 28.

7 | REFLECTIONS ON LEARNING FROM (BUT NOT STUDYING WITH) DIANA ECK | LUCINDA MOSHER

45 Eck, "Prospects for Pluralism: Voice and Vision in the Study of Religion," in *Journal of the American Academy of Religion* 75, no. 4 (December 2007): 768.

46 Ibid., 746.

47 Ibid., 751.

ENDNOTES

48 Ibid., 763.

8 | DIANA ECK'S OVERTON WINDOW | LAURIE L. PATTON

49 Diana Eck's *Banaras: City of Light* was still the buzz of the city when I arrived there in October of 1983.

50 Diana L. Eck, *A New Religious America: How a "Christian Country" Became the World's Most Religiously Diverse Nation* (New York: Harper Collins, 2009).

51 See "The 1990's: Cultural Recognition, Internet Utopias, and Multicultural Identities," in Laurie L. Patton, *Who Owns Religion? Scholars and Their Publics in the Late 20th Century* (Chicago: University of Chicago Press, 2019), 67–84.

52 That handbook's descendant can be found at https://pluralism.org/boston.

53 Thomas Tweed, *Buddhism and Barbeque: A Guide to Buddhist Temples in North Carolina* (Buddhism in North Carolina Project, 2001).

54 "At Swearing in, Congressman Wants to Carry Koran," The Pluralism Project, accessed September 15, 2023, https://pluralism.org/news/swearing-congressman-wants-carry-koran.

55 For a discussion of this legacy, see Eboo Patel's 2022 interview with Diana Eck on Interfaith America, accessed September 12, 2023, https://www.interfaithamerica.org/podcast/eck/.

56 Laurie Patton, "Plural America Needs Myths: An Essay in Foundational Narratives in Response to Eboo Patel," in *Out of Many Faiths: Religious Diversity and the American Promise* (Princeton: Princeton University Press 2018), 151–180.

57 Marina Molarsky Beck, "General Education and the Future of Liberal Arts," *The Harvard Crimson*, October 31, 2013.

10 | PLURALISM AS *NOMOS* AND NARRATIVE | WHITTNEY BARTH

58 Pluralism Project at Harvard University, "A New Religious America," The Pluralism Project, accessed June 15, 2023, https://pluralism.org/new-religious-america.

59 Aysha Khan, "Near Boston, a Friendly's-turned-Hindu Temple Serves Holy Offerings to Go," *Religion News Service*, June 4, 2020, accessed June 15, 2023.

60 Azra Haqqie, "Faith Springs from Belief in Brotherhood," *Times Union*, Jan. 6, 2012, accessed June 15, 2023.

61　Tanya Basu, "How Church Sales Reflect the Shifting American Demographic," *The Atlantic*, July 2, 2014, accessed June 15, 2023.

62　A version of this chapter originally appeared as an essay published on *Canopy Forum* (www.canopyforum.org), a digital publication of the Center for the Study of Law and Religion at Emory University as part of a collection of essays and accompanying webinar on "Religion, Property Law, and the Crisis of Houses of Worship." The original essay is available at https://canopyforum.org/2023/05/03/pluralism-and-the-future-of-religious-property/. I would like to thank the *Canopy Forum* team for their editorial assistance. The views expressed are my own and do not necessarily reflect the views of CSLR. Any errors are also, of course, my own.

63　"About," The Pluralism Project at Harvard University, accessed June 15, 2023, https://pluralism.org/about.

64　Religious Land Use and Institutionalized Persons Act of 2000, 42 USC 2000cc, accessed June 15, 2023, https://www.govinfo.gov/content/pkg/STATUTE-114/pdf/STATUTE-114-Pg803.pdf.

65　Department of Justice, "Statement of the Department of Justice on the Land Use Provisions of the Religious Use and Institutionalized Persons Act (RLUIPA)," Dec. 15, 2010, accessed June 15, 2023, https://www.justice.gov/crt/page/file/1071246/download.

66　Daniel P. Dalton, "Recent Developments in RLUIPA and Religious Land Use." *The Urban Lawyer* 49, no. 3 (2017): 533–61. JSTOR, accessed June 15, 2023.

67　"Joint Statement of Senator Hatch and Senator Kennedy on the Religious Land Use and Institutionalized Persons Act of 2000," July 27, 2000, S7774–7775, accessed June 15, 2023, https://www.govinfo.gov/content/pkg/CREC-2000-07-27/pdf/CREC-2000-07-27-pt1-PgS7774.pdf.

68　Eric Treene, "RLUIPA and Mosques: Enforcing a Fundamental Right in Challenging Times, *First Amendment Law Review*, vol. 10, issue 2, Jan. 1, 2012, accessed June 15, 2023.

69　President William J. Clinton, "Statement on Signing the Religious Land Use and Institutionalized Persons Act of 2000, Sept. 22, 2002, accessed June 15, 2023, https://www.govinfo.gov/content/pkg/WCPD-2000-09-25/pdf/WCPD-2000-09-25-Pg2168.pdf.

70　Ibid.

71　Ibid.

72 Ibid.
73 Religious Freedom Restoration Act of 1993, 42 USC 2000bb *et seq*, accessed June 15, 2023, https://www.justice.gov/sites/default/files/jmd/legacy/2014/07/24/act-pl103-141.pdf.
74 494 U.S. 872 (1990).
75 President William J. Clinton, "Remarks on Signing the Religious Freedom Restoration Act of 1993, Nov. 16, 1993, accessed June 15, 2023, https://www.govinfo.gov/content/pkg/WCPD-1993-11-22/pdf/WCPD-1993-11-22-Pg2377.pdf.
76 Ibid.
77 521 U.S. 507 (1997).
78 572 U.S. 352, 356 (2015).
79 Steve Rabey, "RFRA Coalition Frays in Wake of Ruling," *Christianity Today*, Aug. 11, 1997, accessed June 15, 2023.
80 Martin S. Lederman, "Reconstructing RFRA: The Contested Legacy of Religious Freedom Restoration," *Yale Law Journal Forum*, vol. 125, March 16, 2016, accessed June 15, 2023.
81 Marci Hamilton, "Struggling with Churches as Neighbors: Land Use Conflicts Between Religious Institutions and Those Who Reside Nearby," FindLaw.com, Jan. 17, 2002, accessed June 15, 2023.
82 Melissa Rogers and Amanda Tyler, "A Religious Freedom Success Story," Baptist Joint Committee for Religious Liberty, Sept. 22, 2020, accessed June 15, 2023.
83 Ibid. *See also* U.S. Department of Justice, "Update on the Justice Department's Enforcement of the Religious Land Use and Institutionalized Persons Act: 2010-2016," July 2016, accessed June 15, 202.
84 Religious Liberty Act of 1999, Congressional Record, H5580, July 15, 1999, accessed June 15, 2023.
85 Whittney Barth, "Pluralism, Place, and the Local," *Journal of Interreligious Studies* 17, issue 17 (2015), accessed June 15, 2023.
86 Pam Belluck, "Intolerance and an Attempt to Make Amends Unsettle a Chicago Suburb's Muslims, *N.Y. Times*, Aug. 10, 2000, accessed June 15, 2023.
87 Kathleen E. Foley, "Building Mosques in America: Strategies for Securing Municipal Approvals," Institute for Social Policy and Understanding, October 10, 2010, accessed June 15, 2023.
88 Ibid., 10–11.

89   Dalton, *supra* n.11.
90   Emma Green, "The Quiet Religious Freedom Fight that is Remaking America," *The Atlantic*, Nov. 5, 2017, accessed June 15, 2023.
91   Chris Fuchs, "Sikh Congregation Sues Town After Temple Construction Halted," NBC News, Aug. 4, 2016, accessed June 15, 2023.
92   Ibid.
93   Green, *supra* n.35.
94   Robert M. Cover, "The Supreme Court, 1982 Term," *Harvard Law Review* 97, no. 1, November 1983, accessed June 15, 2023.
95   "About," The Pluralism Project at Harvard University, accessed June 15, 2023, https://pluralism.org/about.
96   Diana L. Eck, "Prospects for Pluralism: Voice and Vision in the Study of Religion," AAR Presidential Address, *Journal of the American Academy of Religion* (2007): 1–34, accessed June 15, 2023.

11 | RELIGIOUS PLURALISM AND CIVIC ENGAGEMENT | CHLOE BREYER

97   "Religious Liberty in Law and Practice," Article, 35 *Journal of Church and State*, 367–401 (1993). Article based on undergraduate thesis published in Baylor University Law Journal.
98   Diana L. Eck and the Pluralism Project at Harvard University, *On Common Ground: World Religions in America*, (New York: Columbia University Press, 1997), CD-ROM.
99   Diana L. Eck, *A New Religious America: How a "Christian Country" Has Become the World's Most Religiously Diverse Nation* (San Francisco: HarperSanFrancisco, 2001).
100 "About," The Pluralism Project at Harvard University, https://pluralism.org/about.
101 "Becoming the Buddha in LA," The Pluralism Project at Harvard University, https://pluralism.org/becoming-the-buddha-in-la.

12 | THE CORRIDOR | LAWRENCE COHEN

102 Diana L. Eck, *Banāras: City of Light* (New York: Knopf, 1982), 25–33, 350–355.
103 J. Barton Scott, *Spiritual Despots: Modern Hinduism and the Genealogies of Self-Rule* (Chicago: University of Chicago Press, 2016).

104 David Boyk, "Collaborative Wit: Provincial Publics in Colonial North India," *Comparative Studies of South Asia, Africa and the Middle East* 38, no. 1 (2018): 89–106. 2008; Lawrence Cohen, "Holi in Banaras and the Mahaland of Modernity," *GLQ: A Journal of Lesbian and Gay Studies* 2, No. 4 (1995); Lawrence Cohen, "Science, Politics, and Dancing Boys: Propositions and Accounts," *Parallax* 14, No. 3 (2008).

105 Diana L. Eck, "India's '*Tīrthas*': 'Crossings' in Sacred Geography," *History of Religions* 20, No. 4 (1981).

106 Eck, *Banaras*, 148–157, 347.

107 Madhuri Desai, *Banaras Reconstructed: Architecture and Sacred Space in a Hindu Holy City* (Seattle: University of Washington Press, 2017).

108 Desai, *Banaras Reconstructed*, 21–27.

109 Diana L. Eck, *Darśan: Seeing the Divine Image in India* (Chambersburg: Anima), 3.

110 Alok Pandey and Saurabh Shukla, "Gyanvapi Case To Continue In Court, Mosque Committee's Challenge Rejected," NDTV News, May 31, 2023, https://www.ndtv.com/india-news/gyanvapi-case-to-continue-in-varanasi-court-mosque-committees-challenge-to-validity-of-case-dismissed-by-high-court-4082042; Sushmita Pathak, "A Hindu-Muslim Dispute Tests Centuries of Interfaith Culture in India's Varanasi." *NPR News*, September 16, 2023.

111 G. L. Gaile, "Towards a Strategy of Growth Paths," *Environment and Planning A: Economy and Space* 9, No. 6 (1977); Albie Hope and John Cox, "Development Corridors," *Economic and Private Sector Professional Evidence and Applied Knowledge Services Topic Guides* (London: United Kingdom Department for International Development, 2015); Sai Balakrishnan, *Shareholder Cities: Land Transformations Along Urban Corridors in India* (Philadelphia: University of Pennsylvania Press, 2019).

112 Detlef Müller-Mahn, "Envisioning African Futures: Development Corridors as Dreamscapes of Modernity," *Geoforum* 115 (2020): 156.

113 See, for example, OpIndia Staff, "Kashi Vishwanath Corridor: When Shekhar Gupta's *The Print* Tried Fuelling Misapprehensions about the Grand Restoration Project," *OpIndia*, December 14, 2021, https://www.opindia.com/2021/12/kashi-vishwanath-corridor-when-theprint-fuelled-misapprehensions-about-restoration-project/, for Patel's deployment of the rationale of encroachment.

114 Kabir Agarwal, "In Modi's Varanasi, the Vishwanath Corridor Is Trampling Kashi's Soul," *The Wire*, January 23, 2019; Riddhish Dutta, "Fact Check: Were Temples Destroyed to Build Kashi Vishwanath Corridor? Old Karnataka Video Shared with Lies," *India Today*, April 26, 2022.

115 Eck, *Banāras*, 304–323.

116 Nita Kumar, *The Artisans of Banaras: Popular Culture and Identity, 1880-1986*, (Princeton: Princeton University Press, 1988).

117 Kajri Jain, *Gods in the Time of Democracy*, (Durham: Duke University Press, 2021).

118 Tulasi Srinivas, *The Cow in the Elevator: An Anthropology of Wonder*, (Durham: Duke University Press, 2018).

119 Sanjay Srivastava, "Urban Spaces, Disney-Divinity and Moral Middle Classes in Delhi," *Economic and Political Weekly* 44, no. 26/27 (2009): 341–342.

120 I am grateful to Jennifer Peace and Ellie Pierce for the provocation to write this essay and to Diana Eck for a lifetime of reaching and inspiration. I thank Deepak Mehta for first suggesting I pay closer attention to shifting relations of mosque and temple in Varanasi. Understandings of these relations are contested, and I am grateful to numerous persons in Varanasi who I do not name—scholars, pilgrims, priests, shopkeepers, and residents of the city—for their kindness in talking with and guiding me: given this contestation, I do not wish to extend any hurt this essay may engender on to others. I have tried to render disparate civil and religious understandings and experiences of the Corridor with what care this essay's brevity allows and apologize if either my language or intellectual commitments here cause undue offense.

13 | LIKE A RIVER | REBECCA KNEALE GOULD

121 Diana L. Eck, *Encountering God: A Spiritual Journey from Bozeman to Banaras*, (Boston: Beacon Press, 1993), 2.

122 Diana L. Eck, *India: A Sacred Geography* (New York: Three Rivers Press, 2012), 4–5.

123 Eck, *India*, 5.

124 In many cases, both can be true at the same time.

125 See for example Michael McNally, *Defend the Sacred: Native American Religious Freedom Beyond the First Amendment* (Princeton: Princeton University Press, 2020).

ENDNOTES

126 Victoria Loorz, *Church of the Wild: How Nature Invites Us Into the Sacred* (Minneapolis: Broad Leaf Books, 2021), 143.

127 The Wild Church Network can be found at www.wildchurchnetwork.com.

128 Kelly Alley, "Idioms of Degeneracy: Assessing Ganga's Purity and Pollution" in Lance Nelson, ed. *Purifying the Earthly Body of God: Religion and Ecology in Hindu India* (Albany: State University of New York Press, 1998); David Haberman, *River of Love in an Age of Pollution* (Berkeley: University of California Press, 2006); and Eck's discussion of pollution in *India: A Sacred Geography*, 183–188.

129 For an overview of significant precursors to the "religion and ecology" writing that arose in the 1980's, see Rebecca Kneale Gould and Laurel Kearns, "Ecology and Religious Environmentalism in the United States," John Corrigan, ed. *Encyclopedia of Religion in America* (Oxford: Oxford University Press, 2018), 604–646.

130 Rosemary Radford Ruether, *New Woman, New Earth: Sexist Ideologies and Human Liberation* (New York: Seabury, 1975).

131 Rosemary Radford Reuther, *Integrating Ecofeminism, Globalization and World Religions* (Oxford: Rowman and Littlefield,) 76. See also Ruether, *Gaia and God: An Ecofeminist Theology of Earth Healing*, Second Edition (New York: Harper Collins) 26–31.

132 Sallie McFague, *Models of God: Theology for an Ecological, Nuclear Age* (Minneapolis: Fortress Press, 1987); *A New Climate for Theology: God, the World and Global Warming* (Minneapolis: Fortress Press, 2008); and *Blessed Are the Consumers: Climate Change and the Practice of Restraint* (Minneapolis: Fortress Press, 2013).

133 See, for example, Rabbi Arthur Waskow, *Torah of the Earth: Exploring 4,000 Years of Ecology in Jewish Thought*, 2 Volumes (Woodstock, VT: Jewish Lights Publishing, 2000); Rabbi Arthur Green, *Seek My Face: A Jewish Mystical Theology* (Woodstock, VT: Jewish Lights Publishing, 2003); and Ellen Bernstein, *The Splendor of Creation: A Biblical Ecology* (Cleveland: Pilgrim Press, 2005).

134 "Reflections on the Energy Crisis: A Statement by the Committee on Social Development and World Peace," (Washington, DC: United States Catholic Conference, 1981), 10.

135 Documents issued by official Catholic bodies historically build arguments on the precedent of prior Catholic teaching. Thus, it is not surprising that the authors of this text use *Gaudeum et Spes*, with its focus on

modernity and global responsibility as its foundation. Issued by Pope Paul VI on December 7, 1965. *Gaudeum et Spes* ("Joy and Hope"), the Pastoral Constitution on the Church in the Modern World, was the last and most globally oriented of the four constitutional statements coming out of the Second Vatican Council of 1965.

136 Laurel Kearns, "Religion and Environmental Justice" in *Religions and Environments: A Reader in Religion and Ecology*, Richard Bohannon, ed. (London: Bloomsbury, 2014).

137 It is worth noting that the early Deep Ecology critique of Christianity revealed a lack of attentiveness to the Christian eco-theology that was also emerging in this period. It took time for these two conversations to become aware of each other and to adjust their claims accordingly.

138 By "religious environmentalism," I mean such developments as: the founding of institutions, the issuing of formal religious declarations and the growth of individuals expressing ecological commitments in explicitly religious terms such as "Creation Care." See Gould and Kearns, "Ecology and Religious Environmentalism in the United States."

139 Francis, *Laudato Si*, (Washington, DC: United States Conference of Catholic Bishops, 2015). Leonardo Boff, *Cry of the Earth, Cry of the Poor* (Maryknoll, NY: Orbis Books, 1997).

140 The structure of NRPE has changed over time and the current (2023) constituents of NRPE are the National Council of Churches of Christ (NCC) in partnership with Creation Justice Ministries, the U.S. Conference of Catholic Bishops, the Evangelical Environmental Network, the Jewish Council on Public Affairs in partnership with COEJL and the Jewish Social Justice Round Table. See www.nrpe.org.

141 This legacy remains, however, as the founders of the Evangelical Environmental Network are always quick to insist: "we worship the Creator, not the Creation," a stance that differs significantly from that of Victoria Loorz.

142 Address of His Holiness Pope Benedict XVI, "The Listening Heart: Reflections on the Foundations of Law," September 22, 2011. (It is worth noting that Pope Benedict then goes on to discuss *human* nature.) Archbishop Paul S. Coakley and Bishop David Malloy reiterate and build upon Pope Benedict's speech in their World Day of Prayer for the Care of Creation statement "Listening to the Voice of Creation," September 1, 2022. Available at US Conference of Catholic Bishops website.

143 David Haberman, *People Trees: Worship of Trees in Northern India* (New York: Oxford University Press, 2013), 29.

144 Haberman, *People Trees*, 29–30.

145 Mark Wallace, *When God Was a Bird: Christianity, Animism and the Re-enchantment of the World* (New York: Fordham University Press, 2019), 69. While in the 1980's and 1990's McFague's writing was considered "too radical" in some mainline and evangelical contexts, the evolution of the religion and ecology field demonstrates how, in contrast to Wallace's work, McFague's theology might now seem "too tame." McFague's emphasis on metaphor preserves a distance between God and nature wherein we are invited to "try on" the idea of earth as the body of God to see what we might learn, while Wallace's work argues for a passionate embrace of Christian animism. A careful reading of McFague's corpus, however, shows that her theological vision was cautiously, but steadily, moving toward the kind of analysis that Wallace provides.

146 Wallace, *When God Was a Bird*, 69.

147 See, for example, the range of articles in the 2023 (Spring/Summer) edition of the *Harvard Divinity School Bulletin* "Exploring Ecological Spiritualities." This issue emerged out of the inaugural conference of the Program for the Evolution of Spirituality (PES) at the Harvard Divinity School. The PES program is directed by Dan McKanan.

14 | *DARSHANA* | RAHUL MEHROTRA

148 This essay is reprinted with permission from *Religion and Society* 12: 1 (Sep 2021), 15–17.

149 Diana L. Eck, *Banaras: City of Light* (Princeton: Princeton University Press, 1982).

150 Eck, *Banaras*, 58–59.

15 | SHIFTING PATTERNS OF EPIPHANIES | VIJAYA NAGARAJAN

151 For an introduction to the scholarship of the Indus Valley Civilization, see Harappa.com.

16 | RESIDING ON THE HAIR OF ŚIVA, RISING FROM THE FOOT OF VIṢṆU | VASUDHA NARAYANAN

152 I would like to thank the American Council of Learned Societies and the Centre for Khmer Studies for fellowships in 2005 and 2007 for funding

my research. The materials here are drawn from many site visits to Kbal Spean and the many Angkor monuments over a twenty-year period, as well as studying the artifacts at the Musée Guimet, and those under the safe custody of National Conservancy, Siem Reap. I would also like to thank Kobeak Ou for generously sharing his undergraduate thesis. I am grateful to Anand Venkatkrishnan, Shiv Subramaniam, Nilima Chitgopekar, and Frank Korom in helping with references to the Pārvatī-Gaṅgā rivalry in Sanskrit literature and Indian inscriptions.

153 Diana L. Eck, *India: a Sacred Geography* (New York: Harmony Books, 2012), 132–166; Diana L. Eck, *Banaras: City of Light* (New York: Knopf, 1982), 211–250; and Diana L. Eck, "Gaṅgā: The Sacred Ganges in Hindu Sacred Geography," in *Devī : Goddesses of India*, ed. John Stratton Hawley and Donna Marie Wulff (Berkeley: University of California Press, 1996), 137–153.

154 I am grateful to Professor Ashley Thompson of SOAS for kindly clarifying not just the name of Mekong but also on how the name/word "Gaṅgā" is used for water and waterways in Cambodia even today.

155 Eck, *Banaras*, 74.

156 See for instance *Mudraraksasa* 1, translated by Bronner and McCrea, "Poetics," 436. In Kālidāsa's *Meghadūta* ("Cloud Messenger") 1:50, Gaṅgā revels in Pārvatī's jealousy. For Indian inscriptions on Umā-Pārvatī's jealousy, see Chitgopekar, *Encountering Sivaism*, 108.

157 Inscriptions from Cambodia will follow the standard cataloguing system (K. xxx) started by the EFEO in the early 20th century. References to the inscriptions are from Coedès, *Inscriptions du Cambodge*, volumes 1–8, 1937–1966.

158 K. 829, v. 29. Coedès, *Inscriptions du Cambodge*, vol. 1, 33 and 35. The two page numbers from Coedès' volumes in citing the inscriptions in this paper indicate the locations of the original Sanskrit verse and the translations.

159 Goodall, *East Mebon Stele Inscription*, 90, n. 95, 178, n. 289, and 245, n. 420.

160 K. 675. Coedès, *Inscriptions du Cambodge*, vol. 1, 62 and 65.

161 K. 250. Coedès, *Inscriptions du Cambodge*, vol 3, 100.

162 OU, *Brah Ganga*, ii; K. 81. Barth, *Inscriptions Sanscrites*, 16.

163 K. 989. Coedès, *Inscriptions du Cambodge*, vol. 7, 172 and 179

164 K. 834. Coedès, *Inscriptions du Cambodge*, vol. 5, 251 and 258.

165 Eck, "Gaṅgā," 144.

166 The story of Gaṅgā flowing over Viṣṇu's toe when he takes the third step is related in the *Viṣṇu Purāṇa* 2.8.109 (McComas Taylor, *Viṣṇu Purāṇa*,

184), *Bhagavata Purāṇa*, 5.17.1; general references to Gaṅgā flowing from Viṣṇu's foot: *Viṣṇu Purāṇa* 2.2.32, 4.4.20. McComas Taylor, *Viṣṇu Purāṇa*, 156, 290.
167 K. 806. Coedès, *Inscriptions du Cambodge*, vol. 1, 102 and 139.
168 K. 806. Coedès, *Inscriptions du Cambodge*, vol. 1, 139, n.1.
169 Coedès, *Inscriptions du Cambodge*, vol 1, 224.
170 For examples, see Coedès, *Inscriptions du Cambodge*, vol 1, 224 note 1.
171 K. 806. *Inscriptions du Cambodge*, vol 1, 91 and 122
172 IM Sokrithy, "Siem Reap river," 34.
173 APSARA, *Angkor*, 2–3.
174 Jacques, "Kbal Spān," 358–359.
175 APSARA, *Angkor*, 53
176 Kummu, "Water Management in Angkor," 1413.
177 (1). *(ru)dradhārā çivārnāsā gaṅgā ghoṣavatī babhau (2). (lo)kakilbiṣasaṃhartrī pratyakṣan dyunadīva yā* // Jacques translates this into French as: "Torrent de Rudra, rivière de Çiva, cette Gaṅgā s'est manifestée visiblement, bruyante, elle qui détruit complètement les fautes du monde, comme la rivière céleste !" Jacques, "Kbal Spān," 361.
178 IM Sokrithy, "Siem Reap river," 34.
179 Bhattacharya, Sanskrit inscriptions from Cambodia, 31.
180 Evans et al., "A comprehensive archaeological map," 14277
181 Evans et al., "A comprehensive archaeological map," 14282.
182 IM Sokrithy, "Siem Reap river," 34.

18 | SOMANATH AND THE RHETORIC OF "THE SHRINE ETERNAL" | NEELIMA SHUKLA-BHATT

183 Romila Thapar, *Somanatha: The Many Voices of a History* (New York: Verso, 2005), 10–13.
184 J.D. Parmar, "Somnath," Shree Somnath Trust Virtual Library, accessed August 22, 2023, https://vartman.somnath.org.
185 Diana L. Eck, "India's 'Tīrthas': 'Crossings' in Sacred Geography. *History of Religions* 20 (4, 1981): 324.
186 Thapar 2005: 39–51.
187 Kanaiyalal Maneklal Munshi, *Somnath, the Shrine Eternal: Souvenir Published on the Occasion of the Installation Ceremony of the Linga in the New Somanatha Temple on May 11, 1951*. Bombay: Somnath Board of Trustees.
188 Thapar 2005; Neelima Shukla-Bhatt, "Somanath, the Shrine Eternal?

Perceptions and Appropriations of a Temple" (unpublished manuscript, 2001).

189 Diana L. Eck, *India: A Sacred Geography* (New York: Harmony Books, 2012), 220.

190 George Michell, *The Hindu Temple: An Introduction to Its Meaning and Forms* (New York: Harper & Row, 1977), 62, 67.

191 Eck, *India*, 11–12, 454–56.

19 | A LEGACY OF EMBODIED SCHOLARSHIP | HALAH AHMAD

192 Eck, "What is Pluralism," The Pluralism Project at Harvard University, https://pluralism.org/.

193 M.P. Bernhard, "Dining Services 'Mistakenly' Factored Politics into Sodastream Decision, Spokesperson Says," *The Harvard Crimson*, December 18, 2014, https://www.thecrimson.com/article/2014/12/18/HUDS-statement-sodastream/

194 K.A. Swaby, "HUDS suspends purchases from Israeli Soda Company," *The Harvard Crimson*, December 17, 2014.

195 Eck, "What is Pluralism?"

196 A.L. Almore, "'In Harvard, But Not Of It': Harvard, Slavery and the Civil War: A Profile of W.E.B. Du Bois," *The Harvard Crimson*, October 21, 2011, https://www.thecrimson.com/article/2011/10/21/dubois-375-profile/

197 Eck, "What is Pluralism?"

198 See for example: José Casanova, "Rethinking Secularization: A Global Comparative Perspective," in *Religion, Globalization, and Culture* eds., Peter Beyer and Lori Beaman (Boston: Brill, 2007), 101–120; Talal Asad, *Formations of the Secular: Christianity, Islam, Modernity* (Redwood City: Stanford University Press, 2003); Atalia Omer, "The Hermeneutics of Citizenship as a Peacebuilding Process: a Multiperspectival Approach to Justice," *Political Theology*, 11:5, (2010), 650–673.

199 Eck, "What is Pluralism?"

21 | A TRANSFORMATIONAL CONFERENCE | SISSELA BOK

200 Sissela Bok, Diary entry, June 14, 1983.

201 Diana L. Eck, "Women, Religion, and Social Change: Issues and Methods in the Study of Religious Ethics and Social Change," (unpublished article, June 1983) 1.

ENDNOTES

202 Diana Eck, "Women, Religion, and Social Change: Discussion on Violence and Non-Violence, June 15, 1983," (unpublished article, June 1983) 11, 3.

203 Diana Eck and Devaki Jain, *Speaking of Faith: Global Perspectives on Women, Religion, and Social Change* (Kali for Women, 1986), 13.

204 Ibid., 14.

205 Ibid., 13.

206 Alva Myrdal, "Nobel Speech and Lecture," in *Alva Myrdal: A Pioneer in Nuclear Disarmament*, eds., Peter Wallensteen and Armend Bekaj (Berlin: Springer, 2002), 233–252. See also Sissela Bok, *Alva Myrdal: A Daughter's Memoir* (Boston: Addison-Wesley, 1991), 345–6.

207 Myrdal, "Lecture," 252.

208 Alva Myrdal, *The Game of Disarmament: How the United States and Russia Run the Arms Race* (New York: Pantheon Books, 1982), xi–xxiv.

209 Ibid., xii.

210 Sissela Bok, "Foreword," Gandhi, *An Autobiography: The Story of My Experiments with Truth*, tr. Mahadev Desai (Boston: Beacon Press, 1993), xi–xviii.

211 Sissela Bok, *A Strategy for Peace: Human Values and the Threat of War* (New York: Pantheon Books, 1989).

212 Ibid., viii.

213 Sissela Bok, Op-Ed, "Does Peace have a Chance?," *The New York Times*, December 25, 1989.

214 Ibid.

215 See a discussion of the 1993 World Parliament of Religion's document in "Four Approaches to Common Values," in Sissela Bok, *Common Values* (Columbia: University of Missouri Press, 1993), 31–4.

216 Diana Eck, Opening Remarks and Introductions, April 30, 2003, (unpublished article).

217 Eck and Jain, *Speaking of Faith*, 15.

218 Nobel Committee announcement, Oslo, October 6, 2023.

219 Farnaz Fassihi, "Who Is Nargas Mohammadi?," *The New York Times*, October 6, 2023.

22 | BRAIDING EPISTEMOLOGICAL, THEORETICAL, AND METHODOLOGICAL CONTRIBUTIONS | PATRICE BRODEUR

220 For the detailed program, see the following link, accessed September

23, 2023: https://www.mcgill.ca/religiousstudies/files/religiousstudies/LegacyofWilfredCantwellSmith.pdf.

221 On Professor Eck's recollection of her journey with Professor Graham as fellow doctoral students starting in 1969, see: Diana L. Eck, "Fifty Years as Colleagues: Pilgrim's Progress," in *Non Sola Scriptura: Essays on the Qur'an and Islam in Honour of William A. Graham,* eds. Bruce Fudge, Kambiz GhaneaBassiri, Christian Lange, and Sarah Bowen Savant, (London: Routledge, 2022), 305–308.

222 John B. Carman, "Wilfred Smith as an Academic Architect," first presentation at above symposium.

223 Diana L. Eck, "Diana L. Eck on Becoming a More Complex 'We'," *Tikkun,* Vol. 24, No. 1 (2009), 49–50.

224 Seiple, C., & Hoover, D.R. eds., *The Routledge Handbook of Religious Literacy, Pluralism, and Global Engagement,* (London: Routledge, 2021), 9.

23 | DIANA ECK: SHE WHO CHANGED MY LIFE | DHAMMANANDA

225 Korkiat Shatsena (1908–1985), the first person to pave the way for the Democrat party in Trang province, in the southern part of Thailand.

226 As a woman, one needs to be trained two years before taking full ordination, according to the Vinaya prescription.

25 | POTENTIALS OF PLURALISM | NANCY A. KHALIL

227 This essay is based on a presentation delivered at the Pluralism Project 25th Anniversary Conference: *Pluralism @ 25* held at Harvard University September 21–22, 2016.

228 Wendy Brown, *Regulating Aversion: Tolerance in the Age of Identity and Empire,* (Princeton, NJ: Princeton University Press, 2008).

27 | DIANA ECK: THE SINGLE LARGEST INFLUENCE ON INTERFAITH AMERICA | EBOO PATEL

229 To read the speech, "Of Visions, Methodologies and Movements: Interfaith Youth Work in the 21st Century," by Eboo Patel at the Harvard University's Center for World Religions, March 11 2004, hwpi.harvard.edu/files/pluralismarchive/files/cswr2004_patel.pdf?m=1631568943

230 Read the 2006 American Academy of Religion Presidential Address, "Prospects for Pluralism: Voice and Vision in the Study of Religion" at

https://scholar.harvard.edu/dianaeck/files/2006_presidential_address-diana_eck.pdf.
231 Listen to the "Interfaith America with Eboo Patel" podcast conversation, "Can people who worship differently find common ground?" https://www.interfaithamerica.org/podcast/eck/
232 Laurie L Patton, *Who Owns Religion? Scholars and Their Publics in the Late Twentieth Century*, (Chicago: The University of Chicago Press, 2019).

28 | AN ADVAITA VEDĀNTA THEOLOGY OF RELIGIONS| ANANTANAND RAMBACHAN

233 Diana L. Eck, "Preface," in *Encountering God: A Spiritual Journey from Bozeman to Banaras* (Boston: Beacon Press, 1993).
234 Eck, *Encountering God*, 186.
235 Francis X. Clooney, *Comparative Theology: Deep Learning Across Religious Borders* (New York: Blackwell Publishing, 2010), 10
236 *Brahma-Sūtra-Bhāsya of Śrī Śaṅkarācārya*, trans. By Swami Gambhirananda (Calcutta: Advaita Ashrama), 1977. II.ii.32, 426.
237 *Brahma-Sūtra-Bhāsya of Śrī Śaṅkarācārya*, II,ii, 32, 426.
238 *Ibid*. 36, 433.
239 For brief summaries of exclusivism, inclusivism and pluralism see *Encountering God*, 168.
240 *Brahma-Sūtra-Bhāsya of Śrī Śaṅkarācārya*, II.i.3, 305–306.
241 See Govind Chandra Pande, *Life and Thought of Śaṅkarācārya* (Motilal Banarsidass, 1994), 269.
242 Eck, *Encountering God*, 168.
243 Eck, *Encountering God* 193.
244 Paul J. Griffiths, *An Apology for Apologetics: A Study in the Logic of Interreligious Dialogue* (Eugene OR: Wipf and Stock, 2007), 3.
245 See *Eight Upaniṣads with the Commentary of* Śaṅkarācārya, translated by Swami Gambhirananda. 2 vols. Īśa, Kena, Kaṭha, and Taittirīya in vol. 1; Aitaraya, Muṇḍaka, Māṇḍūkya and Kārika, and Praśna in vol. 2. Calcutta: Advaita Ashrama, 1965–1966, 100–102.
246 *Bhagavadgītā with the Commentary of Śaṅkarācārya*, trans. by Alladi Mahadeva Sastry (Madras: Samata Books, 1977).
247 Daniel Soars, *The World and God are Not-Two: A Hindu-Christian Conversation* (New York: Fordham University Press, 2023), 17.

248 Eck, *Encountering God*, 66.

29 | BUDDHISM, RELIGIOUS PLURALISM, AND LABOR STRIKES IN HAWAI'I | DUNCAN RYŪKEN WILLIAMS

249 Louise Hunter, *Buddhism in Hawaii* (O'ahu: University of Hawaii Press, 1971), 71.

250 Alan and Take Beekman, "Hawaii's Great Japanese Strike," *Pacific Citizen*, December 23, 1960, B1–8, 23–24, A14.

251 Gary Okihiro, *Cane Fires* (Philadelphia: Temple University Press, 1992), 44.

252 Akemi Kikumura-Yano, *Issei Pioneers* (Los Angeles: Japanese American National Museum, 1992), 27.

253 Roland Kotani, *The Japanese in Hawaii: A Century of Struggle* (Honolulu: Hawaii Hochi, 1985), 45.

254 Hunter, *Buddhism*, 92.

255 Fusa Nakagawa, *Takie Okamura: A Life Lived in Service to Japanese in Hawaii* (Tokyo: Ozorasha, 2015), 88.

256 Okihiro, *Cane*, 49–52.

257 Kotani, *The Japanese*, 59.

258 Quoted in Tomoe Moriya, "Buddhism at the Crossroads of the Pacific," in *Hawaii at the Crossroads of the U.S. and Japan before the Pacific War* (O'ahu: University of Hawaii Press, 2008), 200.

259 Moriya, "Buddhism," 200–201.

260 Kotani, *The Japanese*, 49–50.

261 Moriya, "Buddhism," 49.

262 Kotani, *The Japanese*, 49–50.

263 Hunter, *Buddhism*, 123 and Okihiro, *Cane*, 74.

264 Okihiro, *Cane*, 131.

265 Okihiro, *Cane*, 78.

266 Noriko Shimada, "Social, Cultural, and Spiritual Struggles of the Japanese in Hawaii," In *Hawaii at the Crossroads of the U.S. and Japan before the Pacific War* (O'ahu: University of Hawaii Press, 2008), 155.

267 Kotani, *The Japanese*, 66.

268 Kikumura-Yano, *Issei*, 29.